DIGITAL IMAGE
ACCESS & RETRIEVAL

PAPERS PRESENTED AT THE
1996 CLINIC ON LIBRARY APPLICATIONS OF DATA PROCESSING
MARCH 24-26, 1996
GRADUATE SCHOOL OF LIBRARY AND INFORMATION SCIENCE
UNIVERSITY OF ILLINOIS AT URBANA-CHAMPAIGN

CLINIC ON LIBRARY APPLICATIONS
OF DATA PROCESSING: 1996

Digital Image
Access & Retrieval

Edited by
P. Bryan Heidorn
Beth Sandore

Graduate School of Library and Information Science
University of Illinois at Urbana-Champaign
1997

ISBN 0-87845-100-5   ISSN 0069-4789

Printed in the United States of America
on acid-free paper

Contents

Introduction
Bryan P. Heidorn and Beth Sandore   1

Image Databases:
The First Decade, the Present, and the Future
Howard Besser   11

Exploring New Models for Administering
Intellectual Property:
The Museum Educational Site Licensing Project
Jennifer Trant   29

The Big Picture: Selection and Design Issues
for Image Information Systems
Lois F. Lunin   42

Content-Based Image Modeling and Retrieval
Rajiv Mehrotra   57

Visual Information Retrieval in Digital Libraries
Ramesh Jain   68

Efficient Techniques for Feature-Based Image/Video
Access and Manipulation
Shih-Fu Chang, John R. Smith, and Jianhao Meng   86

Multimedia Analysis and Retrieval System (MARS) Project
Tom Huang, Sharad Mehrotra, & Kannan Ramchandran   100

Finding Pictures of Objects in Large Collections of Images
David A. Forsyth, Jitendra Malik, Thomas K. Leung,
Chris Bregler, C. Carson, H. Greenspan,
and Margaret M. Fleck   118

Using Speech Input for Image Interpretation,
Annotation, and Retrieval
Rohini K. Srihari   140

**Preserving the Past: The Development of a
Digital Historical Aerial Photography Archive**
Donald E. Luman   164

Contributors   171

Index   177

P. BRYAN HEIDORN & BETH SANDORE

Introduction

The last several years have brought about technological advances in computing and digital imaging technology that have immediate and permanent consequences for visual resource collections. This technology is fast becoming a part of routine library operations and is an important facet in the evolution from current print-based to digital libraries. Libraries are involved in organizing and managing large visual resource collections. These collections are now being created to support research and instruction in nearly every discipline. Within the library and information center environment, the same technologies can impact preservation, interlibrary loan, and classroom support. The central challenges in working with digital image collections mirror those that libraries have sought to address for centuries: How do we organize, provide access to, store, and protect the collections to meet user needs at a reasonable cost?

The Thirty-Third Annual Clinic on Library Applications of Data Processing was held at the Beckman Institute on the campus of the University of Illinois at Urbana-Champaign (UIUC) on March 24-26, 1996. The theme of this symposium was "Digital Image Access and Retrieval." Speakers were invited to present papers in three general areas: (1) systems, planning, and implementation; (2) automatic and semi-automatic indexing; and (3) preservation. Although the clinic encompassed three areas of digital imaging, substantially more time was devoted to automatic and semi-automatic indexing and retrieval because the conference organizers felt that this was the area in which there was the strongest need to foster cross-disciplinary interaction. Preliminary reports of the symposium were featured in *Library Hi Tech* (Heidorn et al. 1996). The goal of the clinic was to bring together researchers and practitioners in multiple fields and provide a forum where experts could present their research and engage in creative interaction with participants. Directors of cultural heritage institutions, educators, librarians, systems engineers, computer and information scientists, and content providers were among those who participated in the clinic. The participants explored digital image technology and many facets of its impact on the libraries of today and tomorrow.

If a picture is worth a thousand words, it should not be surprising that it takes at least that many words to index an individual image. Libraries do not have the resources to manually index the extensive digital image collections that they are creating. A similar problem exists in not-for-profit and commercial sectors where visual resources represent a significant component of the information in a collection. While current technology enables cost-effective creation of digital image collections, the cost of manually indexing and describing images remains prohibitive. Technical difficulties and the fluidity of technology that are involved in creating digital collections further complicate the cost issue. There are few well-established practices that can be emulated. In addition to the indexing challenge, other significant unresolved issues include copyright and archiving and preservation of digital material. The authors in this volume are among the pioneers who are charting an uncertain course into this new territory.

The collection of papers that were presented at the Thirty-Third Annual Clinic on Library Applications of Data Processing is arranged in three sections that reflect different aspects of digital image access that were explored at the symposium. The first section, "Systems, Planning and Implementation," contains three papers that provide a framework for exploring these topics. These papers cover the historical, technical, and management issues involved in digital image collection development. The second and largest section includes six papers that address the central issue of automatic and semi-automatic indexing of images. The final section contains two papers that treat the topic of using digital images as replacements for deteriorating originals in the preservation process.

The technology to create digital images and digital image databases is readily accessible. Imaging systems can provide a powerful new tool for transmitting and using information. Visual information permeates our world and will continue to do so with increased technology development. This development ensures that most humans have a very strong bias toward visual information. Consequently, we can expect an ever-growing demand for the technology. We hope that the research and practice reflected at the Thirty-Third Annual Clinic on Library Applications of Data Processing and in this volume will facilitate the evolution within libraries and cultural heritage institutions from print-based, highly unique resources to digital materials that are easily accessible to a broad user community.

SYSTEMS, PLANNING, AND IMPLEMENTATION

In his keynote address, "Image Databases: The First Decade, the Present, and the Future," Howard Besser reminds us how much has been accomplished in the area of digital imaging within such a short time. He also indicates that there is still considerable work left to be done. Howard Besser was involved in library and museum image databases development before many thought image databases were a practical consideration. While that interpretation of the field proved incorrect, it is true that a decade ago the technology was limited. Innovation in several critical technologies, including storage, telecommunications, and processing power, has fueled the current fast pace of development. These technologies will need further improvement before the vision of some current practitioners can be met. Digital bandwidth to the home, for example, is inadequate for image applications. Besser outlines the roles of library and information scientists, both in future developments and in their interaction with other sciences such as computer science and engineering. While the imaging projects of a decade ago did not anticipate a few of today's developments, such as the World Wide Web, these projects were, for the most part, on the right track. From our current perspective, Besser was able to identify crucial areas of future work. Among these are standards and metadata development, image quality issues, and approaches for content-based retrieval. Current projects must take this future into account in order to maximize the useful life of the collections.

Jennifer Trant's paper, "Exploring New Models for Administering Intellectual Property: The Museum Educational Site Licensing (MESL) Project," explores the administrative, technical, and legal mechanisms for the eventual delivery of large high quality collections of museum images to educational institutions. Through the MESL consortium, seven museums and seven universities are cooperating in a two-year project to establish standard practices to accommodate this new potential for distribution of images. There are numerous and complex legal and intellectual property rights issues associated with the migration of rights from original works to reproductions, as well as to surrogates that represent reproductions. This is complicated by the ease with which an exact copy of a digital image can be made and transported, greatly increasing the likelihood of theft. Some models for rights management include: rights holders' collectives, brokerages, rights resellers, consortia, and locator services. At the time of the conference, the MESL project had been underway for one and a half years. Some of the lessons learned from that project will facilitate the organization of new projects.

In the final paper of this section, "The Big Picture: Selection and Design Issues for Image Information Systems," Lois Lunin examines the many factors involved in the planning and design of an image information system. Lunin counsels that, while it is easy to become preoccupied with the technology alone, any digital image delivery system requires much broader planning and analysis of the users' needs and the eventual desired functionality of the system. Before a project begins, it is necessary to identify the users of the system, the images of interest, the source and property rights associated with the images, short- and long-term hardware and software needs, standards, and costs. These proceedings provide a valuable decision-making framework for anyone contemplating the development of an image database for any substantial collection.

P. Bryan Heidorn & Beth Sandore

AUTOMATIC AND SEMI-AUTOMATIC INDEXING

This section of the volume is dedicated to the discussion of research and commercial systems that perform automatic content-based indexing of images. Each paper includes a theoretical discussion of the problem domain and the principles used to solve the problems in that domain. While none of these systems solves the image database problem in its entirety, each makes a unique contribution to progress in the field. In some cases the systems can be used to solve at least a subclass of practical problems. These authors make it clear that one of the significant research questions that remains to be explored is that of mapping from the low level features that are recognized by image processing techniques to the high level and conceptual features of interest to humans. The contributions by Chang et al. and Forsyth et al. represent research that has been supported by the NSF/ARPA/NASA Digital Libraries Initiative Program. It is significant to note that two of the six federally funded digital library research projects focus directly on image processing and retrieval systems.

Rajiv Mehrotra centers his thesis, "Content-Based Image Modeling and Retrieval," on the fact that an image database or any other type of database is only effective if it models the real world in a manner that is attuned to the user's perceptions and needs. For visual resources, this means that a system must be capable of representing image content in terms that are recognizable to users. Some of these features are at a low level and describe image properties, objects, and their attributes. A separate set of features describes application-dependent and user-dependent semantics. Mehrotra points out a distinction between two classes of image retrieval problem. Problems of the first class occur in content-constrained domains where it is possible to define, *a priori*, a semantic domain model. One example of a constrained domain is a part database in a manufacturing application. In these domains, it is possible to construct mechanisms to extract semantic features of any image. The second, more complex problem class is not restricted to a particular set of objects or relations. These heterogeneous collections are more difficult (if not impossible) to quantify with predefined semantics. To address this issue, Mehrotra proposes a generalized model that supports levels of abstraction and dynamic semantics. The model is intended to be flexible enough to support both user-dependent and domain-dependent semantics.

Mehrotra tests his ideas in the prototype system, MUSEUM, which uses separate models for the representation and processing of two- and three-dimensional object shapes. The former is handled by a variety of segment matching while the latter is handled by labeled sequences of vertices. Vertices in 3-D shapes are labeled with features values that are reminiscent of Waltz's (1975) vertex labels of "L," "ARROW," "FORK," and "T." These are normalized into a fixed sequence and used as a retrieval vector, similar to the vector space model sometimes employed in text information retrieval systems.

Ramesh Jain discusses the role of multimedia access in the area of digital libraries. The new material in digital libraries will exist to support text, images, video, audio, animation, as well as other formats. This heterogeneity of format makes it difficult to support queries at the semantic level, particularly where the query requires an integration of media. Yet, it seems clear that users would often want the option to search for information independent of media. A query like "Asteroid impacts on Jupiter in 1995" should return articles and books about the topic but also potentially NASA photos and even data in formats used only by astronomers.

In his chapter, "Visual Information Retrieval in Digital Libraries," Jain introduces a data model called VIMSYS that supports a hierarchical representation of images. The lower levels are reminiscent of the hierarchical structure introduced in manual standards for indexing graphical materials such as the *Art and Architecture Thesaurus* (Peterson, 1990; Whitehead, 1989) and the Library of Congress, *Thesaurus for Graphic Materials* (Library of Congress, 1995). The chief feature of the VIMSYS model is that the bottom two layers pertain to the physical characteristics of a scene that are domain-independent while the top two layers refer to domain-dependent features and relationships in the image. This separation facilitates the movement of the system across domains.

The contribution of Chang et al., "Efficient Techniques for Feature-Based Image/Video Access and Manipulation," focuses on the parallel issues of image and video indexing, retrieval, and manipulation. VisualSEEK is a content-based image query system. The second system, CVEPS (Compressed Video Editing and Parsing System), supports video manipulation with indexing support of individual frames from VisualSEEK. In both media forms, these systems address the problem of heterogeneous unconstrained collections, the second problem class identified by Mehrotra in this volume. In this problem class, low level visual features are extracted from a scene, independent of any domain-specific semantic interpretation. In the case of VisualSEEK, these "low" level features include the complex operations of automatic object segmentation and characterization.

Most other current automatic image systems index on global color or texture. In the cases where object level indexing is allowed, segmentation must be provided by a human. VisualSEEK supports some forms of spatial indexing and query, a feature rare in image indexing systems. A query may include information about the relative location of objects in a scene as well as absolute location. Both automatic segmentation and spatial relations are addressed in the work of Forsyth, et al. later in this volume. There are potential drawbacks to the impressive number of visual characteristics that are supported—e.g., computational complexity and user interface complexity. The greater the number of features supported by a system, the more difficult it becomes for a user to fully exploit the system's resources. Both issues are addressed in the current paper, although both are very much still open research issues.

There are a number of problems that form the center of focus for current domain independent automatic image indexing research. The paper by Huang, Mehrotra, and Ramchandran, "Multimedia Analysis and Retrieval System (MARS) Project," provides a rich discussion of many of these. These issues include: indexing based on global image color and texture, image segmentation, layout, shape descriptors, compression, and multimodal query integration. The most commonly implemented feature among the domain-independent image indexing techniques are global image color and texture indexing. Systems differ in the techniques used, but in all cases the goal is to devise an automatically generated metric which reflects the average or typical color or texture of an entire image independent of objects which may exist in the image. While this is a relatively gross measure, it is useful in some retrieval domains, providing a useful feature in databases where there is a single object in each image. It allows for the recognition of "red" in queries such as "Retrieve all red vases."

Of course, it is useful to provide access to the individual objects in an image as well. This motivates solutions to the image segmentation problem. The current version of MARS uses c-means clustering to identify like regions in the image. Details of the technique can be found in the paper. The general problem for all systems is that humans naturally segment an image into its component objects and frequently wish to query a system about the presence of particular objects in a database or properties of the objects such as their color. The techniques used in MARS are relatively general, allowing for the identification of properties of regions. Object recognition is not performed automatically in this system. Object-specific labels are neither generated nor attached to the identified regions. Indeed this is impossible given the current state of technology. The MARS system can, however, process queries which look for regions of color or texture of a specific size and location.

Once coherent regions in an image have been identified, it is possible to allow queries based on the layout of those regions. Layout refers to the positioning of regions in an image. A query may require that the top half of an image should be red while the bottom half should be dark (as in an ocean sunset). This type of layout relies on global positioning of regions relative to the entire image and is the type performed in this version of MARS. Some systems, such as VisualSEEK, support relative layout constraints in queries. In this query type, the locations of regions are specified in relation to one another and independent of the location on the image. For example, a query of this type may specify that there should be a blue region to the left and above a red and white region (as in an American flag).

MARS uses a Modified Fourier Descriptor (MFS) to support shape similarity search. This technique uses a quantification of the edge of an object. This particular approach has a number of attractive properties, one of which is that it is computationally tractable. The challenge for any system which tries to support automatic shape indexing is to devise a method that is computationally tractable, has descriptive power sufficient to differentiate objects in the collection, is robust under noise, is perspective invariant, and is intuitively accessible to a user. While no system has achieved all of these criteria for shape matching, there are a number of useful approaches to shape description such as the MFS used in MARS.

Because of the size of digital images and video, compression is a major issue. It is necessary to compress images to conserve disk space and to reduce the time needed for transmission. Not quite as obvious is the fact that there is potential to speed up some aspects of image analysis by processing in the compressed domain rather than working in uncompressed formats. This approach is taken using the MPEG compression format in the CVEPS system described by Chang in this volume. MARS uses wavelets.

The richness and diversity of the indexing techniques discussed above introduce their own problem—i.e., how to efficiently integrate this broad spectrum of features into a single query. MARS uses a weighted sum of similarity measures for independent features with the presumption of feature independence.

Some of these issues and others are addressed in the paper, "Finding Pictures of Objects in Large Collections of Images" by David Forsyth et al. One of the most interesting features of this system is the pre-coordination of feature sets to create object detectors such as a horizon filter. Three case studies are presented in this paper. The first demonstrates the use of low level color and texture properties for indexing and classification. This work is distinguished by its attention to segmentation based on color and texture similarity in adjacent subregions. During this process, additional information about the texture properties is extracted allowing for quantification of the spatial relationship between repeated elements in a texture. This is useful for recognition of regions containing patterns such as plaids and prints that occur frequently on clothing as well as repeated patterns that occur in nature. The characteristics of the pattern can be used in indexing and in segmentation. Consistent with Mehrotra's analysis of problem classes, these techniques work best in environments where there are few domain-specific constraints.

The second case study demonstrates the introduction of the geometric constraints which may be exploited when the domain is limited. In this case, the domain is limited to trees. Techniques are developed to recognize the strong vertical axis typical of trees. This is integrated with assumptions of rotational symmetry along the generating axis to help identify the edges of the tree. Additional texture and color properties are used to help with subclassification of the trees—e.g., into conifer and broadleaf forms. The final case study progresses further into domain-specific semantics. A system is discussed which develops a filter to automatically identify naked people in images. Higher level algorithms build on texture based segmentation to identify potential limbs and torso. Geometric constraints of the relative size and orientation of the segments are used to make the classification.

Moving further along the continuum between general broad and shallow techniques to narrow and deep, we arrive at the contribution of Rohini Srihari, "Using Speech Input for Image Interpretation, Annotation, and Retrieval." This paper focuses on the design and implementation of *Show&Tell*, which performs the task suggested in the paper's title. One of the subgoals of the system is to perform the computationally difficult image understanding task of object recognition. As stated earlier, this is an open problem. Here, two techniques are used to constrain the problem and to introduce top-down processing constraints. First, the vision problem is limited to the active area of aerial photography with a constrained set of objects of interest, including buildings and roads. The second technique is novel and represents the primary intellectual contribution of the work. The semantic output of a natural language processing system is used to direct image analysis and the object identification task. This is a semi-automatic indexing and retrieval system where a human provides a verbal and gesture description of objects in an aerial photograph. This description is used to annotate the objects in the image and to direct image processing. Both the natural language processing and the image processing are dependent on a domain-specific world model or ontology.

These human-provided annotations may be used as index terms for later retrieval and are attached to the objects in the segmented image. The output of the image processing is used to fill in details of the semantic model and to augment the image index. The functionality of the system may best be summarized through an example query from the paper, "*Show all buildings to the right of Kelly Laboratory.*"

Parallel techniques are used by Srihari's group in the section on MMVAR: A Multimodal System for Video Annotation and Retrieval. The problem is to allow content-based retrieval in a video database. Here again, natural language annotation is used to direct image processing. In this case, the additional problem of video sequence segmentation is addressed. *WordNet* is used to expand query terms to increase the likelihood of matching the original annotations. Together, the techniques used in *Show&Tell* and MMVAR demonstrate the processing advantages that may be gained by integrating processing in multiple modalities and by exploiting rich domain-specific ontologies.

Taken together, the papers in this section mark the forward edge of research in automatic content-based image indexing and retrieval. We can expect this to be an active area for research and commercialization for the next decade.

PRESERVATION

The final section of this volume contains two papers on preservation as it relates to digital media. The first paper outlines the general issues for any preservation project, the second describes a particular preservation project. In the first paper, "Digital Imaging: Issues for Preservation and Access," Meg Bellinger points out the fallacy of digital incorruptibility. Many factors must be taken into account before reliable digital media can be produced. Digitization projects are just one aspect of a comprehensive preservation plan. As has been reported elsewhere (*Preserving Digital Information: Report of the Task Force on Archiving of Digital Information*, 1996; Lunin, this volume), some of the factors to consider that are identified in this paper are: the quality of the digital image as a factor of resolution, authenticity, verification, bibliographical integrity, preserving and archiving digital media, as well as equipment and standard obsolescence.

If these considerations are addressed, a digitization project can both help preserve a collection and improve access. The digital format has other advantages as well. Donald Luman discusses digitization and digital manipulation in "Preserving the Past: The Development of a Digital Historical Aerial Photography Archive." In preceding papers in this volume, the ease with which digital images can be modified was viewed as a liability of the digital format. This project demonstrates the use of image processing to repair and enhance photography. It also demonstrates how digital representations of archival material can be digitally merged with modern data. In this case, archival images are merged with modern digital orthophotography to provide three-dimensional views of the terrain of the past. These can be compared with the current landscape to evaluate change.

REFERENCES

Library of Congress. Prints and Photographs Division. (Comp. & Ed.). (1995). *Thesaurus for graphic materials*. Washington, DC: LC, Cataloging Distribution Service.

Peterson, T. (1990). Developing a new thesaurus for art and architecture. *Library Trends, 38*(4), 644-658.

Preserving Digital Information: Report of the Task Force on Archiving of Digital Information, commissioned by The Commission on Preservation and Access and The Research Libraries

Group, Inc. Washington, DC: Commission on Preservation and Access. Also available from: <http://lyra.rlg.org/ArchTF/>

Waltz, D. (1975). Understanding line drawings of scenes with shadows. In P. H. Winston (Ed.), *The psychology of computer vision*. New York: McGraw-Hill Book Company.

Whitehead, C. (1989). Faceted classification in the *Art and Architecture Thesaurus. Art Documentation, 8*(4), 175-177.

BIBLIOGRAPHY

Besser, H., & Trant, J. (1995). *Introduction to imaging: Issues in constructing an image database.* Available from: <http://www.ahip.getty.edu/intro_imaging/0-Cover.html>. Santa Monica, CA: Getty Information Institute.

CNI/OCLC Workshop on Metadata for Networked Images, Sept. 23-24, 1996, Dublin, Ohio. Available from: <http://purl.oclc.org/metadata/image>.

Heidorn, P. B., et al. (1996). 33d annual UIUC clinic highlights digital image storage and retrieval. *Library Hi Tech News*, No. 133, June, pp. 1-9.

Mostafa, J. (1994). Digital image representation and access. *Annual Review of Information Science and Technology* (ARIST), 29, 99-135.

Museum Educational Site Licensing Project (MESL). Available from: <http://www.ahip.getty.edu/mesl/home.html>.

Stanford University Copyright & Fair Use site: <http://fairuse.stanford.edu/> This site is sponsored by the Council on Library Resources, FindLaw Internet Legal Resources and the Stanford University Libraries and Academic Information Resources.

Waddington, M. (1989). The AAT application protocol. *Art Documentation, 8*(4), 178-180.

Winston, P. H. (1975). *The psychology of computer vision.* New York: McGraw-Hill.

HOWARD BESSER

Image Databases:
The First Decade, the Present, and the Future

We have seen an explosion of image database developments in the decade since work began on the first multi-user networked system. This paper explores the state of technology a decade ago, revisits one of the earliest systems, identifies current interesting projects, discusses the major issues that are being faced today, and forecasts issues and trends that will emerge in the future. This paper reflects the biases of the author, whose primary interests lie in building image databases of cultural heritage materials, and who was involved in the development of the Berkeley Image Database System (ImageQuery).

TECHNICAL CAPABILITIES IN 1986

In 1986, the idea of large-scale image databases seemed quite far-fetched. By today's standards, storage capacity was minuscule, networks were unbearably slow, and visual display devices were poor. The market penetration was very low for most of the tools needed for image database development.

In the past several years, we have seen a spurt in the growth of image databases. It is now possible to overcome the once insurmountable technological impediments. Recent increases in storage capacity, network bandwidth, processing power, and display resolution have enabled a tremendous growth in image database development. Literally hundreds of such projects have begun in the last few years.

Technical capabilities in 1986 look primitive when viewed from our current perspective. Future forecasters a decade ago wrote about how technological change would eventually make digital image databases viable (Besser, 1987a, 1987b, 1987c; Lynch & Brownrigg, 1986), but few people (even those forecasters) were certain that this would happen within their lifetimes.

In this section, we will examine the technological capabilities of a decade ago, both to try to understand the impediments that were faced at that time and to provide insight into how we might plan today for changes in the coming decade.

Storage

Hard disks had just recently been introduced in personal computers (such as the IBM XT) and were a fairly new idea for desktop machines. A

30 megabyte disk was considered very large for a personal computer. Large disks for mainframe computers (such as the one hosting the University of California's Melvyl system) each had a capacity of about 600 megabytes and were the size of a washing machine. In an environment like this, proposing the development of collections of one megabyte image files sounded impractical, and the advocacy of 50 megabyte files sounded ridiculous. Today it is hard to find a new personal computer with a hard drive much smaller than 100 megabytes, and multi-gigabyte drives are commonplace, and smaller than the floppy drives of a decade ago.

Processors

The IBM AT was the newest personal computer a decade ago. IBM XTs and Apple Macintosh Plus machines had the widest use and the most common processor at the time was the 8086. PCs had an internal memory (RAM) limit of 640K. Mainframe computers, such as the IBM 4300, had 16M-32M of RAM, executed 2 million instructions/second (MIPS), and cost around $1 million. Image processing (which is unbearably slow if one cannot have quick and easy random access to the entire image) was impractical and generally was confined to specialized machines.

Today most computers come with a minimum of 8M of RAM, and desktop machines with more power than the mainframes of a decade ago are cheap and commonplace. Today's machines are fast enough and have enough RAM to hold and manipulate an image without the purchase of specialized hardware.

Networks

Networking within a site was not very common. Wiring to the desktop was usually twisted-pair wires carrying signals for terminals or terminal-emulation. Ethernet wiring had come out just a few years before and was still rare. Wide area networks had not really penetrated beyond the defense industry and large universities. Sites were connected to the predecessor of the Internet (the Arpanet) at approximately 56 Kilobits/sec.

Today, most wiring is designed to carry full-scale networking, Internet access is commonplace, and large to mid-sized organizations tend to be connected to it at speeds of T-1 to T-3 (1.5 Megabits to 45 Megabits/sec.).

Display Devices

Few display devices could handle a wide range of colors. Eight-bit display devices (256 colors) were considered high-end in the PC market and required a special card and monitor. In public lectures, people were surprised to see images of works of art displayed on a computer screen.

Today, 24-bit displays (16 million colors) come as a standard feature on new PCs, and no special cards or monitors are required. Onscreen graphic images are frequently used to promote computer and software sales.

Scanners

A decade ago, scanners were expensive and rare. The only advertisements for scanners appeared in catalogs of instrumentation devices. Scanning software had poor user interfaces, and most scanners required programming skills in order to make use of them. Most software did not permit immediate onscreen viewing of the image, and frequently the user had to scan on one workstation, run programs on the scanned file, and move it to another workstation to view it. Even when attached to a powerful CPU, scanners were slow (a 45 minute scan was not out of the question) and frequently required so much light and accompanying heat that scanning of delicate objects, such as works of art, was impossible.

Today, very good scanners sell for under $500 and are available through most sources that sell computer peripherals. Virtually all scanners come with point-and-click software that quickly displays images on the screen. Today, a scan that takes more than a few minutes is considered unbearably slow, and light and heat exposure are within tolerance levels for most objects.

Compression

The only image compression scheme with wide implementation was the CCITT Group III standard employed in fax machines. Work on defining compression standards for color images was just beginning. With this lack of sophisticated compression standards, individuals developed their own compression schemes, and images compressed using these schemes could not be decompressed by others.

Today compression schemes such as JPEG and LZW are widely accepted standards, and the capability to decompress these files is included in a wide variety of image display and processing software, as well as in generic viewing and browsing tools, such as Web browsers.

Client-Server Architecture

X-Windows was the only client-server architecture with a significant installed base, but its deployment at the time was very small (limited primarily to a small percentage of UNIX-based workstations on major university campuses). Because image database designers could not rely upon distributing processing to the client, most designs had to assume all image processing would be done at the server, and that high bandwidth would be required in order to send compressed files to the client.

Today the widespread deployment of Web browsers permits image display and processing functionality to be off-loaded to the client. This puts less strain on the server and on the use of network bandwidth.

IMAGEQUERY REVISITED

How well did we really understand the problems in 1986, and what functions are still important today? In 1986, UC Berkeley's office of Information Systems and Technology began work on a project to deliver high quality digital images from its Art Museum, Architecture Slide Library, and Geography Department. The developers believe that this software (eventually called ImageQuery) was the first deployed multi-user networked digital image database system. The software was first shown publicly at the conferences of the American Association of Museums and the American Library Association in June 1987.

ImageQuery was an X-Windows-based system with a number of features that were relatively new for the time: a graphic user interface (GUI), point-and-click searching, thumbnail images to permit browsing and sorting, tools for annotation of images, and the linking of images to locations on maps. In addition, ImageQuery was designed for networked accessibility, had client-server features, and permitted Boolean searches. ImageQuery design and features have been described in more detail elsewhere (Besser, 1991b, 1990, 1988a, 1988b; Besser & Snow, 1990). Here we will focus on some key elements from ImageQuery and analyze them with the benefit of a decade of hindsight.

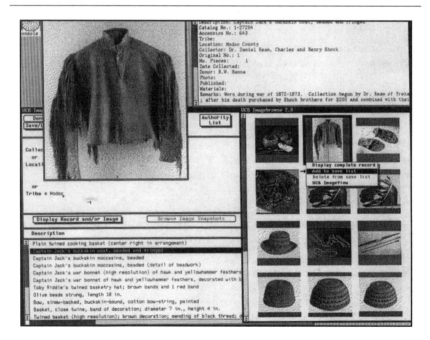

Figure 1. ImageQuery Screendump
(images courtesy of Phoebe Hearst Museum of Anthropology, UC Berkeley)

ImageQuery featured thumbnail images linked to a list of brief records for each image (see the lower-right and lower-left windows in figure 1). Clicking on an image highlighted that image as well as the related text record. Clicking on a text record highlighted the related image. This proved to be a powerful method both for finding the correct image off a list of hits and for quickly identifying an image displayed on the screen.

Each displayed thumbnail image was linked to both a full-text record and a larger version of that image. A pulldown menu (triggered by pointing to a thumbnail image and holding down a mouse button) would give the user the choice of displaying the full image or text (see menu below thumbnail of jacket in figure 1). Again this proved to be a powerful tool to link browsing to fuller information, though in today's environment, small on-screen buttons appear to be more effective than pulldown menus.

ImageQuery's architecture was modular (see figure 2). The user interface sent queries to a database that resided separately, so different databases and structures could serve as the "back-end." For a number of years, ImageQuery could only support back-end structures that had been collapsed into flat files, but eventually capabilities were added to support SQL-type queries. Another limitation of ImageQuery was that the text database structure had to be pre-identified and coded into a short preferences file rather than dynamically discovered.

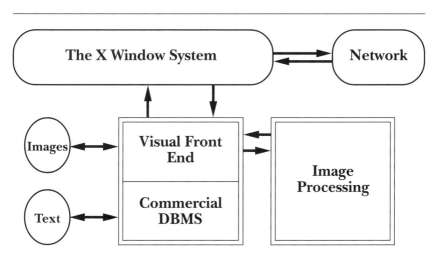

Figure 2. ImageQuery's modular structure

ImageQuery's design incorporating a separate module for text storage and retrieval is still a very powerful idea (see the author's generalized model in figure 3). This allows image database developers to leverage off technical developments in the much larger text-database market which have realized great efficiencies in indexing and retrieval. The modularity also permits external applications to easily access the text portion of the database. The ImageQuery design is part of a movement away from closed nonmodular systems toward the modularization of user interface, query structure, search and retrieval, storage, and the linking of these modules through a set of standards and protocols. This currently popular trend is apparent in the library world with the focus on the Z39.50 standard.

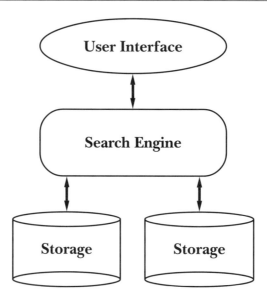

Figure 3. Generalized structural model for Image Database

ImageQuery also employed modularization to link sets of tools for users to view and process images. By pointing to an onscreen image, a user could pull down a menu and choose a variety of image processing tools that could be applied to that image. ImageQuery would then invoke software (such as paint programs for annotation or color-map programs for balancing and altering colors, or processing programs for zooming) that would allow them to analyze or alter the current image.

This idea of linking to external tools is still very important. One can expect that a variety of tools will emerge for image manipulation, for image organization, and for classroom presentation. Image database developers cannot hope to keep up with the latest developments in all these areas (particularly in areas like image processing and display which will respond quickly to software and hardware developments). By providing modular links to external software, image database developers can instead leverage off of the large image processing and consumer markets and the continuous upgrading of functionality that is likely to take place within those markets. But in order to do this effectively, the image database community needs to define standard links it will use to invoke these programs.

The ImageQuery team's idea of links to external tools was part of a broader view of what an image database should be. The team's philosophy was that (particularly in an academic environment) simply providing access to a database was not enough; developers had the responsibility to provide the user with tools to integrate the results of database retrieval into their normal work processes. This was part of a general notion then beginning to emerge within the academic community that libraries, computer centers, instructional designers, and users should be working together to build "scholars' workstations" (Rosenberg, 1985; Moran, 1987). Over the years, these ideas have been implemented in a variety of areas including the capability of downloading records from an online public access catalog into software for handling personal bibliographies and footnotes (Stigleman, 1996), or the development of templates to help instructors build instructional material incorporating images from a database (Stephenson & Ashmore, 1996). A key factor that has enabled the joining of tools to databases is the adoption of standards (Phillips, 1992).

The ImageQuery developers recognized the importance of a client-server architecture, both to assure that the image database could be accessed from a wide variety of platforms, and to put less of a strain on the server and network by off-loading some of the functionality onto client workstations. But the ImageQuery team expected that environment to be an X-Windows based environment. For many years, they waited patiently for a variety of developments over which they had no control—i.e., the porting of X-Windows onto Intel and Macintosh platforms, an increase in the installed base of X-Windows machines, and the development of the X Imaging Extensions (MIT X Consortium, 1993). No one on the ImageQuery development team anticipated the phenomenal growth in World Wide Web browsers that would clearly make this the delivery platform of choice. Web browsers not only solved the multiplatform and central database load problems, but they implemented client functionality in a much more sophisticated way than ImageQuery. Web browser helper applications recognize a variety of image file formats, handle decompression, and can spawn external viewing software (all of which combine to lessen the load on the network and the server and to increase the number of file storage options).

Another key philosophy behind ImageQuery was the implementation of a user interface that would provide a common "look and feel" across all image collections. Prior to ImageQuery, each campus object collection had its own idiosyncratic retrieval system and user interface (Besser & Snow, 1990). Users had to make a substantial investment of time to learn to use one of these retrieval systems, and most appeared reluctant to invest the time to learn a second. The ImageQuery team believed that a common user interface would encourage cross-disciplinary use of these collections, so they designed a system that, on the surface, always appeared the same to the user. Only the names and contents of fields differed from database to database, and an "authority preview" function was developed to permit users (particularly those unfamiliar with valid terms associated with a field name) to view a list of terms that had been assigned within a given field. It is likely that much of the appeal of World Wide Web browsers lies in the fact that they act as a universal interface, providing a common "look and feel" to anything they access. Though a function to preview the actual contents of a field within a database still appears powerful, this has not yet been widely implemented.

There are a number of areas in which the designs for ImageQuery look naïve in retrospect. Though the notion of interoperability still appears important, the functionality to allow searching across image databases of different objects (each having different field names and contents) is vastly more complex than the ImageQuery team anticipated (Besser & Snow, 1990; Besser, 1994b; Beauregard et al., 1994). The ImageQuery team was also naïve in dealing with the issue of scaling up. Though some thought was put into methods for decreasing storage cost and topologies which would limit the impact on a particular server or a particular segment of a network, very little thought was put into issues of how to handle queries that might retrieve thousands of initial hits. ImageQuery did provide for important functionality like visual browsing to narrow query sets (by clicking on the thumbnail images that the user wanted to save), but by itself this would not help the user whose initial query retrieved more than 100 hits. In retrospect, functions like relevancy feedback look critical to dealing with large image databases (see the section on "Retrieval" under the heading "Where Do We Need to Go from Here?").

IMPORTANT RECENT PROJECTS AND DEVELOPMENTS

The landscape today is far different from that of a decade ago. A combination of technological developments and adventurous pioneering projects has paved the way for serious image database development. In recent years, there has been such a rapid explosion in image database projects and developments that any attempt to publish an article compiling these would be outdated before it was printed. Here the author will just make brief mention of the most recent important developments; he sporadically maintains a more current list on the WorldWide Web (Besser,

1996d).

Important issues facing image databases in the recent past have been outlined elsewhere (Besser, 1995a, 1995b, 1992, 1991a; Cawkell, 1993). Guides to building image databases in environments such as cultural repositories have begun to appear (Besser & Trant, 1995). A listserv is now devoted to image database issues (ImageLib Listserv), and the same group at the University of Arizona's Library also provides a clearinghouse of image database products (*ImageLib Clearinghouse*, 1995). An online image database bibliography is also available (Besser, 1996c).

Many hundreds (probably thousands) of collections are at least partially accessible on the WorldWide Web. Photographic stock houses have begun digitizing their images, and there are now well over a dozen commercial vendors with collections of over 100,000 digital images. New competitors (such as Bill Gates's *Corbis,* Kodak's *KPX,* and Picture Network Inc's *Seymour*) are trying to market digital images to a wide variety of markets.

The Museum Educational Site Licensing Project (MESL) has given us the first serious testbed for image databases in a multisite academic environment. Images from seven museums are being distributed and deployed on seven university campuses (Museum Educational Site Licensing Project, 1996). This project is already helping to identify intellectual property issues (see Trant's paper in these Proceedings), standards and issues needed for image distribution (Besser & Stephenson, 1996), and the infrastructure and tools needed to deploy an image database in an environment with many users (Besser & Stephenson, 1996). This project will also help us understand what we will need in order to incorporate the use of image databases into the instructional environment.

The Computerized Interchange of Museum Information (CIMI) project is designed to define interchange issues for the museum environment (CIMI, 1996). Most of the work thus far has taken unstructured and database-generated textual information, that in some way relates to museum objects, and inserted SGML tags into this text so that it conforms to the structured text standard developed by the project team. CIMI's work is likely to provide keen insight into interchange issues involving images and accompanying text.

WHERE DO WE NEED TO GO FROM HERE?

A number of impediments to the widespread deployment of image databases still remain. Some of these will be solved whether or not the library and information science (LIS) communities[1] choose to participate, while others can only be solved by the LIS communities.

Impediments due to the limitations of storage capacity and cost, bandwidth, client-server functionality, and scanner capabilities will be solved without LIS participation. Storage capacity will continue to increase, storage costs will fall, network speeds will accelerate, and client-server functionality will continue to grow. Scanner throughput and reliability will increase, image capture quality (in terms of resolution, bit-depth, and fidelity) will improve, and scanner software will develop even better user interfaces and increased interoperability with image processing and other software. The driving forces behind these changes are a constituent market that is so large that the LIS community probably couldn't have much of an impact even if it tried to.

The LIS community needs to focus attention where it can play a critical role. One such key area is around issues of image longevity. The LIS community has begun to identify issues of long-term preservation and access to digital information in general. The author has participated in a task force on digital preservation issues co-sponsored by the Commission on Preservation and Access and the Research Libraries Group. This task force has put forward the notion of data migration as far superior to data refreshing and has made a variety of recommendations to assure long-term preservation and access of materials in digital form. These include the creation of certified storehouses for cultural heritage materials, development of metadata standards, and development of migration strategies (Waters et al., 1996).

The LIS community also needs to work on ensuring integrity and authenticity of digital information. The widespread use of image processing tools has led to widespread dissemination of "altered" images, particularly over the WorldWide Web. Our community needs to find ways to assure users that an image is truly what it purports to be. This is an area where it might be most promising to intervene in industry discussions about security and control over access to digital information. Security tools like digital signatures, encapsulation, and cryptography might also be adapted to ensure integrity and authenticity. Because publishers and technologists are currently experimenting and developing standards for security, it is critical that the LIS community becomes immediately involved in shaping these standards so that the standards adopted do not preclude extensions which will ensure integrity and authenticity.

Developing Standards for Images

The LIS community must also be deeply involved in development of metadata[2] standards for digital images. In March 1995, this author joined a group of other librarians and computer professionals at a meeting that began to define a core set of metadata elements for digital objects in general. Over the past year, significant work has been done on this *Dublin Core* (Weibel & Miller, 1996), and, a week after this Data Processing Clinic, a second meeting will be held in Warwick, England, to further identify and define metadata elements essential for networked digital information

(United Kingdom..., 1996). Building on this metadata work, the Coalition for Networked Information and OCLC will sponsor a meeting in September 1996 to identify metadata elements specifically relevant to images (for a report of the meeting, see Weibel & Miller, 1997).

Metadata standards for digital images are critical. Current practices for image header information are sufficient to provide most of today's applications with enough information (about file format and compression) to successfully view the image, but it is doubtful that these will be sufficient to view these images a decade from now (let alone view them a century later). Today it is difficult for applications to recognize or view documents created with the most widely used word processing program of a decade ago (Wordstar). We must take the steps necessary to ensure that digital images produced today will be viewable well into the future, and a key step in making that happen is the provision of adequate metadata.

The first set of metadata we need to define is *technical imaging information*. This is the information that applications will need in order to open the image and view it appropriately. For this we will need to include basic information about the image (dimensions and dynamic range), the scheme used to encode the image (file formats such as TIFF, GIF, JFIF, SPIFF, PICT, PCD, Photoshop, EPS, CGM, TGA, etc.), and the method used to compress it (JPEG, LZW, Quicktime, etc.). We will also need to note information about color, including the color lookup table and color metric (such as RGB or CMYK).

A second area for which we need to develop metadata standards is information about the capture process. We need to store information about what was scanned (a slide, a transparency, a photographic print, an original object), some type of scale to relate the size of the scanned image to the dimensions of the original object and/or the item scanned, and the type of light source (full spectrum or infrared). For quality control and accurate viewing, processing information (such as scanner make and model, date of scan, scanning personnel, audit trail of cropping and color adjustments, etc.) is likely to prove helpful.[3] When color management systems improve their handling of onscreen display, having information about the model of scanner used to create an image will be critical in order to view that image with appropriate color correction.

We also need to consider information about the quality and veracity of the image. Who was responsible for scanning (for certain purposes, we might need to distinguish between an image scanned by the Metropolitan Museum of Art and an image of the same object scanned by a teenager on her home scanner)? What source image was scanned (the original, a high quality transparency, or a page out of an art book)? It would also be useful to be able to recursively track the source of the image. Our communities have not yet reached a consensus on whether digital copies are equivalent to other digital copies, particularly if they differ in compression scheme, file format, resolution or bit-depth, or if one is a close-up derived from a portion of the other. We have just begun to identify the issues in image equivalency (Besser & Weise, 1995) and need to come to common agreement on vocabulary with which to discuss this (such as versions and editions). This kind of identification is also critical for us to be able to enter a new stage of networked information where we begin to identify digital information as distinct works (which may reside in multiple locations in the same or different versions) rather than the (very dangerous) current situation where we identify networked information as a particular location in the form of a URL. Separating a work from its location (though URNs and URCs) will be a critical development for networked access to information in the next few years.

Another critical factor involving veracity is to develop ways of assuring that the image is indeed what the metadata contends that it is. Today many images on the World Wide Web purport to be what they are not (Besser, 1996a). As mentioned earlier, systems for data encryption, encapsulation, and digital signatures need to be adapted so that they can help assure authenticity and veracity of images.

The final area that will be important is information about rights and reproduction of the image. It would be advantageous for metadata to note basic information such as use restrictions related to viewing, printing, reproducing, etc. Contact information for the rights holder should also be included. Some of this information should be stored where it cannot be separated from the image (i.e., in the header or footer), while some of the information should be stored where it can easily be accessed by a retrieval program (i.e., in an external database). Because each derivative of an image inherits rights restrictions from its parent but may also convey certain rights to the derivative creator, the rights metadata for a given image might be complex (including a separate set of restrictions on the original, a photographic copy, and a scan of that photographic copy).

Much work still needs to be done in refining each of these areas of image standards. The constituent communities (LIS, commercial imaging, networked information) need to come to some common agreement about these standards. They need to agree on what types of information must be placed in the image header (where it is less likely to become disassociated with the image), what types of information should be placed in an accompanying text record, and what information should be duplicated in both. For each piece of this metadata, these communities must identify a field in which to house it and define a set of controlled vocabulary or rules for filling in that field. Wherever possible, these communities should adapt existing standards to incorporate the needs of images. In some areas, we will have to work with other bodies to make sure the standards they adopt will incorporate our needs, and in other areas we will have to set the standards ourselves. And in many cases we will have to follow the standard-adoption cycle with a strong public relations campaign in order to convince application vendors to implement the standard we adopt.

Image Quality

Because we are still constrained by the technological limitations of storage and bandwidth, we clearly have to separate the issue of the quality of image we capture and save versus the quality of image we choose to deliver today. It is certainly possible (and perhaps preferable) to capture an image at a higher quality than we can afford to deliver, and derive a lower-quality image that we will deliver today. Then, as our technological capabilities improve, we can go back to those stored images and derive better-quality ones (without having to repeat the more costly step of image capture).

We still know very little about image quality needs. In the area of cultural heritage, there has only been one set of serious studies examining the quality of image we need to provide to users (Ester, 1990, 1994). This set of studies (by the Getty Art History Information Program [AHIP]) had a small population, studied a small set of images, and did not examine the effects of compression. But the methodology of this set of studies (identification of the points at which users could not discern differences in image quality, plotting these on discernability/cost axis, and suggesting that delivery systems should choose the quality at the beginning of the various flat points on the curve) is very sound and should prove useful for further studies.

We must be careful not to let the perceptions of our current users affect our long-term custodianship over digital images. We know that users' perception of image quality changes over time and is shaped by the quality of the images they see in their daily lives. In the early 1950s, a grainy 6-bit image on a screen would have looked excellent to a viewer accustomed to black and white television. A decade ago, 8-bit images were really impressive; today they look inferior to people who have 24-bit display capabilities. If high-definition television (HDTV) comes into widespread use, the average person's idea of what constitutes a quality image will again change significantly.

It is perhaps more relevant to seriously explore the use that is made of images in particular domains. In some domains, it will be important for digital images to preserve some of the artifactual nature of the object (such as the paper grain on a manuscript page), while in other domains it will only be important to preserve the information content of the object (such as the words on a page). We need a better understanding of these differences.

We need many more studies like those done at the Getty Art History Information Program, stratified by user type (undergraduate student, faculty researcher, curator, research scientist), domain (art history, archeology, coronary medicine, astronomy), and type of object represented by the image (painting, pottery, X-ray). This will give us some guidance as to the level of image quality we need to deliver to current users. And we need to use what we learn from such studies to distinguish among different classes of purposes for image digitization (preservation, scholarly research, consumer access, etc.).

Retrieval

Because most collections of images have very little textual information already accompanying them, our traditional means of retrieval cannot easily be applied to images (Besser & Snow, 1990). Museums, which collectively house one of the largest bodies of images that do have accompanying text, often assign terms to an image which are not at all helpful to the average layperson. Vocabulary for scientists, art historians, and doctors appears foreign to the average user searching for images.

Few collections anywhere in the world provide item-level access to images using terminology that is useful to the average person or to anyone outside the very narrow domain for which access was designed. While most collections wish to expand their usefulness to other "markets," very few will be able to afford the cost of assigning terms to each individual image within their collections. Two methods for dealing with this appear to hold promise: user-assigned terminology and content-based retrieval.

If we can develop systems for user-assigned terminology, collection managers can rely upon users to assign terms or keywords to individual images. Under such a system, when a user finds an image, the system would ask them what words they might have used to search for this image. Those words are then entered into the retrieval system, and subsequent users searching on these words will find the image. As the number of people using such a system grows, so do the number of access points for many of the images.

It is essential that such systems allow searches against officially-assigned terms both independently of user-contributed terms and in conjunction with them. We can expect two types of searches: one that only looks at terms assigned by catalogers, and the other that looks at both cataloger-assigned terms and at user-assigned terms.[4] Systems like this will also be able to serve as aids to catalogers. One can envision a system where periodically user-contributed terms will be "upgraded" to officially assigned terms by a cataloger (and will then be retrievable by both methods).

As systems like this grow, future users may want to limit their searches to terms assigned by people who they trust (perhaps because they come from the same field, or because they assign terms more reliably). So these systems will likely develop both a searchable "ownership" feature for each term assigned and a "confidence level" that a user can set which applies to a group of owners. Design of systems like this will also have to be sensitive to the privacy of term contributors. Users setting confidence levels for term-assigners may locate these people through basic profiles of their subject expertise and position (but not name), or they may locate them by finding correlations between other term-assigners and how the user him/herself assigns terms to other images (as incorporated in current systems such as *Firefly*).

User-assigned terms are likely to be part of a broader trend that will affect collection access. As resources for cataloging diminish while digitally based material becomes more available, collection managers will begin to rely more heavily upon input from their users. Recently, a professor at the University of Virginia[5] has been contributing information to the Fowler Museum in Los Angeles about the objects pictured in the digital image he is using through the Museum Educational Site Licensing Project. We will have to develop feedback mechanisms to channel information from scholars back into the collections and collection records.

In the past, we have maintained that image-browsing functions will help overcome some of the problems associated with the paucity of associated text (Besser, 1990). But recent breakthroughs in content-based retrieval hold the promise of even more far-reaching effects. Content-based retrieval systems such as Virage, UC Berkeley's Cypress (see discussions of both systems in other papers in these Proceedings), and IBM's QBIC offer users the opportunity to ask the system to "find more images like this one." The two critical pieces to content-based retrieval are *image extraction* (the system's capability of automatically finding colors, shapes, texture, or objects within an image) and *relevance* (the capability to retrieve images in a ranked order in relation to attributes identified [usually as part of the extraction process]).

Currently, some content-based retrieval systems are extending relevance feedback functions to incorporate existing text records in addition to image features, and this will prove to be a very powerful tool for image retrieval. In the coming years, these systems will also need to adapt their measures of similarity to work differently for various user populations (e.g., the meaning of similarity in color or texture may be different for a graphic designer than for an art historian).

Other Issues

In the future, we can expect the emergence of new types of user interfaces. Virtual reality techniques will provide new ways of seeing and navigating through a body of information and provide us with new metaphors for relating to that information.

Another key issue will be the development of analytical tools to view, recombine, and manipulate images. As was explained in the earlier section on ImageQuery, software and learning materials to manipulate images are critical parts in building a Scholar's Workstation. Tools like Mark Handel's (1996) CLens (which lets a user move a digital magnifying glass over an image and move through different registered images [such as infrared or radiograph versions]) and Christie Stephenson and Lara Ashmore's (1996) templates (to help instructors create instructional exercises using images) are critical parts in making image databases useful as more than mere retrieval tools.

A final critical issue is that of scalability. No one has yet built a very large highly used image database. Though we can identify key issues that we know will cause problems (such as how to handle queries that retrieve thousands of hits, or how to migrate images between primary, secondary, and tertiary storage), we really don't know how various architectures and functions will scale up.

CONCLUSION

From reviewing the past, it should be clear that what seem like insurmountable technological impediments can disappear in just a decade. From this we should learn not to let current impediments distract us from seriously moving toward the implementation of image databases for the future. Thinking about how today's impediments might be viewed a decade from now might help us move toward that future without being saddled with the limitations imposed by today's technologies.

This paper has outlined some immediate steps that must be taken in order to move forward. We must move from constructing a *collection* of discrete images to building a library of material that inter-relates and inter-operates. The digital library of the future will not simply be a collection of discrete objects but will also provide the tools for analyzing, combining, and repurposing the objects. Digital objects housed in a library will become the raw material used to shape still newer information objects. Builders of image databases must develop a broad vision that goes beyond merely capturing and storing a discrete set of digital images.

ACKNOWLEDGMENTS

Discussions with Christie Stephenson helped expand upon a number of points in this paper. Clifford Lynch, Cecilia Preston, and Janet Vratney helped identify the technical state of the art in 1986. Steve Jacobson, Randy Ballew, and Ken Lindahl wrote the code for ImageQuery. Maria Bonn provided editorial assistance.

NOTES

[1] For the purpose of this discussion, what we call the "LIS community" consists of a number of different traditional communities: library, information science, cultural heritage, and the general academic communities.

[2] Metadata are "data about data." A cataloging record and a bibliographic citation are both metadata for a book.

[3] At some point in the future, a repository may discover that a particular scanning staff member was color blind to orange or that a scanning device lost its blue sensitivity. This information will help identify (and possibly even restore) problem images.

[4] This is similar to many OPACs today which permit subject searches against cataloger-assigned subject terms but also allow keyword searches which run against words in a number of fields (including Subject).

[5] Benjamin C. Ray of the Religious Studies department. The Fowler Museum does not currently have a curator to cover this domain, and in some ways Ray is effectively acting as a remote curator for them.

REFERENCES

Beauregard, L.; Bissonnette, L.; & Silverman, J. (1994). *Report on Collections and Library Authorities Databases Mapping Project.* Montréal, Quebec, Canada: Centre Canadien d'Architecture, 1993-11-10 (unpublished internal document).

Besser, H. (1987a). Digital images for museums. *Museum Studies Journal, 3*(1), 74-81.

Besser, H. (1987b). The changing museum. In C-c Chen (Ed.), *Information: The transformation of society* (Proceedings of the 50th Annual Meeting of the American Society for Information Science) (pp. 14-19). Medford, NJ: Learned Information, Inc.

Besser, H. (1987c). Computers for art analysis. In R. A. Braden et al. (Eds.), *Visible & viable: The role of images in instruction & communication* (Readings from the 18th Annual Conference of the International Visual Literacy Association). Blacksburg, VA: IVLA.

Besser, H. (1988a). Image processing integrated into a database for photographic images: Applications in art, architecture, and geography. In *Electronic imaging '88,* vol. 2 (Advanced Paper Summaries). Waltham, MA: Institute for Graphic Communication.

Besser, H. (1988b). Adding analysis tools to image databases: Facilitating research in geography & art history. *Proceedings of RIAO, 88*(2), 972-990.

Besser, H. (1990). Visual access to visual images: The UC Berkeley Image Database Project. *Library Trends, 38*(4), 787-798.

Besser, H. (1991a). Advanced applications of imaging: Fine arts. *Journal of the American Society for Information Science, 42*(8), 589-596.

Besser, H. (1991b). User interfaces for museums. *Visual Resources, 7,* 293-309.

Besser, H. (1992). Adding an image database to an existing library and computer environment: Design and technical considerations. In S. Stone & M. Buckland (Eds.), *Studies in multimedia* (Proceedings of the 1991 Mid-Year Meeting of the American Society for Information Science) (pp. 31-45). Medford, NJ: Learned Information, Inc.

Besser, H. (1994a). Image databases. In *Encyclopedia of Library and Information Sciences* (vol. 53, pp. 1-15). New York: Marcel Dekker.

Besser, H. (1994b). *RFP for library information systems for the Canadian Centre for Architecture, Montréal* (unpublished document). Montréal, Quebec, Canada: Centre Canadien d'Architecture.

Besser, H. (1995a). Image databases update: Issues facing the field, resources, and projects. In M. King (Ed.), Going digital: Electronic images in the library catalog and beyond (pp. 29-34). Chicago, IL: Library Information Technology Association.

Besser, H. (1995b). Image databases. *Database, 18*(2), 12-19.

Besser, H. (1996a). *Ethics and images on the net* (World Wide Web site). Available from: <http://sunsite.berkeley.edu/Imaging/Databases/Ethics>

Besser, H. (1996b). *Homepage* (World Wide Web site). Available from: <http://www.sims.berkeley.edu/~howard>

Besser, H. (1996c). *Image Database Bibliography* (WorldWide Web site). Available from: <*http://sunsite.berkeley.edu/Imaging/Databases/Bibliography*>.

Besser, H. (1996d). *Image Database Resources* (WorldWide Web site). Available from: <*http://sunsite.berkeley.edu/Imaging/Databases/*>.

Besser, H., & Snow, M. (1990). Access to diverse collections in university settings: The Berkeley dilemma. In T. Petersen & P. Moholt (Eds.), *Beyond the book: Extending MARC for subject access* (pp. 203-224). Boston, MA: G. K. Hall.

Besser, H., & Stephenson, C. (forthcoming). The Museum Educational Site Licensing Project: Technical issues in the distribution of museum images and textual data to universities. In *Proceedings of the 1996 Electronic Imaging and the Visual Arts Conference*, Fleet. Hampshire, England: Vasari Enterprises.

Besser, H., & Trant, J. (1995). *Introduction to imaging: Issues in constructing an image database.* Santa Monica, CA: Getty Art History Information Program. Available from: *http://www.ahip.getty.edu/intro_imaging/home.html*

Besser, H., & Weise, J. (1995). Don't I already have that image? *Issues in Equivalency of Digital Images* (unpublished paper).

Cawkell, A. E. (1993). Developments in indexing picture collections. *Information Services and Use, 13*(4), 381-388.

Consortium for the Computer Interchange of Museum Information. (1996). World Wide Web Site. Available from: <*http://www.cimi.org*>.

Ester, M. (1990). Image quality and viewer perception. *Leonardo, 23*(1), 51-63.

Ester, M. (1994). Digital images in the context of visual collections and scholarship. *Visual Resources, 10*(1), 11-24.

Handel, M. (1996). *CLens* (Java Applet). Available from: <*http://www.si.umich.edu/~handel/java/Lens/*>.

ImageLib Clearinghouse. (1995). (WorldWide Web site). Available from: <*http://www.library.arizona.edu/images/image_projects.html*>.

Lynch, C. A., & Brownrigg, E. (1986). Conservation, preservation & digitization. *College & Research Libraries, 47*, 379-382.

MIT X Consortium. (1993). *X Image Extensions Protocol Reference Manual* (version 4.1.2). *The X Resource: A practical journal of the X window system* (Special Issue C, January). (O'Reilly & Associates).

Moran, B. (1987). The electronic campus: The impact of the scholar's workstation project on the libraries at Brown. *College & Research Libraries, 48*(1), 5-16.

Museum Educational Site Licensing Project. (1996). *Homepage* (WorldWide Web site). Available from: <*http://www.ahip.getty.edu/mesl*>.

Phillips, G. L. (1992). Z39.50 and the scholar's workstation concept. *Information Technology and Libraries, 11*(3), 261-270

Rosenberg, V. (1985). The scholar's workstation. *College & Research Libraries News, 10*(November), 546-549.

Stephenson, C., & Ashmore, L. (1996). *Examples [using MESL images to teach Art History].* (WorldWide Web site). Available from: <*http://jefferson.village.virginia.edu/uvamesl/example_projects/home.html*>.

Stigleman, S. (1996). Bibliography programs do Windows. *Database, 19*(2), 57-66.

United Kingdom Office for Library & Information Networking and OCLC Online Computer Library Center (organizers). (1996). *Metadata Workshop II* (April 1-3, 1996, University of Warwick, England). Available from: <*http://www.purl.org/OCLC/RSCH/MetadataII/*>

Waters, D., et al. (1996). *Preserving digital information: Report of the task force on archiving of digital information.* Washington, DC: Commission on Preservation & Access. Available from: <*http://www.rlg.org./ArchTF/*>

Weibel, S., & Miller, E. (1996). *The Dublin Core Metadata Element Set Home Page.* Available from: <*http://www.purl.org/metadata/dublin_core*>.

Weibel, S., & Miller, E. (1997). Image description on the Internet: A summary of the CNI/OCLC Image Metadata Workshop, September 24-25, 1996, Dublin, Ohio. *D-Lib Magazine*, January. Available from: <*http://www.dlib.org/dlib/january97/oclc/01weibel.html*>.

J. TRANT

Exploring New Models for Administering Intellectual Property: The Museum Educational Site Licensing Project

Research and teaching in the university would benefit if high-quality museum images and associated information could be made available over campus networks for educational purposes. For this to be possible, however, museums and educational institutions need to define a common framework for information collection, distribution, and use, that respects intellectual property rights. The Museum Educational Site Licensing (MESL) Project has brought museums and universities together to explore these administratvie, legal, and technical issues.

INTRODUCTION

The museum and educational communities have seen the potential for digital imaging and network technologies to make cultural heritage information more broadly accessible. However, the integration of museum digital content into higher education has been hampered by a lack of progress on the definition and administration of intellectual property rights. By their nature, imaging systems require a complex balancing of the interests of numerous rights holders in protecting their intellectual property and the desires of image users to use images in their studies, teaching, and research. A common understanding of rights, permissions, and restrictions and a shared framework for administering rights reflecting broadly accepted terms and conditions for the use of materials would ease the burden of honoring intellectual property rights and enable the educational use of digital materials.

The Museum Educational Site Licensing Project (MESL) brings representative U.S. museums, colleges, and universities together to explore these issues. Their goal is to define the terms and conditions for educational use of museums' digital images and information on campus-wide networks. During this two-year experiment (launched in 1995 by the Getty Art History Information Program {now the Getty Information Institute] in conjunction with MUSE Educational Media), a select group of educational and collecting institutions are collaborating in good faith to study the capture, distribution, and educational use of digital images and their associated texts.

J. TRANT

The partners in the MESL project are developing and testing administrative, technical, and legal mechanisms that could eventually make it possible to deliver large quantities of high-quality museum images and information to all educational institutions. Participants are drafting a model site licensing agreement, exploring models for the collective administration of intellectual property rights, and studying the economics of image creation and network distribution. The project has also provided a vehicle for exploring and promoting the educational benefits of digital access to museum collections through campus networks.

This discussion reports on the first eighteen months of activity in the MESL project (January 1995-June 1996) offering both some preliminary impressions of the participants' experiences to date and an assessment of the issues the project faces in its second year of activity.

INTELLECTUAL PROPERTY RIGHTS IN DIGITAL IMAGES

Uncertainty regarding intellectual property rights has been a barrier in the creation of networked information resources for some time.[1] This problem is exacerbated when visual resources are concerned for a number of reasons. First, the rights in digital images are often multilayered and complex. Simply determining who holds the rights in a particular work is often difficult. This problem is exacerbated when the digitization of existing visual resource collections is contemplated, because these collections have been constructed over time and often lack detailed information about the sources of images. Second, existing rights administration systems are inefficient at best. We are without a comprehensive service that offers rights to museum images. As a result, a disproportionate amount of time and effort is expended in the information location and rights-negotiation process. Third, the legal framework has yet to respond to the changes in technology. A solution to these conundrums is unlikely to come from the legislative arena, as the law is by nature responsive and conservative; a consensus on these issues, which is satisfactory to lawmakers and lobby groups alike, is unlikely to emerge in the short term.

WHICH IMAGE? WHOSE RIGHTS?

Basic picture research has always been one of the primary research challenges in disciplines that depend on the visual as a primary information source. Simply locating works of art that may have passed from private collection to private collection or are held, but uncataloged, in a public collection is a specialist task, requiring much ingenuity and not a small amount of serendipity or sometimes blind luck. Much specialist knowledge is required to negotiate the vast number of information sources to identify the particular images that are relevant to a specific line of inquiry. A large proportion of research is based on the construction of the corpus of a particular creator—the *catalogue raisonnée*. There is still no union catalog or finding aid which indexes available images. Much picture research involves separately contacting numerous institutional collections and requires much expert knowledge to identify appropriate visual resources. Many sources go unnoticed, and a disproportionate amount of time and effort is expended in this information location stage.

Once an image has been found, gaining the rights to use it in a publication or multimedia project is an equally complex task. Much of the confusion regarding intellectual property rights in visual images arises from the many ways that they are created and the many sources for images in educational institutions' collections.[2] Digitizing and using digital images for educational purposes requires an analysis of all the rights connected with each image. Determining the rights inherent in an image requires an understanding of the source of the image, the content portrayed, and the nature of the image (whether it is an original visual image or a reproduction).

Visual images can be original works themselves, they can be reproductions of other copyrighted works or, if a reproduction includes original elements, they can be both. Often a digital image is many "generations" removed from the original work that it reproduces. For example, a digital image may have been scanned from a slide, that was copied from a published book, that printed a photographic transparency, that reproduced an original work of art. Each stage of reproduction in this chain may involve an additional layer of rights. The rights in each of these images may be held by different rightsholders; obtaining rights to one does not automatically grant rights to use another. Existing visual resource collections are comprised of many types of images, each with particular rights or layers of associated rights. Digitizing such a collection requires a commitment to the identification of rightsholders and the negotiation of rights to convert an image into digital form.

Figure 1 offers a schematized (and simplified) representation of the sources for digital images.

An *original visual image* can be defined as a work of art or an original work of authorship (or part of a work) fixed in a visual medium. Original visual images may be in digital or analog form. Examples of original visual images include graphic, photographic, sculptural, and architectural works as well as stills from motion pictures or other audiovisual works. The rights in an original visual image are defined in Section 106 of the U.S. Copyright Act as the right to reproduce the work, to prepare derivative works based on it, to distribute copies of the work, to perform the work, and to display it in public.[3]

A *reproduction* can be defined as a copy, in digital or analog form, of an original visual image. The most common forms of reproductions are photographic, including for example, prints, 35 mm slides, and color transparencies. If a reproduction is legally made (i.e., with the permission of the rightsholder in the original work) and includes copyrightable elements, it can be eligible for its own copyright protection, which must be considered in addition to the rights inherent in the original visual image.[4] The original visual image shown in a reproduction is often referred to as the "underlying work." Many digital images reproduce other works. Digital images can be reproductions of either original visual images—e.g., when an original work is scanned directly—or of other reproductions—e.g., when a scan is made from a transparency reproducing a work of art.

A *published reproduction* is a reproduction of an original visual image appearing in a publication. Examples of published reproductions include a plate in an exhibition catalog that reproduces a work of art or a digital image appearing on a CD-ROM. Separate copyrights may exist in the publication, the reproduction, and the original visual image.

In some cases, such as copystand photography, a published reproduction may have been further reproduced, creating a *copy of a published reproduction*. As these types of copies are often mechanical in nature, they may not be copyrightable in themselves. However, rights in the original visual image, the reproduction, and the publication must still be considered.

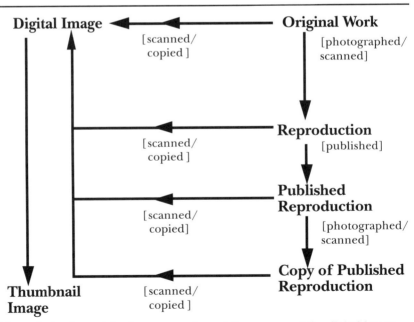

Figure 1. A schematicized representation of the sources of the digital image

In this example, a *digital image* is a single still image stored in binary code—i.e., bits and bytes. Examples of digital images include bit-mapped images (encoded as a series of bits and bytes each representing a particular pixel or part of the image) and vector graphics (encoded as equations and/or algorithms representing lines and curves). A digital image can be an original visual image, a reproduction, a published reproduction, or a copy of a published reproduction; determining in what manner a digital image was created will determine the rights associated with it.

A *thumbnail image* is a small-scale reproduction of a digital image, often used in an online catalog or image browsing display to enable identification of an original visual image. Thumbnail images are of low resolution and quality (often averaging between 100 x 100 to 256 x 256 pixels) and are considered to be of limited commercial or reproductive value. While there are still rights associated with thumbnail images, they are often distributed more freely than higher quality images as a visual reference to the original work and as a marketing tool.

Visual resource collections in educational institutions often number tens of thousands of images, generally photographic slides, which may be original visual images, reproductions, published reproductions, or copies of published reproductions. The images in visual resource collections have been acquired from a wide variety of sources—i.e., by purchase, donation, or through copy-photography or original photography. Collections have been built over an extended period of time, and it is often impossible to trace the sources of images acquired by purchase in the past or to identify if a work is indeed still available in order to negotiate rights. This complexity makes the conversion of existing visual resource collections into digital form problematic.

Even if it is possible to identify who holds the intellectual property rights to an image, locating that rightsholder may be a very difficult task and negotiating the rights an arduous process. Within museums, rights administration procedures are now based on a print model of publication and distribution and are focused on the single image. Each image often requires a separate request with its own forms and permissions to negotiate. Museums are without a single fee scale, and the fees that are charged are also based on the print model. What may have seemed reasonable for a high quality art book containing at the most fifty images seems unreasonable for a multimedia publication containing ten times that many images.[5] In addition, each museum has defined its own terms and conditions under which an image can be used. As a result, a content user has to negotiate (and renegotiate) with many separate institutions in order to build up an archive of usable content. This redundancy adds a level of overhead to the rights acquisition process which impedes the use of large numbers of images and may serve as a deterrent to the negotiation of rights to use images.[6]

DIGITIZATION OF COLLECTIONS

These restrictive forces are in clear opposition to an increased demand for multimedia content in the educational community. Experiments in using new technologies are maturing to become new tools for providing increased access to research resources. Where in the past, for example, undergraduate art history students were unable to use institutional slide libraries for review after class, collections of digital images made available online enable consultation both on- and off-site at a time convenient to the student.

The creation of digital image collections in a systematic and uniform way offers a real benefit to the educational and research community, enabling the creation of teaching resources to support the curriculum and providing a source of quality content to support the integration of new technology into teaching and research. However, the digital conversion of existing slide collections is not necessarily an ideal solution. Slides may be of uncertain age or many generations removed from the original work and therefore of limited quality. Rights in the original visual images and their reproductions may be uncertain and their use restricted. In addition, documentation may be incomplete. The ability to acquire quality digital images from a reliable source, accompanied by authoritative textual descriptions, would be of significant value to the educational community.

MUSEUM/UNIVERSITY COLLABORATION

The Museum Educational Site Licensing (MESL) Project was established to respond to the need for educational access to high quality rights-cleared museum images and accompanying texts. The project brings museums (as information providers) and universities (as information users) together to define the terms and conditions for the educational use of digital resources drawn from museum collections. It is exploring an alternative method for distributing digital content drawn from museum collections to the educational market.

Museums are in a position to offer the educational community a quality information package of text and image—in effect a multimedia description and analysis of the works of art in their collections. Under appropriate licensing terms, it would be possible to make this depth of knowledge about museum collections available for research and teaching. What is required is a contractual arrangement under which museums could supply content to educational institutions at predictable terms and for a reasonable cost.

Bringing the information providers and the information users together to prototype a licensing agreement also offers a means to address the uncertainty of the legal framework. Rather than having to rely on the courts to define the application of old laws to new technology, both parties can negotiate a mutually beneficial licensing agreement. The terms and conditions for this license are being established through experimentation, entered into in a good-faith spirit of cooperation, and that will result in a contractual agreement that meets the needs of both sides.

Museums and universities have been ideal partners in this experiment. In addition to the obvious attraction—i.e., that museums have content that universities want—there are other factors that have contributed to the success of the MESL experiment. Both share a common culture of teaching and learning. This common focus has enabled the definition of licensing terms that enable a full range of educational uses. In addition, museums and universities are both information users and information providers. Museums often engage in research that requires the consultation and use of images in other collections; universities hold collections of unique materials in their libraries' special collections and in campus museums. This duality has enabled the negotiation process, as participants have been able to see issues from both sides.

The participants in the MESL project were selected in a competitive call for participation issued in the fall of 1994. Fourteen participating institutions[7] (seven universities, and seven museums or collecting institutions) were chosen to represent a broad range of sizes and governance structures. Technological experience was also highly ranked, as it was seen as an essential precondition for full project participation. Each institution has fielded an interdisciplinary project team: museum teams include members from the curatorial, registration, photo services, and administration departments along with the museum library and research centers; university teams include faculty, instructional technology, library, and campus computing and administration representatives.[8] The project is managed by the Getty Art History Information Program and advised by a management committee.[9]

Between January 1995 and June 1997, MESL participants will focus their attention on defining the terms and conditions for the educational use of museum digital content and exploring appropriate technical and administrative mechanisms for enabling the distribution of high quality information. This will require the balancing of the requirements of rights holders and rights users and addressing a number of technological and pedagogical challenges.

NEEDS OF RIGHTS HOLDERS AND RIGHTS USERS

As information providers and rights holders, museums' paramount concern is maintaining the integrity of the original works of art that they preserve and interpret in trust. A distribution system must, therefore, ensure the accuracy of the information distributed and provide adequate protection from alteration or unauthorized copying. It must also acknowledge both the artist and the collection and offer some sort of remuneration for the intellectual property created by the museum.

As information users, universities require easy access to a large body of high quality material from a central or coordinated source. Materials should be predictably high quality and available under a reasonable fee structure, according to common terms and conditions, regardless of source. High administrative overheads and processing costs should be avoided, and the materials licensed should be of uniform quality.

ADMINISTERING INTELLECTUAL PROPERTY RIGHTS

An effective and efficient system of administering intellectual property rights is key to the development of educational use of museum digital content. Establishing such a system depends on the definition of a set of standard terms and conditions for the use of quantities of material, the development of equitable pricing models, and the creation of a framework within which it is possible to negotiate rights efficiently.

Traditionally, rights are assigned by holding individuals or institutions for the specific use of a particular work.[10] This kind of licensing, focused on the individual item, is difficult to adapt to the in-depth research requirements of higher education, where access to a broad range of material is essential and depth of content may be as critical as access to a particular work. MESL is exploring a model whereby museums offer *collections* of material to universities under a single site license. A range of digital images and information from museum collections is made available under the same terms for use by all members of a campus community.

Many pricing structures and systems being developed to support digital commerce are premised on a "pay-per-bit" or "pay-per-view model." This type of transaction-based pricing did not fit well with the educational goals of the MESL project. It was feared that per-use charges would inhibit access and discourage the exploration of a new kind of information. In addition, participants did not have the monitoring systems in place that would be required to gather individual usage statistics. Finally, as we were introducing a new resource to the campus community, it seemed impossible to predict usage levels and therefore derive realistic pricing models.[11] The pricing model that MESL is exploring is based on a *subscription*—a predictable fee paid for unlimited use of a defined information set.

There are a number of models for the administration of license terms and fees, each with its own pros and cons. These can be characterized as:

1. **The rights holder's collective model.** A collective body acts for rights holders and represents their interests to copyright users. Often a standard set of terms and conditions with a single fee scale is applied, regardless of the information supplier or user. Examples of this type of organization include the Copyright Clearance Center (CCC) that acts for publishers, and the American Society of Media Photographers (ASMP) that represents photographers.

2. **The brokerage model.** A third party administers rights for a fee, which is often charged as a percentage of the license fee negotiated for the use of intellectual property. The terms of each transaction may vary. Examples include Picture Network International (PNI) or the Kodak Picture Exchange (KPX).

3. **The rights reseller model.** A third party acquires rights and then resells them, with or without consulting the original rights holder. Examples include Corbis Media and stock photo agencies.

4. **The consortium model.** A membership organization, such as Research Libraries Group (RLG), agrees to exchange information for mutual benefit.

5. **The locator service model.** Not truly a rights administering body, a locator service acts as a finding agency, passing requests through to rights holders, which define the terms and conditions of use and negotiate licenses individually. An example includes Academic Press's planned Image Directory (ID) service.

Each of these administrative models has pros and cons, often trading simplicity in administrative structure for flexibility in licensing terms. MESL participants are examining these models to see which would best serve the needs of museums and universities and best satisfy the requirements for integrated information location and intellectual property rights acquisition services. Any organization founded on one of these models would also have to resolve the legal terms of the license agreement and the technical framework for information collection and distribution.

MESL PROGRESS TO DATE

The participants in MESL adopted an experimental methodology to explore the issues of licensing museum digital intellectual property for educational purposes. Over the course of the two-year project, the participating collecting institutions agreed to make a significant number of images from their collections available for educational use on the campus networks of the participating educational institutions. This allowed the project participants to gain real experience with the technical issues associated with the digital distribution of museum information and to develop a framework of use within which to define and test the terms of a model site-license agreement.

LICENSING AGREEMENT

As a basis for their collaboration, all participating MESL institutions signed a cooperative agreement.[12] This document outlined the goals of the experiment and defined the responsibilities of each participant. It also outlined the terms and conditions for the use of museum information on campus networks—i.e., the first draft of the terms and conditions of a site license.

MESL institutions desired to fashion terms that would enable the broadest possible use of museum digital intellectual property within the educational context, but which protected the investment museums have made in its creation. MESL information may be distributed over the campus network for *educational use* only, including research, teaching, and student projects. Any commercial use or redistribution beyond the bounds of the campus is not permitted.

In the next year, the cooperative agreement will be rewritten as a set of model site-license terms.[13] These will address the use of museum information for educational purposes but will not define the legal framework for a licensing body or the technical framework for information collection and distribution.[14]

INFORMATION COLLECTION AND DISTRIBUTION

Each MESL collecting institution agreed to make at least 1,000 images and associated information available to the educational participants over the course of the project. Images were supplied in as high a quality as the participating museum was comfortable releasing and in the file format they had available. Text was reformatted according to a project-defined data dictionary.[15] This information was collected by the University of Michigan, duplicated, and distributed to participating educational institutions.[16] Each university then made its own decisions regarding deployment of that data on its campus network.

This strategy acknowledged the diverse nature of the technological infrastructures on each of the participating university campuses. By separating the content from the deployment systems, it has been possible to leverage the investments already made on each of the campuses. This also acknowledges the heterogeneous nature of the participating insitutions and the difficulty of developing consensus on a common deployment strategy at the outset of the project.

USE OF MUSEUM INFORMATION

From its outset the MESL project has encouraged the broadest possible use of the information made available. As well as supporting teaching and research in Humanities disciplines (including art history, history, anthropology, cultural and religious studies), museum information has been used in multimedia development, (including communications and interface design analysis), and information and computer science (including research into image database access, image description, search and retrieval, and image processing). For example, in the first year of the project MESL images have also been used in joint studio and art history projects at the University of Maryland, a Religious Studies course at the University of Virginia, an Information Science course at the University of Michigan, a history of Photography course at the University of Illinois, an Art History course at American University, and the Art Humanities course required for all undergraduates at Columbia University.

EVALUATION

The second year of the MESL project will focus on evaluating and documenting the experience of making over 8000 museum images available on campus networks. This will include profiling the distribution systems developed on each of the campuses, assessing the interface choices and delivery options made in each MESL implementation, gathering statistics about use, conducting a study of the benefits of the availability of the information and working with faculty and students to assess the impact of integrating new technologies into the curriculum.

The distribution system will also be documented, and a report developed which offers recommendations regarding technical standards and requirements based on the MESL experience, and outlines areas for future exploration. The impact of the project on museum documentation procedures will also be studied, and requirements for information export from collections documentation systems defined. The Andrew W. Mellon Foundation has also funded a study of the economics of the distribution of visual information which will use the MESL project as a case study, and examine the costs and benefits of the introduction of new technologies to manage visual resource collections.

These evaluative reports will provide a clear statement of the costs and benefits of introducing digital museum informaiton into the educational community.

CONCLUSION

There are many potential benefits for research and teaching if high-quality museum images and associated information can be made over campus networks for educational purposes. For this to be possible, however, museums and educational institutions need to define a common framework for information collection, distribution and use. The MESL project has brought together museums and universities to explore the administrative, legal and technical issues underlying the development of a new model for the distribution of museum intellectual property for educational use. In the first eighteen months of the project, through the experimental distribution of over 8,000 museum images and associated information, MESL participants have demonstrated both the feasibility and the desirability of such an alliance. In the project's second year, this experience will be codified and reported, and the results shared.

The success of the Museum Educational Site Licensing Project has been built upon the contributions and enthusiasm of its participants. Project teams have actively embraced the challenges that developing a new distribution model has placed on their technical infrastructures, reassessed conceptions of information distribution and licensing, and redesigned curriculum to take advantage of new resources. As a result, the students in MESL institutions have had an unprecedented opportunity to explore, in depth, parts of the collections of significant U.S. museums. This glimpse of the potential for new technology to bring knowledge and appreciation of cultural heritage to a new generation whose interest is essential for its preservation, it is in itself justification for the struggle to redefine our methods of providing access to collection, and should provide sufficient motivation for both museums and universities to face the challenges of redefining their traditional approaches to the negotiation of intellectual property rights.[17]

NOTES

[1] The participants in the meeting which launched the Getty AHIP Imaging Initiative urgently expressed this: "Imaging and copyright issues are on a collision course" states the report of their discussions (*Initiative on Electronic Imaging and Information Standards*, Meeting Report, Getty Art History Information Program [AHIP] March 3-4, 1994).

[2] This section is based on discussions and draft texts of the *Guidelines for the Fair Use of Visual Image Archives* developed by the Image Archives, working group of the Committee on Fair Use (CONFU). I have been an active participant in these discussions and have drafted portions of that text. I would like to thank other participants in that process, particularly Mary Levering of the U.S. Copyright Office, for their contribution to my understanding of these issues. The rights defined for each of these image types are those which apply under U.S. law. While the issues are similar in other legal jurisdictions, the legal framework and the nature of the rights assigned by copyright and other intellectual property legislation vary from country to country. Creating intellectual property management frameworks that work in an international context is a significant challenge being addressed by projects such as IMPRIMATUR, an initiative of the Euorpoean Union, which has U.S. representation in the form of the Interactive Multimedia Associaion (IMA).

[3] In addition, the moral rights of the creator (as defined in Section 106A) must be considered.

[4] As of this writing, there has yet to be a determination as to whether the digitization process involves sufficient creativity to be a copyrightable work (as is the case with

reproductive lithography) or if it is mechanical in nature and without creativity (as is the case with photocopying) and therefore does not produce a protected work. Given the amount of skill involved in the creation of an accurate scan and the need for accuracy and fidelity in the process (color balancing, cropping, etc.), there is a strong argument, voiced by major suppliers of digital images including Corbis Media and Luna Imaging among others, that reproductive digital images are indeed copyrightable.

[5] When discussing the transaction costs for the identification and acquisition of intellectual property rights, Joseph Lebersole estimates that "as much as ninety percent of the costs of a multimedia work may be allocated to these problems. Something will have to be done to keep new industries from strangling before they come even close to reaching their potential" (Joseph L. Ebersole, *Protecting Intellectual Property Rights on the Information Superhighways*, A Report for the Information Industry Association, March 1994, p. 84).

[6] This issue is explored in more depth by D. Bearman & J. Trant, Museums and intellectual property: Rethinking rights management for a digital world (Special issue: Copyright and fair use: The great image debate). *Visual Resources*, 12(3-4).

[7] **Participating Museums**: Fowler Museum of Cultural History at the University of California, Los Angeles; The George Eastman House, Rochester, NY; The Harvard University Art Museums, Cambridge, MA; The Library of Congress, Washington, DC; Museum of Fine Arts, Houston, TX; The National Gallery of Art, Washington, DC; The National Museum of American Art, Washington, DC.

Participating Universities: American University, Washington, DC; Columbia University, New York; Cornell University, Ithaca, NY; University of Illinois at Urbana-Champaign, IL; University of Maryland, College Park, MD; University of Michigan, Ann Arbor, Dearborn, and Flint, MI; University of Virginia, Charlottesville, VA.

[8] The configuration of each team varies, depending on local circumstances and interests. Full lists of project team members can be found on the MESL WWW site: http://www.gii.getty.edu/mesl

[9] The MESL Management Committee is comprised of Maxwell Anderson, Art Gallery of Ontario and Information Technology liaison for the Association of Art Museum Directors; David Bearman, Archives and Museums Informatics; Howard Besser, University of California, Berkeley; and Clifford Lynch, University of California, Office of the President, and is chaired by Jennifer Trant, MESL Project Director.

[10] A good example of this kind of arrangement is the *Sample License Agreements for CD-ROM Production* distributed by the American Association of Museums.

[11] Elsewhere I have also developed further philosophical arguments in favor of subscription-based pricing rather than "pay-per-use." See J. Trant. (1995). *The Getty AHIP Imaging Initiative: A status report* (presented at EVA 95 and reprinted in *Archives and Museum Informatics*, 9[3], specifically pp. 267-269).

[12] The text of the agreement is available on the MESL WWW site: http://www.gii.getty.edu/mesl

[13] The agreement has already provided the basis for the collaboration of the members of the Art Museum Image Consortium (AMICO), an initiative of the Association of Art Museum Directors (AAMD) to provide collective licensing of works from member institutions' collections. See http://www.amn.org

[14] Defining the administrative framework for a collective licensing body and the technical framework for information collection and distribution have fallen beyond the bounds of the current MESL project. In addition, technical specifications would be best dealt with as a schedule appended to the agreement, as this would provide the flexibility required to respond to changing circumstances. These issues were discussed in detail at the spring 1996 MESL Participants' Meeting (report available on the MESL WWW site).

[15] Available on the MESL WWW site (see note 12).

[16] A full report of the issues raised in the first year of information collection and distribution has been prepared by Howard Besser and Christie Stephenson for presentation at the EVA Conference, London, July 1996.

[17] A full list of the courses taught during the project can be found on the MESL WWW site.

LOIS F. LUNIN

The Big Picture: Selection and Design Issues for Image Information Systems

A digital image is just one visible part of an image information system. What takes place behind the screen in order to display that image is the focus of this discussion. Many factors influence the planning and design of an image information system including its purpose, types of images, users and use, desired functions and features, and equipment and software. Also to be considered are file conversion and preparations in case of disaster as well as many social and ethical issues in the use of the system. Relatively new techniques for access and retrieval by image content are being explored with some systems now available. While these new mathematically oriented computer-based systems might, in time, help to alleviate some costly human processing, text documentation will still be necessary to identify the image and to describe such elements as the historical context or the social environment in which the image was created.

INTRODUCTION

Electronic image information systems appear to have emerged from a period of infancy in the mid-1980s to reach active adolescence one decade later, probably because they offer the promise of greater efficiency and lower cost, and because they give a greater richness of the information within the image. Though imaging in early 1996 was listed as a $2.59 billion industry (Haimila, 1996) and has become an everyday procedure in science, medicine, industry, business, museums, and government, there are still many opportunities for imaging to flourish in new directions. One of today's frontier areas is the access and retrieval of electronic images by their content—that is, by the shape, color, texture, pattern, etc.— within the image rather than by surrogates such as title, artist, or subject.

The image, however, is only part of the picture. What takes place behind the scenes to produce that electronic image is what this article is about—i.e., the selection and design issues that go into building the information system that will access and retrieve digital images efficiently, clearly, and relevant to the search request while at the same time meeting the standards set for the system. Not included in this article is a discussion of hardware, software, or vocabulary control except to indicate where they fit into the general system considerations or, as in the case of display, affect the quality of the image.

What goes into the design of an information retrieval system is not new. Many of the principles that we learned in designing textual information retrieval systems decades ago are still basic today to the success of a project. A review of some of those principles appears in the following sections. Image information systems, however, do have requirements beyond those needed for text, and some of those will be discussed. Also see Lunin (1987) for comparisons of conventional and image databases. In addition, several ethical and social issues having to do with the use of image information systems are described briefly.

ABOUT IMAGES

When we are dealing with electronic images, we are handling a digital representation of an object whether that object is a photograph, painting, drawing, or page of text. Because the image is in digital form, we can manipulate it; enhance it; alter its original colors; reduce its size or enlarge it; and store, print, or send it over networks. To process and transmit images methodically, we need a system.

PLANNING THE IMAGE INFORMATION SYSTEM

Systems analysis is still a basic requirement in planning for an image information system (Lunin, 1990). Figure 1 lists some fundamental aspects.

Overall
    Purpose
    Types and number of images
    Source
    Users: who, how many, types
    Use: when, how, what, where
    Applications
    Access
    Legal issues
    Types of software needed
    Who helps?
Functions and Features
    Indexing/retrieval
    Performance criteria

Storage
    Integration
    Scanners
    Network
    Costs
    Flexibility
    Standards
Display
    Quality
    Service/support
Imaging System Vendors
File Conversion
Preparation for Disaster

Figure 1. Considerations in the design of an image information system

---

Overall

Purpose—Why do you or your organization want to have/use image information? What do you expect as the main benefits of installing the system—e.g., to use an image surrogate in order to protect the original images which may be old and rare? To make it possible for many people to be able to access the image simultaneously? To have near instant access to each image, thus saving the cost and time of searching a manual file, finding and removing what you want to use, then refiling it? Do you want to reduce storage space requirements (as in filing cabinets)? Is better document security a consideration?

Types of Images—What kind of images will be entered into the system? What is the size of the collection, current acquisitions, and anticipated items? Are the items in black and white or in color? And are they all one size or in various shapes, sizes, and forms? Are they in good condition or are they fragile, stained, bent, or torn?

Source of the Images—Where does the image originate? Does it include information about copyright, permissions to use, and restrictions in use?

Users—Who will use the images? How many people and how often? Will the images be used in-house or online? What levels of users do you anticipate: workers in the office, those in the field, visitors, novices, or experts?

Use—How will people use the system and when—daily? around the clock? What will be the frequency of access? The expected speed of access? Will users want to print or download to another system or both? How many users might there be simultaneously? Will they want to browse? Will they want to view images in various sizes and levels of resolution? Will they want functions such as zoom, color change, or annotation? Besser and Trant (1995) discuss use in some detail.

Applications—Will the system be set up for specific topics or for general subjects in many domains? For example, in medicine, will users want images about a particular disease, such as arthritis, or will they want all topics as those in a national library of medicine or consumer health agency?

Access—What categories of information or access points must be searchable? In addition to words in text, identification numbers, keywords, and category, it is now possible in some prototype systems as well as a few on the market to retrieve by color, iconic shapes, and position of elements within the image.

Legal Issues—Will the users have the right to print or download? As Besser (1995) has pointed out, it is necessary to build enforcement of those rules into the systems (more about legal issues appears later in this discussion in the section on social and ethical issues).

Types of Software Needed—Among the software required are programs to integrate a text database, browse thumbnails, and view individual images in detail. And, as Besser and others have pointed out, the integration between text management and browsing tools is still in its infancy; presently, systems have to be glued together rather than linked seamlessly in a sophisticated text management system to high quality image browsers.

Who Helps?—In building the system, consider what groups within your organization should be involved and at what point in the analysis and planning. Also, determine if you want to build your own system, lease one, or purchase.

Functions and Features

Indexing/Retrieval—It is necessary to determine the functions and features desired for the system. For example, do you want full-text searching as well as image retrieval? If so, do you want the images and the text to be retrieved at the same time? Do you want to be able to annotate images as you view them? How do you want to index the images—via a thesaurus or other vocabulary control that you presently use or will you need to construct a new vocabulary control? Do you wish to be able to search the content of the image without the use of such aids as keywords, descriptors, identifying numbers, name, type of image, or title?

In what format will the images be stored—in the record with text or separately? And what about the display—thumbnail, medium scale, full-scale image, or all? And will you need them in black and white, gray scale, or full color? Will you want the image on the screen, in print, or moved to another digital form? And at what resolution?

Performance Criteria—What performance criteria are the most important to you? Landford (1991) has raised many of these issues. For example, she asks what image scanning speed is wanted and at what image resolution? What average search speed and what display resolution and number of visible pixels are required? And what average image retrieval speed is needed? What image print speed is desired? What image compression ratio is wanted and should it be lossy or lossless?

Storage—What will be your document/image storage capacity and environment (CD-ROM, hard disk, juke box, client-server, etc.)? To a large extent, that depends upon the size of the collection and its integration with other databases in the organization.

Integration—What amount of custom integration with other systems is desired? Should it be with your collection management system, online public access catalog, publishing system, and/or other business or administrative systems (Besser, 1995)? Will you want to integrate with other technologies—micrographics? telecommunications? connectivity with other computer systems? (Lunin, 1990).

Scanners—What kind of scanner will be used—desktop? flatbed? high volume? See Besser and Trant (1995) for a brief overview of image capture and of the selection of scanners.

Network—What are the network requirements within the organization or enterprise? What bandwidth is called for; what standards will be followed? As Besser and Trant (1995) have pointed out: "Because image files are so large, the construction of a networked image database is likely to affect system resources significantly. Therefore, systems architecture and network topology become significant concerns" (p. 33).

Costs—Must the system operate under some cost constraints and, if so, what are they? Image information systems can be costly and perhaps more than an organization can afford. Is it necessary for the system to pay for itself or can it be underwritten by other sources?

What are the implementation costs? Can one use any hardware or software that is currently available? Can you assign staff to the project, either temporarily or on an ongoing basis? Row (1995) raises several issues: what level of training, learning, and organizational change will the new system require? The cost of implementing the technology is fairly easy to estimate but often it is not the largest cost. Training, organizational change, and possible disruption can increase costs enormously. What is the estimate for the total costs of entry, including preparing the materials for scanning, checking the quality of the scans, refiling the original material, indexing the image, and entering the new information into the system?

Flexibility—As for the systems that you are considering, are they flexible? Can they be altered easily and adapted to changing needs? Because it is often impossible to know exactly what you will need until the system is up and running, it is often advisable to do a pilot project that includes all aspects. As Row advises, once installed, a malleable system can be modified to suit individual needs at a time when one really knows what is needed.

Can the system be expanded to add new functions such as batch scanning and full-text search and perhaps some activities you cannot now anticipate? As technology evolves, can you incorporate innovations? Is the system scalable? Can you go from a few to many hundred workstations without an unbearable strain on the system that affects speed and capacity? Will the current system tolerate migration to a system for the entire organization with support for a wide range of functions and computing platforms and different services?

The foregoing questions are not new. With some exceptions that relate specifically to images, we have asked these kinds of questions in the creation of text information systems during the past thirty-five years or more. Yet, as noted by other papers delivered during this conference, in some ways images are far more challenging than text.

Standards—In the last sentence in his article in *Database*, Besser (1995) states: "For a digital image database to be useful beyond a single short-term project or beyond a narrow user base, the database must be constructed according to common standards in both technical and descriptive areas" (p. 19). To ensure that data will be interchangeable among systems, national and international standards for image file formats and compression methods have been developed and maintained by industry and other collaborative bodies. Sources for information about standards and methods for describing images are listed in Besser and Trant (1995).

Display

One of the most important aspects of an image information system is the display—it is the face of the system the user sees. Meadows (1995) lists eleven things to look for in an imaging display: Among these are:

- image legibility;
- color or gray scale;
- size of display screen (at least 20 inches diagonal);
- resolution of at least 1600 x 1200 pixels;
- dot pitch of at least 0.28 mm; and
- refresh rate of a minimum of 70 Hz.

Meadows advises that one should not buy a display based on specifications alone. The product data sheets are useful but not good indicators of image quality. And, most important, he adds, is to try a product before you buy. Evaluate the display in your own work environment with your own applications and with the controller you will use. Choose a complete display subsystem from a single source. "Display devices are currently the weakest link in the image quality chain" state Besser and Trant. Also, they note that: "Each model of display and printing device renders color slightly differently" (p. 30).

Quality—Look closely at the image quality. Meadows (1995) discusses three factors that affect image quality that do not appear on data sheets. These factors are focus, convergence, and contrast. "[S]ee if the characters are crisp and if the black-to-white transitions are sharp." Look at the focus in all areas of the screen to make certain that the edge focus is as good as the center. Convergence is how the red, green and blue guns align to form pixels. "Bad convergence shows characters with red, green, or blue edges" which can be distracting" (p. 46). Contrast is important in viewing black and white documents. Because subtle differences become apparent only with extended use, Meadows recommends that, before purchase, users should work several hours on different displays, choose their favorites, and then tell why. Young (1995a) also advises the purchaser to be prepared to spend more money on an imaging display than on a monitor used for viewing word processing files because of the need for higher refresh rate, better resolution, and larger size.

Service and Support—Find out about service and support and the company's commitment to their product before you buy. See if on-site servicing is available. Read the fine print and look for multiyear warranties. This is very important because many companies today are merging or going out of business. Meadows's (1995) advice: "Look for a display with a 50,000 to 70,000 hours demonstrated MTBF [mean time before failure]" (p. 46) and choose a dependable vendor who has a proven track record and financial strength to stay in the business for a long while.

Imaging System Vendors

If you are going to use vendors, Landford (1991, pp. 39-44) and others offer general questions to use in talking with those vendors. For example, ask the vendor to show you exactly how their company would handle your application. Find out how many installations they have. Ask on which computer systems their system runs and its compatibility with other systems. Learn what upgrade paths they provide.

Determine whether the system is easy to use and to maintain. What does their price include? How long before you can have your system up and running? What happens if your system goes down? What kinds of support do they then provide? What resources does their company use for quality assurance? How many keys can you assign to the image and can you name the ones you want to use? And what about the reliability of the system?

Landford also suggests talking to organizations using the system. Ask the people there: If you could make the decision over again would you choose the same system and why? What are the system's main strengths and shortcomings? How easy is it to use? How well did the system integrate with, or connect to, your existing hardware/software? And how good was the vendor's training and customer support?

File Conversion

Most organizations have existing files that they will want to convert to digital form. It is important to estimate correctly the size of the file. Because some documents and images are in less than perfect condition, it is necessary to know how to improve their quality—e.g., how to eliminate extraneous marks, curled edges, and stains. Young (1995b) warned that a serious mistake companies make is estimating how long it will take to complete the job of backfile conversion.

Using a service bureau can also offer advantages:

1. hardware and software support;
2. no productivity losses—your staff keeps working at their regular jobs during conversion;
3. no new employees (temporaries) who learn how to do the work and then leave for a new skilled position;
4. quality of the work;
5. experience in conversion;
6. document preparation (not all materials are ready for scanning);

7. media choices: WORM, CD-ROM, etc.
8. other services should you want them: OCR, ICR, etc.;
9. on-site conversion. This saves the expense of shipping materials and, in addition, you're around to supervise and check;
10. document tracking;
11. accurate time frames: a timetable for the work;
12. no expensive equipment purchases: no capital investment if you do not use the equipment in the future (Young, 1995b).

The cost of conversion depends on many factors: volume, document quality, document size, indexing, your location, time of year, the bureau's workload, your expectations and requirements, shipping, and so on. Service bureaus will try to give you a "vague quote to cover unknowns." Beware of one common practice of quoting low and charging high for any changes. Know in advance what each change will cost. "Talk to people who have done backfile conversions and ask them what changes they had made—and how much each cost" (p. 46).

Compare quotes that you receive. Each bureau has a way of quoting, and items in one quotation might not appear in another. Items that might or might not be included in a quotation are:

- The initial set up: does it include all equipment? Is there an extra charge for new equipment and how much is it?

- Document preparation: Do staples need to be removed and how many? How many folded corners need to be unfolded? If you do it yourself, is what you save worth it in your time?

- Indexing: Do you have an indexing system or do you need to build one? If there's much data entry needed, it might be less expensive to contract out. Make certain that the quotation includes "full indexing."

- Clean-up: Make certain that noise removal is in the quotation.

- Skewed images: Will the service bureau correct the skew in the scanning?

- Sizes: If the material to be scanned is in a variety of sizes, the charge will be more than if it is all one size.

- Re-scan: If you want 100 percent image quality control, that will be expensive. Many service bureaus negotiate an "acceptable" quality control level which means that they will check every first, tenth, or 100th image. The cost can be huge if you want 100 percent accuracy, but also consider the cost if your system is filled with poor images.

- Quality control contract: Put into the contract that you want to check the input periodically.

TIME WARNER'S PHOTO CONVERSION

If all of these details are beginning to feel fairly overwhelming, look at Time Warner's project to digitize more than 20 million photos (Bielski, 1995). Their goal: to digitize and store those photos in a customized system to support research, magazine republishing, and eventually, on-line versions of the publishing group's magazines including *Time, Sports Illustrated, People,* and *Entertainment Weekly.*

They also need to process the accompanying text for each image, which will be the job of catalogers. The photos will be tagged with identifying text for retrieval. Once implemented, the system will be able to support up to 300 queries simultaneously. The company estimates that all the Time Warner magazines use up to 100,000 new photos annually.

Isolating particular types of images of a much photographed subject is another required capability—e.g., to easily sift through 10,000 or more photos of a well-known person such as Bill Clinton or Barbra Streisand by designating body position, facial expression, or social context.

BEING PREPARED FOR DISASTER

While you hope you never have a flood, hurricane, fire, or explosion hitting your organization, nevertheless, experience teaches us that these events do occur and that systems can be wiped out during a disaster. Prevention is critical but sometimes not possible. Recovery—and as quickly as possible—should be planned for. Preparedness should include routine management tasks as well as recovery from any major injuries to the network and database systems. Document all system information and know how to operate immediately after a disaster (see Lunin, 1994):

- Define your recovery assumptions. List the key ones. For example: personnel should have access to the hard copy files within twenty-four hours.
- Identify and list key departmental functions and the activities performed by each department. List priorities.
- Identify procedural implications. List activities that can be delayed, postponed, or performed manually.
- Identify departmental interfaces. List internal and external departmental interfaces by the functions of each department.
- Identify critical applications. List mainframe, mini- or PC-applications and/or software required to support departmental functions department-wide such as e-mail.

Levels of documentation should include user, as well as technical, procedures. Know where your vendors are located and whether they are still in business. If this is not possible, know who can provide the needed service and where that vendor is located. "Don't wait for an emergency to find out that the plan won't work. Assess the plan periodically. Revise it as necessary. Review the plan every 12 months" (Lunin, 1994, p. 58).

NEW DIRECTIONS FOR IMAGE RETRIEVAL BASED ON CONTENT

New developments for access, search, retrieval, filtering, and categorizing image information are in the works. Some of these developments were shown and discussed at RIAO (1994). Also, Web innovators are being encouraged to create applications and services that exceed the features and functionality of the first generation of Web sites (Feder, 1996). Because of the many directions that research and development are taking are described in other papers in these proceedings, only a few not covered at the 1996 Clinic on Library Applications of Data Processing are described briefly here to add to the sense of breadth of ongoing work.

At RIAO 94, a conference organized by Centre de Hautes Etudes Internationales D'Informatique Documentaire (C.I.D., France) and the Centre for Advanced Study of Information Systems, Inc. (C.A.S.I.S., U.S.), researchers and practitioners from many countries focused on still photographs as well as the extraction and representation of the content from clips and images to satisfy the needs of a wide range of users and purposes (see Lunin, 1995 for coverage of that meeting).

M.I.T.'s Media Streams uses an iconic annotation language to represent knowledge about the video content. Using stream-based annotation of video content together with memory-based representation, researchers can capture the semantic structure of the video. Special tools have been developed that understand enough about the content to help with the annotation process. Determining whether and how clips are similar is an ongoing challenge.

One such software tool, Photobook, takes measurements of image features such as brightness, edges, textures, etc. It then uses a mathematical calculation to obtain a compact description of the set of images concerning their prominent characteristics. One application of "Texture Photobook" is used in the fashion industry.

Another challenge for image database tools like Photobook is how best to describe object shapes. A new mathematical method called modal matching is based on the idea of describing objects by their generalized symmetries.

IBM's Almaden Research Center has been studying ways to query large online image databases using the image content as the basis of the queries. Examples of content are color, texture, shape, size, orientation, and position of image objects and regions. Query is by image example; retrieval methods use similarity rather than exact match (Lunin, 1995). For more information see Layne (1994), RIAO (1994), Mostofa (1994), and Svenonius (1994).

SOCIAL AND ETHICAL ISSUES

The selection and design of an image access and retrieval system raises many social and ethical concerns, among them accuracy, integrity, authentication, and intellectual property rights.

Header Information

When an image has been produced or scanned into the system, the record's header should contain information about the make of scanner used, the date of the scan, and the identification of the scanning personnel. Other data should include file size, image quality, compression, file format, layered architecture, terminology, technical information, and intellectual property rights (Lunin, 1994b. See also Figure 2). Many issues arise concerning what might happen to an image once it is produced. Discussion of some of these issues follows.

Header information

Accuracy

Integrity

Authentication

Giving credit

Intellectual property

Re-use of images

Off-color images

Figure 2. Social and ethical issues

Accuracy

When accessing information on the Internet, many questions arise. Is the information accurate and are access and use of this information appropriate (Smith & Bellman, 1996)? If the image comes from a respected library or repository, more confidence can be felt about its accuracy.

Researchers can—and have—altered, edited, adjusted, refined, etc. scientific images without leaving a trace in order to fit their hypothesis. Whether to allow any image manipulation or even cosmetic change is becoming a real source of anxiety, for example, to federal agencies such as the Food and Drug Administration, which relies on scientific images in evaluating drugs for approval. The need is seen "for a clear record of what has been done to an image, from editing to data compression. Without such a record, the image's scientific value becomes questionable" (Anderson, 1994).

Integrity

Related to integrity is whether the image is in its entirety or whether bits have been left out in either purposeful or accidental compression or other activity. Has new information somehow crept in that does not belong to the original image? These are serious concerns and the header information provided in a record might help to check on the accuracy of the image.

Authentication

Who really produced the image? Because images can be obtained from databases in various locations and changed or seen in a draft of a work put out by the creator for comments by colleagues, it is difficult to know if the image is in its final form or is still in a working stage and whether it came from the creator or someone who has obtained the image and then altered it.

Giving Credit

An image obtained from the Internet and used in a report should acknowledge the source as clearly as possible, just as print documents should be acknowledged. Also, there is a real issue concerning payment owed for materials obtained on the Internet. In some cases there is a fee for use, although collection mechanisms have not all been worked out (Smith & Kallman, 1996).

Intellectual Property

Generally, anyone who copies the images or text of another person or publisher or organization without permission is guilty of copyright infringement. That person is also subject to actual damages, statutory damages (potentially in the hundreds of thousands of dollars), and impoundment of the infringing materials, and more (Roberts, 1994).

In the recent current legal environment, copyright infringement has occurred when copyrightable subject matter exists, the infringer must have had access to it, and there is substantial similarity between the original work and the allegedly copied work. Roberts (1994) explains that any copying by exact means such as photocopying, photographing, or other direct recording is not considered an original work.

What are the image processing implications?

If the image processing involves extensive and difficult techniques to achieve an image that is different from the original, such as pixel-by-pixel manipulation of stored data, the image processor may have reached the stage of an independently copyrightable work. Any such work, however, must still pass the test of no "substantial similarity" that will be put to a jury. If, however, the *market* for the new work created from the copying of the original work is different from that of the original creators' and a substantial amount of complex technical work was done by the person copying the original work to give rise to a new image, infringement will not necessarily be found. (Roberts, 1994, p. 93)

The study "Intellectual Property and the National Information Infrastructure" (NII) recommended that this type of electronic transmission of networks be brought under the definition of distribution to avoid any issue of whether this right is somehow not covered by copyright law. Of importance in the imaging area is the thought that importation via transmission of images without the permission of the copyright holder is an infringement of the rights of the copyright owner. "The report noted that copyrighted works should be freely available but not available for free" (Roberts, 1995a, p. 82). While this clever wording states a good principle, the author of the article states that "it does not help those colleges and universities wishing to access and use images in a database, which are accessible over the NII, to use that information without claims of infringement" (Roberts, 1995a, p. 82).

Reuse of Images

The re-use of "owned images" raises some other thorny points. Who is allowed to adapt images in the age of re-purposing? "If you are the commissioning party and owner of the copyright, you control the image reuse. Otherwise, artists are free to reuse their images and customers for those images, should not be surprised by such legal use" (Roberts, 1996).

Off-Color Images

And what about off-color images—and this does not mean fuschia when the color should have been purple. Such images pose a new liability problem. Essentially, the creator should know the contents of the database and whether the contents might possibly be offensive to those who access it.

"A key aspect of your liability is what you knew about not only the contents of your database, but of the laws of the individual jurisdictions from which users might access your information" (Roberts, 1995b, p. 88). If there is any moral in this story, writes Roberts, it is either:

1. Understand the contents of your database well, attempt to find objections to the content and take steps to limit the dissemination

of the information only to those jurisdictions where the contents would be legal; *or maybe it's*

2. Pay no attention to the contents of your database. Do not become involved in contributions to it, do not inspect it in any way, and simply be a vehicle in which information can be disseminated to third parties. (p. 88)

DESIGNING THE WAY TO THE FUTURE

Electronic image systems are here now and will become increasingly prevalent. It is obvious that further research and developments in hardware and software will occur and that content retrieval systems will become widely available. An image system with access and retrieval by content offers a radical departure in the way we can deal with images. It also shifts much of processing from humans to computer operations with both positive and negative effects, some of them social and ethical.

The steps in setting up an image access and retrieval system are specific and complex, and increasingly there is more known about the special requirements for designing efficient and effective systems. Thus, system analysis will continue to be important in the design of such systems.

While developing information technology offers the opportunity to do almost incredible things with images, the technology cannot supply the interpretation that can be offered by carefully selected verbal descriptions (Lunin, 1994b). Text documentation will continue to be needed to identify and describe such elements as historical context or the social environment in which the image was produced, while the image itself will speak to us in a way that verbal language cannot.

REFERENCES

Anderson, C. (1994). Easy-to-alter digital images raise fears of tampering. *Science, 263*(January 21), 317-318.

Besser, H. (1995). Getting the picture on image databases. The basics. *Database, 18*(2), 12-16, 18-19.

Besser, H., & Trant, J. (1995). *Introduction to imaging issues in constructing an image database.* Santa Monica, CA: The Getty Art History Information Program.

Bielski, L. (1995). 20 million photos will be digitized at Time Warner: The image database of the future begins. *Advanced Imaging, 10*(10), 26, 28, 91.

Feder, J. (1996). New directions for image recognition: Toward image content-based retrieval for the World Wide Web. *Advanced Imaging, 11*(1), 26, 28.

Glanz, J. (1995). Computer processing gives imaging a sharper view. *Science, 269*(September 8), 1338.

Haimila, S. (1996). 1995 good, 1996 better. *IW* (*Imaging World*), (January 1), 21.

Landford, A. G. (1991). *Choosing the right imaging system.* Silver Spring, MD: Micro Dynamics, Ltd.

Lunin, L. F. (1987). Electronic image information. In M. E. Williams (Ed.), *Annual review of information science and technology* (chapter 6, pp. 179-224). Amsterdam, The Netherlands: Elsevier Science Publications.

Lunin, L. F. (1990a). Integrating images with the information system. *Bulletin of the American Society for Information Science, 16*(5), 21, 22.

Lunin, L. F. (1990b). Image databases: Some today, more tomorrow. *Bulletin of the American Society for Information Science, 16*(3), 35.

Lunin, L. F. (1994a). Museums: Spreading their images in a telecom world. *Information Today,* (November), 54.

Lunin, L. F. (1994b). Analyzing art objects for an image database. Chapter 3. In R. Fidel, T. B. Hahn, E. M. Rasmussen, & P. J. Smith (Eds.), *Challenges in indexing electronic text and images* (pp. 57-72). Medford, NJ: Learned Information, Inc.

Lunin, L. F. (1995). Cutting edge image and multimedia retrieval systems at RIAO 94. *Information Today,* (January), 37.

Layne, S. S. (1994). Some issues in the indexing of images: In perspective on imaging. *Journal of the American Society for Information Science, 45*(3), 583-588.

Meadows, T. (1995). 11 things to look for in an imaging display. *Imaging Magazine, 4*(8), 44-46, 48.

Mostafa, J. (1994). Digital image representation and access. Chapter 3. In M. E. Williams (Ed.), *Annual review of information science and technology* (pp. 91-135). Medford, NJ: Learned Information, Inc.

Okon, C. (1995). Image recognition meets content management for authoring, editing & more. *Advanced Imaging, 10*(7), 60-62.

RIAO 94. (1994). *Intelligent multimedia retrieval systems and management.* (Conference proceedings on Intelligent Multimedia Retrieval Systems and Management, Rockefeller University, New York, October 11-13, 1994 (Vol. 1, pp. 1-774). New York: Rockefeller University.

Roberts, J. L. (1995a). Intellectual property and the National Info Infrastructure: New rules for the road? *Advanced Imaging, 10*(10), 81-82.

Roberts, J. L. (1995b). Racy images cross borders: Your new liability problem ... Or what? *Advanced Imaging, 10*(6), 87-88.

Roberts, J. L. (1994). So you've got a new scanner: Psst ... Ever heard about copyrights? *Advanced Imaging, 9*(4), 94, 93.

Roberts, J. L. (1996). Re-use of "owned" images: Who can adapt images in the age of re-purposing? *Advanced Imaging, 11*(2), 56-58.

Row, M. (1995). Seven things to look for in a departmental imaging system. *Imaging Magazine, 4*(10), 124-125.

Smith, H. J., & Kallman, E. A. (1996). Ethics for Internet users. *Beyond Computing, 4*(2), 16, 17.

Young, M. (1995a). An insider's guide to picking the right monitor. *Imaging Magazine, 4*(8), 35-38.

Young, M. (1995b). Why should you use a service bureau for your backfile conversion? *Imaging Magazine, 4*(5), 36-38, 40, 42, 44, 46, 48, 50.

Workshop RIAO '94. (1994). Multimedia information representation and retrieval. Unpublished paper presented at a conference cochaired by A. Pentland, K. Haase, & P. Aigrain, Oct. 11, Rockefeller University, New York City.

RAJIV MEHROTRA

Content-Based Image Modeling and Retrieval

A database system models and manages an abstracted real world (or mini-world) pertinent to the problem at hand in terms of alphanumeric data. The semantic associated with any piece of alphanumeric data is known to or derived by the users of the database. This conventional approach to data modeling and management is not well suited for the effective management of imagery data. In an image database management system, the desired information/semantics associated with the imaged mini-world needs to be automatically (or semi-automatically) extracted and appropriately modeled to facilitate content-based retrieval and manipulation of data. In this article, the key issues in content-based image data modeling and retrieval are discussed. A system called MUSEUM is briefly presented to illustrate some of the approaches used to resolve the main challenges of conent-based data modeling and retrieval.

INTRODUCTION

Several application areas have emerged that require effective and efficient management of image data. Examples of such application areas include digital library, medicine, defense, space exploration, law enforcement, environmental monitoring and control, museum or historic collection management, electronic publishing/advertising, education, and entertainment. In most of these areas, several large repositories of image data already exist and only a very small fraction of collected data is ever analyzed due to the lack of effective image database management techniques. The growing list of applications combined with the advances in the areas of image analysis and database management caused an ever increasing interest in image database systems over the last decade. The major hurdle was posed by the memory and the computational requirements of an image database management system. The common saying, "an image is worth a thousand words" turned out to be an understatement. In recent years, rapid improvements in computer hardware, memory management, and display devices have made it feasible to develop practical and user-oriented image database management systems.

The management of image databases involves a close interaction of database and machine vision technologies. Unfortunately, until recently, almost all reported efforts in the development of image database management technology did not consider this close interaction. As a result, some of the key issues were ignored by both the scientific communities resulting in systems with very little practical applications. Most of the proposals from the database community were extensions of the conventional database model that treated images as an appendix to the alphanumeric data. In these systems, pointers (or references) to images are allowed as attributes and very limited processing and analysis of image contents is involved. In other words, images and alphanumeric data are not treated equally since image data-based constraints cannot be employed for data retrieval/selection (Grosky & Mehrotra, 1992). However, some of these efforts assumed that the machine vision community would provide the desired content-based image processing and analysis methods (Aslandogan et al., 1995). The image analysis activities of the machine vision scientific community completely ignored the database-related issues (e.g., image representation, analysis, and recognition in a large and flexible database environment). It is now clear that conventional approaches to database management and image analysis are not well suited to the management of image and other nonalphanumeric data (Grosky & Mehrotra, 1992; Grosky, 1994). The key challenges are posed by the contents of the images to be managed. Image databases are of little use without content-based image data description and retrieval. In the following sections, the challenges posed by the imagery data from the viewpoints of data modeling (description) and data retrieval are discussed.

CONTENT-BASED IMAGE DATA MODELING

A database represents an abstracted real world (mini-world) pertinent to the problem at hand in terms of its entities and relationships. Every piece of datum in a database conveys some application domain-dependent information (or semantics). In a traditional database, the information about the modeled mini-world conveyed by a piece of alphanumeric data is known to, or derived by, the users. In an image database, raw images by themselves are of limited use unless the embedded application- or user-dependent semantics can be somehow extracted and used in image data retrieval and manipulation. In other words, information about the imaged mini-world contained in images needs to be extracted and appropriately modeled in the database (Grosky, 1994; Grosky & Mehrotra, 1992; Gupta et al., 1991). Therefore, an image database management system must be capable of representing images in terms of their contents (image properties, objects and their attributes, and relationships among objects) and the associated application- and user-dependent semantics and knowledge. From the modeling viewpoint, the content-based image databases can be broadly classified into two groups:

1. *Mini-world associated with images is known*—In an image database of this type, the images are of a known (or fixed) mini-world. In these cases, the objects, scenes, events, and visual concepts that can appear in an

image are known a priori. There is usually only one application domain-dependent interpretation of each database image. Therefore, the contents of any database image can be represented by a predetermined modeling scheme. For some application domains, model-based techniques can be employed to extract (automatically or semi-automatically) the desired content-based image representation and to process content-based image retrieval queries. An image database for a manufacturing application (containing images of parts, components, tools, machineries, and products) is an example of such a database.

2. *Unknown and variable mini-world*—The images in such a database do not belong to any fixed mini-world and there is no a priori knowledge about the objects, scenes, and events that can appear in images. A database of a family's picture collection, a database of an explorer's image collection, or a database of images of a museum's collection are examples of such image databases. In such a database, most images are very different from other database images in terms of their contents. Therefore, in general, a predefined set of objects and relationships cannot be used to describe all the database images. Also, model-based image processing and analysis approaches are not directly applicable. Instead, capabilities to dynamically describe (or associate a mini-world) with each of the database images and to manipulate these descriptions is essentially required. In such a database, image processing and analysis methods are needed to interactively or automatically develop models for objects, events, and scenes found in the user-defined mini-world of an image. Such models can then be used in a model-based approach to partially and fully represent other images in terms of previously modeled objects, events, and scenes and to facilitate content-based image information manipulation and retrieval.

In general, the interpretation of an image or a visual concept (e.g., beautiful or serene) may vary from user to user. Therefore multiple user- or application-dependent mini-worlds (interpretations) can be associated with each of the database images. Each user can be characterized by the collection of his/her descriptions (or models) of objects, events, scenes, and concepts. Such user profiles can be effectively used to develop user-oriented descriptions of database images and to process a user's queries in accordance with that user's profile. For example, a user's definition of the concept "colorful" should be utilized to respond to his/her queries like, "retrieve all colorful pictures and retrieve database images at least as colorful as a given query image." If the definition of "colorful" does not exist in that user's profile, then the definition provided by another user, whose profile is found to be most similar to the current user, can be selected to create the corresponding response.

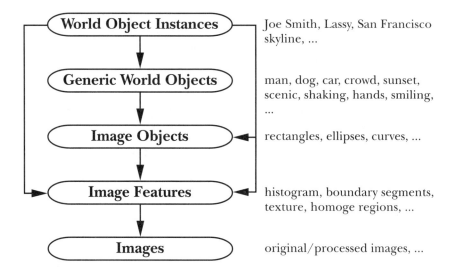

Figure 1: Levels of Abstraction in MUSEUM

It should be clear from the above discussion that image contents pose several challenges with respect to the representation or the modeling of images. We are currently developing an image database system which utilizes a data model called MUlti-SEmantic Unstructured data Model (MUSEUM). MUSEUM resolves the above-mentioned modeling issues and it has the following key features:

- a generalized object-oriented model capable of representing both the structured data (i.e., images with a known mini-world) as well as the unstructured data (i.e., images where the mini-world is dynamically associated);

- ability to dynamically associate, compose, and modify data (image) description;

- flexibility of switching from one view of an image, a group of images, or the entire database, to the other and to simultaneously access and manipulate multiple views of an image, group of images, or the entire database; and

- effective management of user profiles derived from their definitions of abstract concepts and descriptions of mini-worlds.

In MUSEUM, database images and visual concepts are described using a multilevel abstraction hierarchy. The main levels of abstraction are shown in figure 1. At the lowest levels are database images or example images. At the next level of description, an image is characterized in terms of its properties such as background/foreground colors, dominant colors, histograms, and texture properties. Description of images in terms of objects—such as image regions, boundary segments, and contours— and relationships among them forms the next level of abstraction. At the next level of abstraction, images are described in terms of generic objects, relationships, and concepts such as man, dog, car, crowd, horizon, sunset, cloudy, colorful, and smile. At the highest level of abstraction, images are described in terms of specific instances of the generic world objects. For example, a man may be described as Joe Smith, a dog may be described as Lassie, an image may be described as the San Francisco skyline. The image descriptions at any of these abstraction levels can be multilevel and can be derived from—or mapped to—the descriptions at the lower levels of abstraction. In MUSEUM, this multilevel description of images is composed of two parts—i.e., mandatory part and optional part. The mandatory description components are found in all database images, whereas the optional description components are image and/or user-dependent. The mandatory and optional description components are dependent on the nature of the image database. For example, descriptions of images of a fixed mini-world image database may not have any optional description components.

CONTENT-BASED IMAGE RETRIEVAL

The central task of any database management system is to retrieve records/objects that satisfy a set of specified constraints. In image databases, an important class of data retrieval is content-based retrieval of images. In content-based retrieval, images whose contents satisfy the specified constraints are retrieved or selected. Content-based image retrieval queries can be classified into two broad classes:

1. *Queries involving no image processing/analysis*—in these queries, no processing or analysis of database images is required and no query images are given. Examples are: (1) retrieve all images containing at least one automobile in front of a house, (2) retrieve pictures containing a smiling man. The symbolic descriptions (automatically extracted and/or user specified) associated with database images are used to select the desired images. These queries can be processed using traditional approaches.

2. *Queries involving image processing/analysis*—these queries involve one or more images that are processed to extract the associated desired symbolic information. The extracted description is compared against the description of database images to select images that satisfy the

specified constraints. Examples of such queries are: (1) retrieve all images containing one or more objects similar to the object in a given query image, (2) retrieve all images that are similar to a given query image in terms of image color and texture features.

To efficiently process content-based image retrieval queries, various levels of descriptions of database images need to be organized in efficient secondary storage-based index structures. These indexes are searched to find descriptors and hence images that satisfy the specified constraints. Complex queries can be efficiently processed using the incremental refinement process. An incremental refinement process starts by selecting images that satisfy a subset of the specified constraints. This initial response is refined in several stages until all the remaining constraints are satisfied. For example, consider a facial image database. To retrieve facial images similar to a query facial image, first the nose of the query face nose must be used to select facial images with a similar nose. This initial response can be refined by selecting other features in the query face one by one—e.g., hair region, mouth, eyes, and so on. The user can review the response at each stage of refinement and select the query feature for the next stage of refinement or elect to terminate the refinement process. Query processing by incremental refinement can be used with a multiresolution image representation scheme. In this case, the initial response to a query can be generated using a coarse representation, and this response can be refined using finer (less lossy) representations.

To illustrate the key steps involved in the design of a content-based image retrieval system, we consider the problem of shape similarity-based image retrieval (Flickner et al., 1995; Gary & Mehrotra, 1995; Grosky & Mehrotra, 1990; Jagadish, 1991; Petland et al., 1994). In shape similarity-based queries, constraints are therefore specified in terms of similarity of shapes. An example is, "retrieve images that contain at least one shape similar to the given query shape." In this case, the key issues to be resolved are:

- *Shape representation*—how can the shapes present in an image be represented? How can the selected representation be extracted automatically or semiautomatically from images?

- *Shape similarity definition*—what criteria or measures should be used to automatically determine the similarity or dissimilarity of two shapes? The similarity measure should be consistent with the human interpretation of shape similarity.

- *Access or index structures*—how should shapes and related representations be organized to enable efficient searches for shapes that satisfy the specified shape similarity-based constraints?

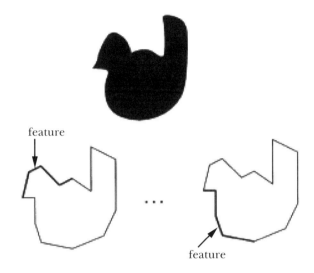

feature

...

feature

Figure 2. A shape and its structural feature.

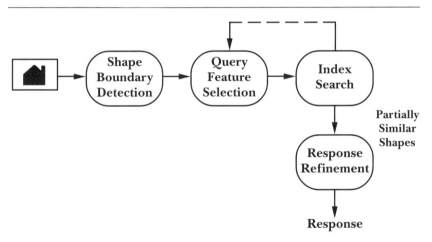

Figure 3: Two-dimensional shape similarity-based query processing

In MUSEUM, a two-dimensional (i.e., almost flat) object image is represented by an ordered set of boundary points (e.g., maximal curvature points or vertices of the polygonal approximation). Each shape is further represented by a set of structural features, which is a fixed size set of adjacent points (or line segments) of its representation. A shape and its structural features are shown in figure 2.

Each structural feature is represented as a point in a multidimensional space. Similarity between two structural features is measured by the Euclidian distance between the corresponding points in the multidimensional space. Any multidimensional point access method (Nievergelt et al., 1984, p. 84; Robinson, 1981; Seeger & Kriegel, 1990) can be used to organize the structural features of all the shapes in the database. Associated with each structural feature is a list containing information about where, and in which shape, that structural feature appears. The key steps involved in processing a shape-similarity-based query are shown in figure 3.

The boundary-based query shape representation is first developed, and then a structural feature, called the query feature, is selected (automatically or by the user). The index is searched to find structural features that are similar to the selected query features, and the list of database shapes associated with these similar features form the initial response (called the set of partially similar shapes). This initial response is then refined by a global comparison of the query shapes with each of the shapes in the initial response. Shapes that are found to satisfy the specified global similarity constraints form the final response to the query. Further details of this technique can be found in Gary and Mehrotra (1993) and Mehrotra and Gary (1995).

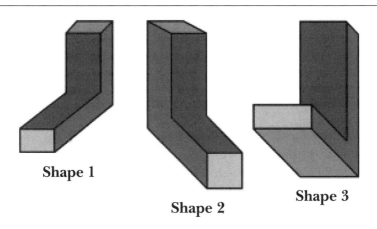

Shape 1

Shape 2

Shape 3

Figure 4. Qualitatively Similar and Different Three-Dimensional Shapes

MUSEUM also supports shape-similarity-based retrieval of images of three-dimensional objects (Mehrotra & Gary, 1996). Similarity of images of three-dimensional shapes is determined by their qualitative appearances in their respective image. Qualitative appearance of a three-dimensional object in an image is defined by the visible surfaces (or faces) and their qualitative characteristics. For example, in figure 4, shapes 1 and 2 are considered qualitatively similar as they have qualitatively similar visible surfaces. Shape 3 is considered to be qualitatively different from the other two.

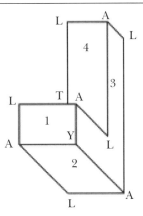

Figure 5. Labeled image of an L-shaped object

In MUSEUM, an image of a three-dimensional shape is represented by a character string composed of substrings, each representing the qualitative appearance of a region in the image in terms of its vertex types. Figure 5 shows an image of an L-shaped object with labeled vertices. The qualitative appearance of this shape is represented by the character string

ALALALTL:ALTAY:AYAL:AYALAL:ALATL,

where ":" (colon) is the region string separator. In this string, the first substring (i.e., the character string before the first ":" character) represents the silhouette region, and the following four substrings respectively represent regions labeled 1, 2, 3, and 4.

Two shape images with the same character string representation are considered to be qualitatively similar. If only some of the leading substrings match, the corresponding shapes are considered to be partially similar. The degree of similarity is determined by the number of matching leading substrings. In this case, a suitable extension of any efficient string-matching index structure can be used to organize the database of shapes and their representations.

A shape-similarity-based query is processed in two stages as shown in figure 6. In the first stage, the query shape representation is used to search the index structures to find the string with the most number of matching leading substrings. The database shapes associated with this string form the initial response. Then if requested, this initial response is refined by retaining shapes having character string representations that completely match the query shape character string.

Note that there is always a loss of information in a content-based representation of images. There is a trade-off between the memory and computational requirements and loss of information. The memory and

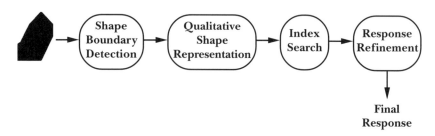

Figure 6. 3-dimensional shape similarity-based retrieval

computational requirements are higher for finer representation schemes. The quality of image representation directly determines the query response quality (i.e., number of images in a query response that are not consistent with the user's interpretation). Multiresolution image representation combined with query processing by incremental refinement provides a scheme in which the trade-off between the response quality and query processing time can be controlled by the users.

CONCLUSION

Recent advances in several digital computation technologies have made it possible to store and manage large repositories of imagery data. In recent years, it has become clear that such image databases are useful only if the database management schemes permit content-based retrieval of images. Image content and associated interpretations pose several challenges. In this discussion, key database design issues pertinent to content-based modeling (representation) and retrieval of images have been reviewed.

REFERENCES

Aslandogan, Y. A.; Thier, C.; Yu, C. T.; Liu, C.; & Nair, K. R. (1995). Design, implementation, and evaluation of SCORE. In *Proceedings 1995 IEEE Data Engineering Conference* (pp. 280-287). Taiwan.

Flickner, M. et al. (1995). Query by image and video content: The QBIC system. *IEEE Computer, 28*(9), 23-32.

Gary, J. E., & Mehrotra, R. (1993). Similar shape retrieval using a structural feature index. *Information Systems, 18*(7), 525-537.

Grosky, W. I. (1994). Multimedia information systems—A tutorial. *IEEE Multimedia, 1*(1), 12-24.

Grosky, W. I., & Mehrotra, R. (1990). Index-based object recognition in pictorial data management. *Computer Vision, Graphics, and Image Processing, 52*(3), 416-436.

Grosky, W. I., & Mehrotra, R. (1992) Image database management. In M. C. Yovits (Ed.), *Advances in Computers* (vol. 35, pp. 237-253). New York: Academic Press.

Gupta, A.; Waymouth, T.; & Jain, R. (1991). *Semantic queries with pictures: The VIMSYS model* (Proceedings of the 17th International Conference on Very Large Databases) (pp. 69-79). Barcelona, Spain.

Jagadish, H. V. (1991). *A retrieval technique for similar shapes* (Proceedings ACM SIGMOD Conference on the Management of Data) (pp. 208-217). Denver, Colorado.

Mehrotra, R., & Gary, J. E. (1995). Similar-shape retrieval in shape data management. *IEEE Computer, 28*(9), 57-62.

Mehrotra, R., & Gary, J. E. (1996). *A technique for retrieval of similar images of three-dimensional objects.* Unpublished technical report, University of Missouri—St. Louis.

Nievergelt, J.; Hinterberger, H.; & Sevcik, K. C. (1984). The grid file: An adaptable symmetric multikey file structure. *ACM Trans. on Database Systems, 9*(1), 38-71.

Petland, A.; Picard, R. W.; & Sclaroff, S. (1994). Photobook: Tools for content-based manipulation of image databases. In W. Niblack & R. Jain (Eds.), *Storage and retrieval for images and video databases II* (pp. 34-47). Bellingham, WA: SPIE.

Robinson, J. T. (1981). *K-D-B-tree: A search structure for large multidimensional dynamic indices.* (Proceedings ACM SIGMOD Conference on the Management of Data) (pp. 10-18). Ann Arbor, MI.

Seeger, B., & Kriegel, H. P. (1990). *The buddy tree: An efficient and robust access method for spatial database systems.* (Proceedings of the 16th International Conference on Very Large Databases) (pp. 590-601). Brisbane, Australia.

RAMESH JAIN

Visual Information Retrieval in Digital Libraries

The emergence of information highways and multimedia computing has resulted in redefining the concept of libraries. It is widely believed that in the next few years, a significant portion of information in libraries will be in the form of multimedia electronic documents. Many approaches are being proposed for storing, retrieving, assimilating, harvesting, and prospecting information from these multimedia documents. Digital libraries are expected to allow users to access information independent of the locations and types of data sources and will provide a unified picture of information. In this paper, we discuss requirements of these emerging information systems and present query methods and data models for these systems. Finally, we briefly present a few examples of approaches that provide a preview of how things will be done in the digital libraries in the near future.

INTRODUCTION

The nature of documents is rapidly changing. A document in a computer is a combination of text, graphics, images, video, and audio. This revolution in the nature of documents, obviously brought on by the technology now available, has resulted in a major change in the role and nature of libraries. Digital or electronic libraries will allow access to information anywhere, anytime, and in the most desired form. Researchers in digital libraries are developing techniques to cope with this major change in the basic nature and functionality of libraries.

Another major change in the nature of libraries will be due to the amount of information available in a library. In fact, the basic notion of a centralized physical library is slowly disappearing. The World Wide Web has resulted in a transparent linking of worldwide information sources. Most of these information sources on the Web are currently multimedia documents. The amount of information on the Web is already beyond easy access without powerful search tools, and it is increasing exponentially. A library can now be considered a means of access to this vast resource on the Web. The libraries of the future will be similar to the World Wide Web than to the traditional physical library. This change results in some very interesting challenges. The most important challenge is to find the right information in this huge body of data.

In order to search digital libraries, many search tools are emerging, and these have become common on the Web. These search engines, which currently work only for text, help users by preparing data directories that assist in finding all documents relevant in the context of specified key words. Arguably, search engines have played a significant role in the popularity of the Web. Without these tools, we would be wasting significantly more time chasing links on the Web.

Since most documents are now multimedia, search tools for nontextual information will be required. Without search and organization methods for nontextual information, it will be very difficult to use digital libraries.

In this paper, we discuss visual information retrieval methods. We discuss the nature of visual information (graphics, images, and video) and present the techniques being developed to retrieve this information. In a digital library, these tools will work closely with textual searches. In this paper, however, the focus will be only on visual tools.

INFORMATION IN DIGITAL LIBRARIES

A few decades ago, traditional libraries had only books; they were the only mechanism to store and communicate data, information, and knowledge. Technological advances in several fields have made it possible to store and communicate other forms of knowledge as easily as books. A major reason for this is the multimedia revolution. The power of multimedia systems originates in the fact that disparate information can be represented as a bit stream. This is a big advantage because every form of representation, from video to text, can be stored, processed, and communicated using the same device—a computer. By reducing all forms of information to bit streams, we can start focusing on information rather than the sensor used to acquire it and the communication channel used to transport it. We can also use an appropriate presentation method to supply information to a user.

Most information in computers used to be alphanumeric and was already at a higher symbolic level. In multimedia systems, different types of information—images, text, audio, video, and graphics—are used. These media provide information in disparate representations and at different levels, ranging from signal (audio) to symbol (graphical). To combine and compare two information sources, it is essential that both information sources are understood, and this understanding should be at a level where we can compare and contrast information independent of the original representation medium. This is true for us, and if we want computers to seamlessly deal with disparate information sources, then we will have to do this for computers also. In digital libraries, computers should be able to distinguish each form of information. Strictly syntactic knowledge about video, audio, graphic, or any other form of data makes them just a communication channel. The most attractive feature of current multimedia systems is that, even with very little semantic information, they make different forms of information available in one environment. This facility is an enormous step in the right direction. By bringing all this information into a computing environment, we are developing systems that can deal with this information in a very flexible way.

Images, video, audio, and other information representation have a large volume of data. Technology is progressing rapidly to deal with the required storage and bandwidth problems. These information sources represent low-level information. When considered as a bit stream with the meta information, the explicit semantic information content in these sources is very low. This poses a serious problem in accessing these information sources. Humans are very efficient in abstracting information and then interacting with humans and other devices at a high level. This allows high bandwidth interactions among humans and between human and machines.

Multimedia systems currently have this semantic bottleneck. Techniques must be developed to add semantics to the data acquired from disparate sources in disparate forms. Since documents in digital libraries will be complex, tools to deal with information independent of its overall representation will become essential. A user may just ask a question and the answer may be available in the library in either text, image, graphics, or tabular form. The answer must be provided independent of the representation. In some cases, the answer may be partially available in different forms, and then these partial results must be combined at different information levels to provide the answer.

In this discussion, we consider the semantics of image and video data. No effort is made to address techniques that combine partial information from several sources. We will focus on how to represent information in images and how to organize images and related information to provide answers to a user from a database.

NEW DATABASE OPERATIONS

A digital library should allow the storage, communication, organization, processing, and envisioning of information. It should facilitate interactions by using natural interactions, which include multimedia input and output devices and use of high-level domain knowledge by a user.

Domain knowledge should be so much a part of a system such that a user feels that the system is an intelligent aide. A user should be able to articulate queries using terminology commonly used in his field and should not have to worry about the organization of information in the system.

The system should allow for powerful navigation tools. The user will use vague natural language, and that should be understood by the system to let a user navigate through the system. The nature of queries will be fuzzy not due to the laziness of the user but due to the nature of information and the size of the database. A general query environment will be like the one shown in figure 1. A user looking for certain information, for example, about a person who he vaguely recalls, specifies important things he remembers about the person. This specification may be that she has big eyes, wide mouth, long hair, and a small forehead. Based on this information, candidate people's pictures are retrieved. The user can then select the closest person that matches the query and modify the query by either specifying features or by using graphical and image-editing tools on the photo. This refines the query image, which is then sent to the system to provide new candidates to satisfy the query. Thus a query is incrementally formulated starting with the original vague idea. This process will terminate when the user is satisfied.

Due to the nature of data, several levels of abstraction in the data, and temporal changes in the data, the types and nature of interactions in such systems will be richer than those in a database or image processing system. We loosely refer to all interactions initiated by a user as queries. The types of queries in such systems can be defined in the following classes:

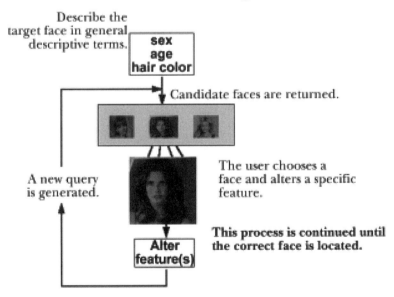

Incremental Queries

Describe the target face in general descriptive terms.

sex age hair color

Candidate faces are returned.

The user chooses a face and alters a specific feature.

A new query is generated.

Alter feature(s)

This process is continued until the correct face is located.

Figure 1. This figure shows that the queries in digital libraries will be incremental in nature. These queries will facilitate navigation and browsing of data.

1. *Search.* Search is one of the most commonly used operations in digital libraries. A user may want to search a library for specific images or documents containing some pictorial information. Tools should be provided to search based on this information. As discussed later, meta features are used to provide some information about images. In many applications, queries can be formulated to search specific images using only meta data. These queries can be answered, in most cases, using conventional database queries. In fact, many early image databases and browsers were designed using this approach.

   A search based on some image or object attributes is more common. To answer these queries, one may have to use visual attributes of images for the search. A major difference in these queries will be the fact that similarity becomes a central operation rather than conventional matching. Techniques to evaluate similarity are an active research topic in many fields of science and technology (Santini & Jain, in press). Many approaches have been proposed to compare several attributes to evaluate the similarity of two objects. In addition to the decision on what attributes to select, a very difficult decision is how to combine those attributes. Methods to combine attributes are domain dependent and subjective. It is clear, however, that in dealing with images and similar data sets, similarity rather than matching will be a key function in searching.

2. *Browse.* When a user approaches a library, the most common operation is browsing documents to locate those that may contain the information of interest. A user may have a vague idea about the attributes of an entity, relationships among entities in an image, or overall impression of an image. Such ideas are formed due to the overall appearance of the image rather than very specific objects and relations among them. In such cases, the user may be interested in browsing the database based on an overall impression or appearance of images rather than searching for a specific entity. The system should allow formulation of fuzzy queries to browse through the database. In browsing mode, there is no specific entity for which a user is looking. The system should provide data sets that are representative of all data in the system. The system should also keep track of what has been shown to the user. Some mechanism to judge the interest level of the user in the data displayed should be developed and this interest level should be logged to determine what to display next.

3. *Temporal Events.* It is estimated that videos will be a major source of information in digital libraries. The number of videos has been rapidly increasing, and video is becoming an integral part of compound documents. In video sequences, one may want to retrieve images based on some events taking place in the sequence. A typical query of this

type may be: Show me all sequences in which player *X* was blocked by player *Y*. These queries will require temporal analysis of video sequences in terms of the events of interest. Some primitive spatio-temporal features must be computed and stored in the database to answer questions concerning events of interest to users.

Abstractions in spatio-temporal space are not yet understood well enough to automatically extract them from video sequences. Though some techniques have been developed to represent relative time ordering of two events, representations for abstraction of events need to be developed to allow users to articulate questions related to temporal events.

4. *Integrated Queries.* Users are interested in getting information independent of the medium. Thus, in a document, the requested information may be either in text, image, graphics, or video form, and the system should provide the information without a user knowing the medium. This facility will require an abstraction of information from every media into one unified representation. We do not know of any efforts being made in this area yet.

DATA MODEL AND VISUAL FEATURES

Information in an image exists at several abstraction levels and should be accessible at these levels. The data model used to store this information must allow the existence of information at these multiple levels. Several data models have been proposed (e.g., see Gupta, 1991). Here we discuss one model that allows explicit representation of abstract levels in images. The VIMSYS data model uses a hierarchical representation of data using various levels of semantic interpretation that may satisfy the needs of digital libraries (Gupta et al., 1991). This data model is shown in Figure 2. At the image representation (IR) level, the actual image data are stored. Image objects (such as lines and regions) are extracted from the image and stored in the image object (IO) layer with no domain interpretation. Each of these objects may be associated with a domain object (DO) in that layer. The semantic interpretation is incorporated in these objects. The domain event (DE) layer can then associate objects of the DO layer with each other, providing the semantic representation of spatial or temporal relationships. This hierarchy provides a mechanism for translating high-level semantic concepts into content-based queries using the corresponding image data. This allows queries based on object similarity to be generated without requiring the user to specify the low-level image structure and attributes of the objects. Another very important aspect of this representation is that the first two levels, IR and IO, are domain-independent levels and the other two, DO and DS, are domain-dependent levels. We do not know any system yet where this goal of clearly organizing domain-dependent and domain-independent components can be cleanly partitioned and implemented. We believe, however, that this is a worthwhile target. The architecture discussed below is motivated by this desire.

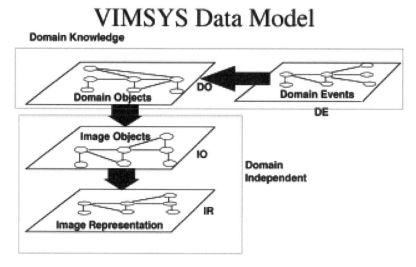

Figure 2. A four-level data model to capture different levels of abstractions in visual information systems is shown here. The image levels are domain independent, the other two levels depend on the domain.

These ideas have been used to develop several systems for the retrieval of images and video information in our group (Gupta et al., 1991; Bach et al., 1992; Swanberg et al., 1993a). Here we discuss each of the system components briefly. In the following discussion, we will discuss this architecture in the context of images and video, but our concepts are applicable to any kind of data.

TYPES OF FEATURES

Features must be extracted from input images and stored in the database. As is well known, different applications may require different features (Jain et al., 1995). Since the features must be stored at the time of data entry, one must carefully decide which features will be used in a system. We consider that all features must be classified in one of the following classes:

1. F_u. This set contains the features which are commonly referred to as meta-features. Some of these features can be automatically acquired

from the associated information on images. These features may include the size of the image, photographer, date taken, resolution, and similar additional information. This group also contains other features that can be called user-specified. Values are assigned to these features by the user at the time of insertion. Many of these features can be read by the system either from the header, file name, or other similar sources. These features cannot be directly extracted from images.

2. F_d. This set contains the features which are derived directly from the image data at the time of insertion of the images in the database. Values are automatically calculated for these features using automatic or semiautomatic functions. These features are called derived features and include those that are commonly required in answering queries. These features are stored in the database.

3. F_c. This set contains the features whose values are not calculated until they are needed. Routines must be provided to calculate these values when they become necessary. These features may be computed from data at the query time. These are called query-only features or computed features.

The first two types of features are actually stored in the database. Metadata can be frequently read from other sources or should be manually entered. Which feature should be in F_d and which should be in F_c is an engineering decision. One must study frequently asked queries and determine the required features. This determines the set to which a particular feature should belong.

The system interface encourages users to formulate queries using metadata and derived features as much as possible. It reluctantly allows use of computed features. To access data, the system can purge the search space significantly using metadata and derived features and then apply computed features to only this reduced set of images. This strategy allows flexibility while maintaining a reasonable response time. The system may be able to predict wait time using number of images from which computed features must be extracted.

INTERFACES

Users of digital libraries will have disparate backgrounds. As a result, the interfaces to these libraries should be such that any novice can use intuitive methods. The operations used in these interactions must require almost no knowledge of the organization of the data and information. Many of these operations cannot be conveniently performed using traditional interfaces. Here we discuss some general issues in designing interfaces for digital libraries. Interactions with libraries are likely to be multimedia. Due to the nature of the data and several abstraction levels, it is expected that users will require multimodal interface mechanisms.

Our focus on visual queries in digital libraries must allow facilities to formulate the following interactions:

- *General Search*: In general, there will be two modes of navigation in libraries: locating and browsing. In the location mode, a user knows what he or she wants and the goal of the queries will be to get precisely that information. Also in the location mode, many queries may be symbolic because what is required can be articulated using meta data. Some location queries may require visual data. It is expected that search queries will deal mostly with meta data. For these queries, some query language, possibly a variant of SQL, may be used.

- *Query by Pictorial Example (QPE)*: A very powerful expression of a query is to point to a picture and expect that the system will show all pictures similar to the example. This approach is easy to use but very complex to implement. The system must use certain features and some similarity measures to evaluate other pictures that are similar to the example. Effectively, the system must rank all data with respect to the example and then display pictures that are closest to the example. Interestingly, this has been very popular in designing image databases (Niblack et al., 1993).

In QPE, features and similarity measures must be clearly defined for use in retrieving images. Similarity judgment has been a difficult problem and continues to attract the attention of several researchers (Santini & Jain, in press). The most interesting fact about similarity measures is that they are domain dependent and very subjective. Assuming that we have identified a measure that is acceptable to a user for his or her domain, we face some interesting problems in QPE. All images are compared to the example to evaluate their similarity. This is possible in those cases where the size of the database is such that computations can be done in a reasonable time. When the size of the database grows such that it is not possible to accommodate all data in main memory and such computations become impractical, one must resort to indexing techniques.

Indexing techniques for spatial data have been developed (Jagadish, 1991; Niblack et al., 1993; Samet, 1984). These techniques are very limited when it comes to addressing the problem of similarity indexing. Techniques like TV-trees are a good step in the right direction but lack several important features (Linet al., 1994).

- *Query Canvas:* Queries may be formulated by starting with an existing picture, scanning a new picture, and modifying these by using the visual and graphical tools available in common picture editing programs, such as Adobe Photoshop. One may cut and paste from several images to articulate a query in the form of an image. It is also possible to start from a clean image and then draw an image using different drawing tools. The basic idea in this approach is to provide a tool to define a picture that may be used in a QPE. This approach allows a user to define a picture that they are looking for using visual tools. This will provide users with a visual query environment.

- *Containment Queries:* In many cases, a user may point to an object or circle an area in an image and request all images that contain similar regions. These queries seem simple and will be if complete segmentation of images is performed and all region properties are stored. Most image database systems store only global characteristics of an image. In these cases, one is looking for all images that are a superset of the region attributes. Once all such images are retrieved, some other filtering techniques could be developed to solve this problem.

- *Semantic Queries:* All the above queries were based on image attributes. In most applications, an image database is likely to be prepared for a specific domain-dependent application, such as human faces, icefloe images, or retinal images. It is important that users can then interact using domain-dependent terms. It is common that people may describe a person using terms like big eyes, wide mouth, small ears, rather than the corresponding image objects.

  Semantic queries require extensive use of domain knowledge. Domain knowledge is necessary both in defining features that will be used by the system and in interpreting user queries. Most image database systems either considered domain knowlede implicitly by defining features or ignored it (Faloutsos et al., 1994). The role of explicit knowledge in image databases is discussed in (Gupta et al., 1991; Swanberg et al., 1993a; Swanberg et al., 1993b).

- *Object Related Queries:* These queries are semantic and ask for the presence of an object. These queries may deal with three-dimensional objects. Since three-dimensional objects are difficult to recognize using automated techniques, these queries may become very complex. Three-dimensional object recognition is a very active research area in machine vision. Queries based on recognizing objects in a query image may be, therefore, very difficult to execute.

- *Spatio-Temporal Queries:* In video sequences, and in many other applications where pictures are obtained over a long period, a user may want to get answers to some spatio-temporal events and concepts. Answers to such questions may require complete analysis of all video sequences and storing some important features from there. Considering the fact that methods to represent temporal events are not well developed yet, this area requires much research before one can design a system to deal with spatio-temporal queries at the natural language level.

EXAMPLE SYSTEMS

In this section, we present some emerging approaches in visual information retrieval. The information may be retrieved either based on global image properties or on object characteristics. We discuss approaches for both these systems and present example systems.

Image Databases

When one looks at an image, some global impression is formed. This impression is based on some general characteristics of images. Even in those cases where one may be interested in objects in images, global characteristics may help. This is due to the fact that, in the context of the library, many images will contain only one object of interest, and this object will be photographed in relatively controlled conditions. Thus, one may design a powerful system just by considering basic image features. Some very basic image features are color, texture, and shape. Grayscale images are considered here as a special case of color. On first examination, it appears that one should consider attributes of objects in images. From machine vision literature, it is clear that segmentation is a difficult problem (Jain et al., 1995). While dealing with a diverse set of images which are acquired under varying conditions, segmentation may be very difficult. In such cases, one may want to completely ignore domain knowledge and build a database only using image attributes. These attributes may be computed for complete images or for their predefined areas.

Many systems have been designed using image-only attributes. QBIC from IBM uses color, texture, and manually segmented shapes (Faloutsos et al., 1994). QBIC was the first complete system to demonstrate the efficacy of simple attributes in appearance-based retrieval of images from a reasonably sized database. The use of shape in QBIC is problematic, however. Shape is defined for individual segments which must be obtained manually. This also creates an artificial situation in the database because, for each manually obtained segment, one must consider a separate record in the database. Thus if an image has N objects, the database must contain $N + 1$ records—one for the image and one each for N segments. Shape measures on complete images are not satisfactory because shape is defined for an image region. Some heuristics have been proposed, but much remains to be done in this area.

Color is considered a global characteristic. Most systems rely on color histograms. Some kind of histogram matching is done to determine similarity of two images. Histogram-based approaches clearly ignore spatial proximity of colors and hence may result in erroneous results. In most cases, however, histogram-based matching is quite effective.

Texture poses a more difficult problem. Most systems use global measures of texture and try to assign some texture attribute to images. These attributes are then used for evaluating similarity of texture in images. Most images contain different types of texture in different parts of the image. The global texture attributes, therefore, could be misleading. These systems use only the first two levels of the VIMSYS data model. Since both of these—IR and IO—levels are domain independent, these image databases are domain independent. Users of these systems must supply the semantics in these systems. The semantics can be provided by using color and texture attributes of objects of interest. One may filter using these attributes and then use domain-dependent features on remaining images to retrieve desired information.

An example of an image database that provides tools to organize and retrieve information using image level information is the PinPoint system

Figure 3. A screen shot of PinPoint showing the query window and all images retrieved using QPE. Notice that a user can adjust weights of features and the feedback to the user is instantaneous.

developed at Virage. This system extracts features to characterize images using color, texture, structure, and composition. These features can be combined using distance functions. This system treats keywords also like features by using a thesaurus to compute distances between keywords in the query and stored images. The weights of the features can be changed to retrieve similar images using different similarity functions. We show a screen shot of this system in Figure 3. This shot shows all images retrieved as similar to the example image, which is the best matching image and hence appears as the first image in similar images. If the images are created using the query canvas, shown in Figure 4, then one can articulate a query by cutting and pasting and by other image manipulation operations. It must be mentioned that this system has no domain-level knowledge.

Interestingly, even without any domain knowledge in this system, users very quickly learn to retrieve images of their choice by using an example image and appropriate weights of the features provided in the system. The system uses color, texture, and structure as features of an image. In color, both global colors, and automatically segmented segments and their locations, defined as composition, are used. For texture, several properties

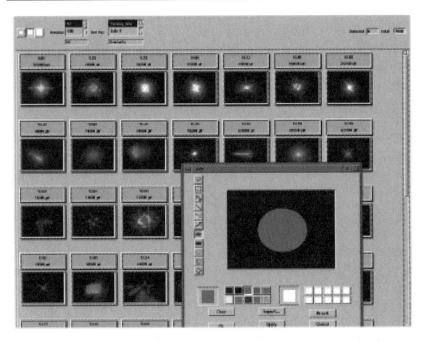

Figure 4. The query canvas allows a user to articulate a query using visual means. One can cut and paste from images and use image manipulation programs to articulate a query.

are computed using standard texture features and are combined to represent an overall measure of the texture. Structure addresses shapes and location of edge segments. It is interesting to see that these purely image-based features, when combined with hand drawn queries on a canvas or an image selected for QPE, perform quite effectively in retrieving semantically relevant objects. This strongly suggests that by defining a pictorial alphabet and suitable rules to use this alphabet, it may be possible to develop powerful domain-dependent systems.

Semantic Knowledge: The Xenomania System

One can use domain knowledge to extract features at insert time and interpret user queries using domain knowledge and statistical characteristics of the information in the database. Many projects in academia and industry address these issues. Here we demonstrate some of these ideas using a face retrieval system called Xenomania implemented at the University of Michigan (Bach et al., 1992).

Xenomania was an interactive system for the retrieval of face images and information. It allows a user to locate a specific person in the database and retrieve the person's image and other information. The user can describe the target face in general terms—e.g., shape of eyes, nose, length of hair—to begin the location process and to retrieve the initial results. After that, the target face may be described using these general terms or by using the actual image contents of the retrieved faces. All aspects of the architecture described above are incorporated into this system (this system is described by Bach et al. [1992]).

We chose the interactive face identification problem because of the lack of well-defined image objects and features and the heavy dependence on both predefined domain knowledge and extensive user participation. Although much work has been done toward modeling of facial features, it is still very difficult to accurately extract and evaluate these features over a variety of faces and situations and even more difficult to assign semantic attributes to these features which are meaningful to users. This application exploits the demands for both extensive predefined domain knowledge and user-incorporated knowledge at every step of processing.

Xenomania relied very heavily on previous research in the field of face recognition. Much work was done regarding the psychological aspects of face recognition which provided a basis for our initial implementation. Many automatic face recognition systems have also been developed. The Xenomania project, however, was not a face recognition system but rather an image database system used for interactive face retrieval. Some face-recognition systems have approached the problem from strictly an image processing point of view with little or no emphasis on descriptive representation of faces. These systems do not incorporate the user for describing the face or guiding the query refinement once the recognition process has been initiated. The most successful face reocgnition system is based on eigenfaces (Pentland, Moghaddam, & Starner, 1994; Pentland, Picard, & Sclaroff, 1994). This system is also influenced by image recognition approaches. In an eigenface-based system, one can specify an image and the system will retrieve all images that are similar to that. It may be interesting to combine eigenfaces with the descriptive approach used in Xenomania.

Domain Knowledge

As in any image management application, we are faced with the difficulty of determining which attributes are important for each domain object, and how to accurately represent these attributes in the system. However, this is an attractive problem from our point of view, because it gives us the opportunity to investigate different types of object and feature representations. For instance, there are several attributes about an eye that may be important. Individual eye attributes such as area and width will be necessary, as will relative attributes such as the width of the eye compared to the height of the eye. Spatial attributes such as distance between the left eye and the right eye are also important and must be incorporated into the system. Other objects, such as eyebrows, may require entirely different attributes than those for eyes to be maintained in the system. We have based much of our initial implementation on research that has been done to evaluate which facial features and attributes are best suited for face identification and differentiation.

Many image databases are likely to be for specific applications and hence will require strong domain knowledge. The domain objects should be described using the image alphabet or image objects in the VIMSYS model. This task will require close interactions among database designers, image processing experts, and domain experts.

VIDEO DATABASES: TV NEWS ON DEMAND

Video is rapidly becoming the preferred mode of receiving information and video is certainly the most vivid medium for conveying information. Video has gained tremendous popularity since it appeared on the scene. As is well known, television has been one of the most influential inventions of this century. As a result, the last decade has seen rapid growth in camcorder use in all aspects of human activities.

Video is the most impressive medium for communicating and recording events in our life. Its use is limited, however, by its basically sequential nature. To access a particular segment of interest on a tape, one must spend significant time searching for the segment. Video databases have potential to change the way we access and use video.

By storing each individual shot in the database, one can then access any individual frame based on the content of the shot. Each shot can be analyzed to find what is contained in each shot. Frames in each shot can be analyzed to find events in it. By segmenting videos into shots and analyzing those shots, one can extract information that can be put into a database. This database can then be searched to find sequences of interest.

Video databases can be useful in many applications. One application is news on demand. Suppose that each sequence is analyzed and the information in it is stored in a database with pointers to the relevant frames. This database then can be used to view the news of choice to the depth desired by a user and in the sequence desired. We are implementing such a system in our laboratory (Swanberg et al, 1993a; Swanberg et al., 1993b; Hampapur et al., 1994a; Hampapur et al., 1994b). Details of segmentation of the sequence, architecture of the system, role of knowledge in such a system, and all other aspects have been presented in Swanberg et al., 1993a; Swanberg et al., 1993b; and Hampapur et al., 1994. It must be mentioned here that many other systems of this type are being implemented in other places.

The architecture for the video database is composed of four major components: input, database, query environment, and knowledge base. The input module is further divided into two major components: a sequence segmentation subsystem and a feature detection subsystem. The knowledge module has a video object schema definition subsystem to help a user enter knowledge into the system for a specific application. The video object schema definition subsystem provides tools to model the video object schema for an application based on the operators available in the input and query processing systems. Based on the video object schema, the feature detection subsystem analyzes a video frame sequence to extract structure and the semantic information about each object of interest in the video. The extracted objects and related semantic information are then stored in the feature database. According to the video object schema definition, a user query interface is automatically customized. A user can also navigate the video object schema defined from the video object schema definition subsystem as well as its associated video object data through the user query interface.

CONCLUSION AND FUTURE RESEARCH

We have discussed some basic issues in visual information retrieval and presented some example systems. As is clear from these examples, these systems are in the early stages of development, but there is growing research interest in this area. Many powerful approaches are being developed for image and video databases. It is clear that these approaches should work very closely with textual and audio search techniques. We believe that, as research in these areas progresses, we will see the emergence of powerful multimedia information retrieval techniques. These techniques will allow a user to articulate their queries using the medium of their choice and will retrieve information from distributed multimedia libraries. The next few years are likely to result in significant progress in this area.

ACKNOWLEDGMENTS

The research and ideas presented in this paper evolved during collaborations with several people in the InfoScope project. I am thankful to everyone who actively participated in the project. I want to particularly thank Jeff Bach, Shankar Chatterjee, Amarnath Gupta, Arun Hampapur, Bradley Horowitz, Arun Katkere, Don Kuramura, Saied Moezzi, Edna Nerona, Simone Santini, Chiao-Fe Shu, Deborah Swanberg, David White, and Terry Weymouth for collaboration in different aspects of this work.

REFERENCES

Bach, J.; Paul, S.; & Jain, R. (1992). An interactive image management system for face information retrieval. *IEEE transactions on knowledge and data engineering, 5*(6), 619-628.

Faloutsos, C.; Barber, R.; Flickner, M.; Hafner, J.; Niblack, W.; Petkovic, D.; & Equitz, W. (1994). Efficient and effective querying by image content. *Journal of Intelligent Information Systems, 3*(3/4), 231-262.

Gupta, A.; Weymouth, T.; & Jain, R. (1991). Semantic queries with pictures: The VIMSYS model. In *Proceedings of the 17th International Conference on Very Large Databases* (pp. 69-79). Barcelona, Spain: Morgan Kaufmann Publishers.

Hampapur, A.; Jain, R.; & Weymouth, T. (1994a). Digital video indexing in multimedia systems. In *Proceedings of the Workshop on Indexing and Reuse in Multimedia Systems. Proceedings of the 12th National Conference on Artificial Intelligence.* Seattle, WA: American Association of Artificial Intelligence Press.

Hampapur, A.; Jain, R.; & Weymouth, T. (1994b). Digital video segmentation. In *Proceedings of the ACM Conference on Multimedia.* Association of Computing Machinery.

Jagadish, H. V. (1991). A retrieval technique for similar shapes. In *Proceedings of the ACM SIGMOD International Conference on the Management of Data* (pp. 208-217). Denver, CO: ACM.

Jain, R.; Kasturi, R.; & Schunck, B. (1995). *Machine vision.* New York: McGraw-Hill, Inc.

Lin, K-I.; Jagadish, H. V.; & Faloutsos, C. (1994). The TV-tree: An index structure for high-dimensional data. *VLDB Journal, 3*(4), 517-542.

Niblack, W.; Barber, R.; Equitz, W.; Flickner, M. D.; Glasman, E. H.; Petkovic, D.; Yanker, P.; Faloutsos, C.; & Taubin, G. (1993). The QBIC project: Querying images by content, using color, texture, and shape. In W. Niblack (Ed.), *Storage and Retrieval for Image and Video Databases: Vol. 1908: SPIE Proceedings* (pp.173-187). Bellingham, WA: SPIE.

Pentland, A.; Moghaddam, B.; & Starner, T. (1994). View-based and modular eigenspaces for face recognition. In *Proceedings of the IEEE Computer Society Conference on Computer Vision and Pattern Recognition* (pp. 84-91). Seattle, WA: IEEE Press.

Pentland, A.; Picard, R. W.; & Sclaroff, S. (1994). Photobook: Tools for content-based manipulation of image databases. In W. Niblack & R. Jain (Eds.), *Storage and Retrieval for Image and Video Databases II: Vol. 2185: SPIE Proceedings* (pp. 34-47). Bellingham, WA: SPIE.

Samet, H. (1984). The quadtree and related hierarchical data structures. *Computing Surveys,* *16*(2), 187-260.

Swanberg, D.; Shu, C. F.; & Jain, R. (1993a). Architecture of a multimedia information system for content-based retrieval. In P. V. Rangan (Ed.), *Network and operating system support for digital audio and video: Third international workshop proceedings.* Berlin: Springer-Verlag.

Swanberg, D.; Shu, C. F.; & Jain, R. (1993b). Knowledge-guided parsing in video databases. In *Electronic imaging: Science and technology proceedings* (pp. 13-24). San Jose, CA: IST/SPIE.

Swanberg, D.; Weymouth, T.; & Jain, R. (1992). Domain information model: An extended data model for insertions and query. In *Proceedings of the Multimedia Information Systems* (pp. 39-51). Tempe, AZ: Arizona State University, Intelligent Information Systems Laboratory.

White, D., & Jain, R. (1996). Similarity indexing with the SS-tree. In *Proceedings of the IEEE 12th International Conference on Data Engineering* (pp. 516-523). Los Alamitos, CA: IEEE.

SHIH-FU CHANG, JOHN R. SMITH, & JIANHAO MENG

Efficient Techniques for Feature-Based Image/Video Access and Manipulation

This paper describes our recent work on content-based visual query with emphasis on automatic visual feature extraction, efficient feature indexing, and feature-assisted search and browsing. Efficient techniques for manipulating compressed videos are included as well. We will discuss several research prototypes, including VisualSeek, which is a Java-based WWW application supporting localized color and spatial similarity retrieval; CVEPS (Compressed Video Editing and Parsing System), which supports feature-based indexing and editing of video in the compressed domain; and a hierarchical news video browsing and indexing system.

INTRODUCTION

Efficient and effective methods for indexing, searching, and retrieving images and videos from large archives are critical techniques required in visual information systems (VIS) applications. Users need a more powerful method for searching images than just traditional text-based query (e.g., keywords). Manual creation of keywords is too time-consuming for many practical applications. Subjective descriptions based on users' input will be neither consistent nor complete. Also, the vocabulary used in describing visual contents is usually domain specific.

There is a recent effort, called content-based visual query (CBVQ) (Niblack et al., 1993; Jain, 1992), aimed at effective solutions to the above problem. Before a discussion of the technical issues involved in the CBVQ, we first briefly discuss its relationships with other image indexing/retrieval approaches.

There are several possible ways of indexing and retrieving visual material. From users' point of view, the more methods available, the higher the flexibility they can exercise and adapt to the specific information they are seeking. However, from the system designer's point of view, different methods imply different cost and efficiency. It is important to achieve good overall system performance. The traditional keyword-based retrieval methods can be extended to more general semantic-level descriptions such as "a red car in front of a house" or "a person running on the beach." This type of retrieval requires semantic information given by users in the indexing stage. The second type of query allows users to specify a complete image or an image region as the query key. Specific images can be retrieved based on similarity with the input image itself or the image features derived from the input image. This is usually called a query by image example. The last type of query is feature-based image retrieval. Visual signal features are extracted in the indexing stage and compared in the search stage to find the "similar" images/videos. Typical features include texture, color, shape, object layout, motion, camera operations, face, logo, associated audio and speech, etc. Some features are for still images and others are for videos although, in general, all still image features are applicable to video as well. The formulation of input features to the search engine can be provided by user's raw data (e.g., drawing and sketch) or user's selection from system templates. The population of feature sets from each image or video in the database can be automatic or semi-automatic (i.e., with user assistance). Knowledge of the application domain also helps significantly in developing reliable automatic retrieval techniques.

In CBVQ, the term "content" refers to the structure and semantics of images and videos at various levels, ranging from pixel patterns, physical objects, spatial/temporal structures, to high-level semantics of the visual material. The content-based approach is not intended as a replacement for the keyword approach. Instead, it is considered as a complementary tool, particularly for applications which have large data collections and that require a fast search response. Provision of the content-based visual retrieval techniques also brings in new synergy between the text-based information and the visual information of the same material. Fusion of different information channels (text and visual in this case) has been used to achieve performance improvement in multimedia databases such as news archives (Srihari, 1995).

A content-based visual query system requires several key components, including:

- choice of effective visual features and their integration with textual indexes;
- visual feature extraction (automatic or semi-automatic) and object segmentation;
- design of effective discrimination measures;
- efficient indexing data structure for high-dimensional feature space;
- efficient user interface for query specification and visual browsing;
- association with domain knowledge and other data types;
- exploration of functionalities in the compressed domain; and
- evaluation criterion and methodologies.

The above broad list reflects the broad cross-disciplinary nature of this area. However, to achieve the goal of searching images/videos based on visual content, a very challenging issue is visual content analysis and automatic extraction of "prominent" features. The definition of "prominence" may depend on the actual application requirements, but a general bottom-up approach is as follows: start with a rich set of automatically extracted low-level generic visual features, then derive high-level semantics by applying the domain knowledge provided by users or applications.

We focus on issues directly related to image/video processing and associated algorithms for efficient indexing, computation, and visualization for improving overall system performance. Several groups have reported promising work in this area (Niblack et al., 1993; Pentland et al., in press; Zhang et al., 1993; Dimitrova & Golshani, 1994; Yeo & Liu, 1995; Hampapur et al., 1995; Mehrotra & Gary, 1995; Stone & Li, 1996; Sawhney et al., 1995). We contrast our work with others by using a fully automatic process for localized feature extraction (e.g., local color and texture regions), compressed-domain feature extraction without full decoding of compressed images/videos, and efficient user interfaces for users to specify localized features and their spatial layout.

We will describe two example prototype systems of content-based visual query—VisualSEEk and CVEPS. VisualSEEk is a fully automated content-based image query system which allows users to search images by localized colors and their spatial layout. It includes a Java-based Web interface for interactive visual content specification, integrated visual/textual search, and performance evaluation. It is the first CBVQ system which supports local content specification and integrated query using visual feature and spatial layout. CVEPS (Compressed Video Editing and Parsing System) is a software prototype of a video indexing and manipulation system which supports automatic video segment decomposition, video indexing based on key frames or objects, and compressed video editing. It is the first software-based system supporting both indexing and manipulation of compressed video. The compressed domain approach provides great benefits in reducing computational complexity, storage space requirements, and improving picture quality. Implementation of a simple editing function—e.g., random cut and paste—can be improved in speed by about 100 times by using the compressed-domain approach.

VISUALSEEK

VisualSEEk is a new content-based image query system that provides for querying by both image region visual properties and spatial layout. VisualSEEk is a hybrid system in that it integrates feature-based image representation with spatial query methods. The integration relies on a recently proposed representation of color regions by color sets (Smith & Chang, 1996). Color sets provide for a convenient system of region extraction through back projection. In addition, a decomposition of the quadratic form of the color set distance function consists of terms that are easily indexed. This allows for the efficient computation of color set distance and the indexing of color sets. As a result, unconstrained images are decomposed into near-symbolic images which lend themselves to efficient spatial query.

CONTENT-BASED IMAGE QUERY

A recurring problem in image database research is how to efficiently retrieve items from the database that optimize some function. In content-based image query applications, this function approximates the perceptual similarity between the user's query image and target images in the database. In general, when the database is large and the image features have many dimensions, the exhaustive search of the database is not computationally expedient. Furthermore, recent approaches toward content-based image query have neglected two important aspects of visual perception—spatial information and spatial relationships.

SPATIAL IMAGE QUERY

A significant aspect of discriminating among images depends on the spatial locations and relationships between objects or regions within the image. However, the problem of content-based image query is only exacerbated by introducing multiple image regions and spatial information into the query process. This is due to the combinatorial explosion resulting from comparison among multiples of regions or objects. On the other hand, by representing images symbolically, spatial query methods compare the spatial relationships of symbols. However, spatial queries do not consider the similarity of the "symbols" such as that based upon visual features of objects or regions.

JOINT CONTENT-BASED/SPATIAL IMAGE QUERY

In VisualSEEk, we propose a new system that provides both feature comparison and spatial query for unconstrained color images. To illustrate (see figure 1), each image is decomposed into regions which have feature properties such as color, texture, and shape and spatial properties such as location and spatial relationships. The most desirable image query system allows users to query by both visual features and spatial properties. Recent approaches for image retrieval do not provide for both types of querying. The QBIC system (Niblack et al., 1993) provides querying of manually segmented regions by color, texture, and shape but not by spatial relationships. The Virage system (Bach et al., 1996) allows querying of only an image's global features such as color, composition, texture, and structure.

 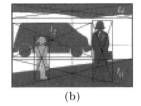 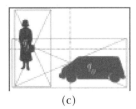

(a) (b) (c)

Figure 1. Query decomposition (a) target image, (b) regions with both feature and spatial properties, $T = \{\hat{t}_0, \hat{t}_1, ..., \hat{t}_4\}$, (c) query image, $Q = \{\hat{a}_0, \hat{q}_1\}$.

To solve the problem of integrating content-based and spatial image query, we decompose the parameters of the image distance function into two classes—intrinsic and derived variables. Then we design the representations for intrinsic variables such as region color, spatial location, and size to require minimal computation in matching. For example, color matching is achieved efficiently through color sets. Furthermore, the intrinsic variables are indexed directly to allow for maximum efficiency in queries. In this way, a query specified by the user is translated into pruning operations on intrinsic variables. The derived variables, such as region-relative locations and special spatial relations, are resolved only in the final stage of the query. This is because these evaluations have the highest complexity. The pruning performed by the queries on the intrinsic variables reduces the number of candidate images that need to be evaluated at the final stage.

UNIQUE FEATURES OF VISUALSEEK

VisualSEEk has joint image feature/spatial querying; automated region extraction; and direct indexing of color features. The VisualSEEk project has also emphasized several unique objectives in order to enhance the functionality and usability of image retrieval systems: (1) automated extraction of localized regions and features (Smith & Chang, 1996a), (2) querying by both feature and spatial information (Smith & Chang, 1996b), (3) extraction from compressed data (Chang, 1993), (4) development of techniques for fast indexing and retrieval, and (5) development of highly functional user tools. The VisualSEEk client application was developed in the Java language to allow for maximum functionality, client platform independence, and accessibility on the World Wide Web. As illustrated in Figure 2, VisualSEEk consists of several components: the set of user tools, the query server, the image and video retrieval server, the image and video archive, the meta-data database, and the index files. Currently, the VisualSEEk system allows searching on a test bed of 12,000 miscellaneous color images. The users can search for images using color and spatial attributes.

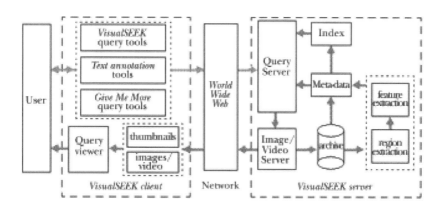

Figure 2. VisualSeek system architecture.

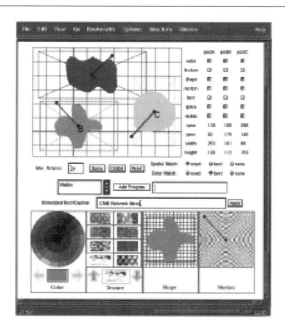

Figure 3. VisualSEEK user interface provides tools for sketching query regions, assigning region properties and positioning regions to form joint content-based/ spatial image queries.

QUERY FORMULATION

The joint color/spatial queries are formulated graphically by using the VisualSEEk user tools as illustrated in figure 3. The user sketches regions, positions them on the query grid, and assigns them properties of color, size, and absolute location. The user may also assign boundaries for location and size. The relationships between regions are diagrammed by connecting regions. In this way, the interface provides for queries that include region features and combinations of both absolute and relative placement of the regions.

VISUALSEEK QUERIES

We present some example joint content-based/spatial queries in VisualSEEk. In the first example (see Figure 4[a]), the query (top) specifies the absolute location of a single region. The retrieved image (bottom) has the best match in features (color and size) to the query region and falls within the "zero distance" boundary diagrammed in the query. In the next example (see Figure 4[b]), the query specifies multiple regions. The retrieved image provides the best match in terms of the features and absolute spatial locations of the query regions. In the next example (see Figure 4[c]), the query specifies the spatial relationships of regions. The retrieved image has three regions that best match the features of the query regions and their spatial relationship satisfies that specified in the query. Finally (see Figure 4[d]), the query specifies both absolute and relative locations of regions. In this query, the match to the region positioned by absolute location (top left region in the query image) considers both the features and location of this region. The match to the other regions (the bottom two regions in the query image) at first

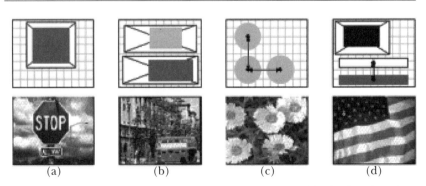

(a) (b) (c) (d)

Figure 4. Example VisualSEEk queries (a) single region with absolute location, (b) two regions with absolute locations, (c) multiple regions with relative locations, (d) multiple regions with both absolute and relative locations.

considers only the features of these regions. In the last stage of the query, the spatial relationship of the regions is evaluated to determine the match.

The discrimination of images is only partly provided by features such as color, texture, and shape. Another important component is based upon the spatial locations and relationships of objects and regions within the images. The VisualSEEk system provides for the retrieval of images by image features and by the spatial locations, relationships, and sizes of color regions. In VisualSEEk, the image feature computation is efficiently integrated into the spatial querying methods. In the future, work will extend the VisualSEEk system to support other image features, such as texture and shape, in the task of joint feature-based/spatial image query.

CVEPS

CVEPS is a functional software-based prototype system for compressed video editing, indexing, and browsing. It provides automatic tools for video segment (i.e., shot) decomposition, special effect detection (e.g., zoom, panning, dissolve), moving objects extraction, key frame/object indexing, and nonlinear editing, mostly in the compressed domain without full decoding of the original compressed streams. By using the compressed-domain approach, real-time performance is achieved even with software implementation.

The compressed-domain approach offers many great benefits. First, implementation of the same manipulation algorithms in the compressed domain will be much cheaper than that in the uncompressed domain because the data rate is highly reduced in the compressed domain (e.g., a typical 20:1 to 50:1 compression ratio for MPEG). Second, given most existing images and videos stored in the compressed form, the specific manipulation algorithms can be applied to the compressed streams without full decoding of the compressed images/videos. Third, because full decoding and re-encoding of video is not necessary, we can avoid the extra quality degradation that usually occurs in the re-encoding process. We have shown earlier that for MPEG compressed video editing, the speed performance can be improved by more than 100 times, and the video quality can be improved by about 3-4 dB if we use the compressed-domain approach rather than the traditional decode-edit-reencode approach (Meng & Chang, 1996).

The primary compression standard used in CVEPS is MPEG (MPEG-1 or MPEG-2). But the underlying approach and techniques are general enough to be applied to other video compression standards using transform coding and/or interframe motion compensation.

In order to allow users to manipulate compressed video efficiently, two types of functionalities are required: (1) key content browsing and search, and (2) compressed video editing. The former allows users to efficiently browse through, or search for, key content of the video without decoding and viewing the entire video stream. The key content refers to the key frames in video sequences, prominent video objects and their associated visual features (motion, shape, color, and trajectory), or special reconstructed video models for representing video content in a video scene. The second type of functionalities, video editing, allows users to manipulate the object of interest in the video stream without full decoding. One example is to cut and paste any arbitrary segments from existing video streams and produce a new video stream which conforms to the valid compression format. Other examples include special visual effects typically used in video production studios.

SYSTEM COMPONENTS

CVEPS consists of three major modules: parsing, visualization, and authoring (see Figure 5). In the parsing module, MPEG-compressed video is first broken into shot segments. Within each shot, camera operation parameters (e.g., zooming, panning) are estimated. Then moving objects are detected and their shape and trajectory features are extracted.

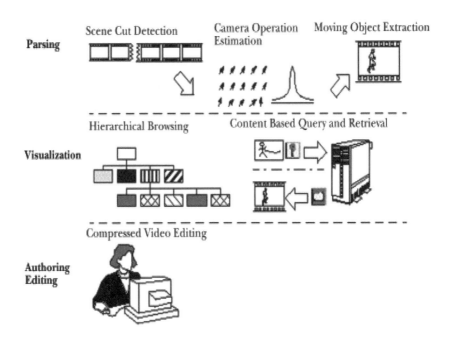

Figure 5. CVEPS System Overview.

In the visualization module, the scene cut list and the camera zoom/pan information are used to extract key frames for representing each video shot. For example, a zoom-in video shot may be represented with the first frame of the shot and a detailed zoom-in frame or a video mosaic.

The key frames can be browsed with the hierarchical video scene browser based on scene clustering described in the next subsection (Zhong et al., 1996). Our content-based image query system, VisualSEEk, can be used to index and retrieve key frames or video objects based on their visual features and spatial layout. In the authoring module, we provide tools for cutting/pasting of arbitrary MPEG video segments and adding special effects such as dissolve, keying, masking, and motion effects (variable speed, stroke motion, etc.).

Scene Clustering

We have developed scene clustering techniques to help users to browse and search efficiently important content in a video sequence. Each scene can be assumed to have consistent video content in most cases, except special situations like fast changing foreground and fast camera motion. Therefore, at the scene level, visual characteristics can be explored to classify various video scenes and derive higher-level semantics. Given a large collection of video sequences, a hierarchical scene-browsing interface will be useful for users to quickly browse through the content contained in a long video sequence or multiple video sequences.

The hierarchical scene browsing system (Zhong et al., 1996) takes the list of detected scenes from CVEPS and organizes them into multiple levels according to three different criteria: (1) temporal order, (2) story (e.g., news story), and (3) visual features. Organization based on the temporal order groups scenes into multi-level clusters according to their sequential order in time. N consecutive scenes form a basic segment in the lowest level, M segments form a class in the next level, and so on until all scenes are included. This hierarchy ensures a fully balanced organization with the same number of scenes in each class.

The second browsing mode uses the knowledge of story boundary and groups all video scenes contained in the same story into a class. This allows users to quickly view different stories in a long video program without going through the low-level scenes. This is particularly useful in situations where users need to quickly find a particular story from a large video archive to meet short deadlines.

The third browsing mode organizes scenes based on their visual features. Users may want to find related scenes from different programs (e.g., related news of different days). Scenes with similar visual features (e.g., color, motion, and faces) may be assigned to the same class if their visual similarity is sufficient. One useful example is to find all anchorperson scenes automatically. This allows automatic detection of the news story boundary without user intervention. Currently, our system has implemented scene clustering using primitive features—i.e., by color and motion. Advanced features will be incorporated later.

REMOTE ONLINE EDITING

The client-server model used in CVEPS provides for economic design of the client's editing terminal. Users may use a lightweight viewing station to connect to a powerful CVEPS server. The emerging WWW technology also provides a very powerful platform for remote online editing. With a Java-enabled Web browser, the user can first browse through the keyframes in a video stream; query and retrieve desired video clips; and preview and edit video at a low resolution. Upon completion, the client software will generate a standard Edit Decision List (EDL). The EDL is sent to the server for generating a full resolution video. The CVEPS server will handle most of the computing-intensive tasks, such as stream parsing, and any required coding process. Once the actual manipulation and rendering of desired special effects is finished, users can request retrieval of the full-resolution video for stream download or real-time display. Note that multiple EDLs can be stored for the same video sequences before the final rendering. Final video output should be produced from as original a video source as possible to minimize multiple-generation quality loss.

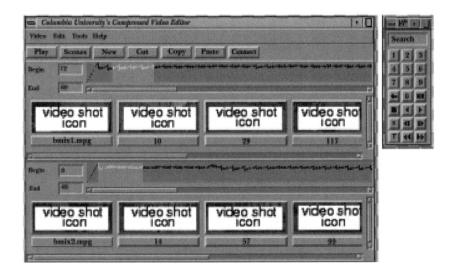

Figure 6. The Compressed Video Editing and Parsing System User Interface.

CVEPS PROTOTYPE

We have developed a prototype of the CVEPS with a C/Unix/Motif graphic user interface (see figure 6). Every time an MPEG video is opened, its corresponding video buffer status is plotted against a timeline. This allows us to monitor and verify the bit rate of any video stream produced in CVEPS. The video bit rate needs to conform to some specification in MPEG and the parameters set in the encoded stream to avoid decoder abnormality (e.g., decoder buffer overflow or underflow).

The user may run the scene cut detection to extract a list of keyframes representing video shots. At any time, the user may invoke the MPEG software viewer and the interactive VCR control panel to do random search, step forward, fast forward/reverse, etc. The user can also use the mouse to highlight the time-line to select arbitrary video segments and apply "copy, cut, and paste" operations. The CVEPS also provides options of inserting special effects—such as dissolve, fade in/out, and wipe—between the connected segments.

CONCLUSION

We have discussed innovative and efficient techniques for image/video indexing, retrieval, and manipulation in large visual information management systems. We presented two working systems, VisualSEEk and CVEPS, to illustrate our unique research approach in content-based visual query and manipulation.

VisualSEEk is a new content-based image query system that provides for querying by both image region visual properties and spatial layout. Unconstrained images are decomposed to local regions with prominent visual features (color, texture) by automatic tools. Spatial relationships are indexed with direct data structures to support efficient spatial queries.

CVEPS demonstrates advanced video indexing and manipulation functions in the compressed domain. The video parsing tools support automatic extraction of key visual features—e.g., scene cuts, transitional effects, camera operations (zoom/pan), shape, and trajectories of prominent moving objects. These visual features are used for efficient video indexing, retrieval, and browsing. The editing tools allow users to perform useful video composing functions and special visual effects typically seen in video production studios. We contrast our compressed-domain approach with traditional decode-process-reencode approach with a quantitative and/or qualitative performance comparison.

ACKNOWLEDGMENTS

This work was supported in part by the National Science Foundation under a CAREER award (IRI-9501266), by IBM under a Research

Partnership (Faculty Development) Award, and by sponsors of the AD-
VENT project of Columbia University. The scene clustering and hierar-
chical video browsing system includes joint work with Di Zhong and Horng
Jiang Zhang.

REFERENCES

Arman, F.; Hsu, A.; & Chiu, M.-Y. (1993). *Image processing on compressed data for large video databases.* Unpublished paper presented at the Proceedings of ACM Multimedia Con-ference, June 1993.
Bach, J. R.; Fuller, C.; Gupta, A.; Hampapur, A.; Horowitz, B.; Humphrey, R.; Jain, R. C.; & Shu, C. (1996). Virage image search engine: An open framework for image manage-ment. In *Symposium on electronic imaging: Science and technology—storage & retrieval for image and video databases IV* (vol. 2670), San Jose, California, February 1996.
Brodatz, P. (1965). *Textures: A photographic album for artists and designers.* New York: Dover.
Chang, S.-F. (1993). *Compositing and manipulation of video signals for multimedia network video services.* Unpublished doctoral dissertation, University of California—Berkeley, August 1993.
Chang, S. -F. (1995). *New algorithms for processing images in the transform-compressed domain.* Unpublished paper presented at the SPIE Symposium on Visual Communications and Image Processing, Taipei, May 1995.
Chang, S. -F.; Eleftheriadis, A.; & Anastassiou, D. (In press). Development of Columbia's video on demand testbed. *Journal of Image Communication* (Special Issue on Video on Demand and Interactive TV).
Chang, S. -F., & Smith, J. R. (1995). *Extracting multi-dimensional signal features for content-based visual query.* Unpublished paper presented at the SPIE Visual Communications and Image Processing, Taipei, May 1995 (Best Paper Award).
Chang, S.-F., & Messerschmitt, D. G. (1995). Manipulation and compositing of MC-DCT compressed video. *IEEE Journal of Selected Areas in Communications* (Special Issue on Intelligent Signal Processing), *13*(1), 1-11.
Dimitrova, N., & Golshani, F. (1994). *Rx for semantic video database retrieval.* Unpublished paper presented at the ACM Multimedia Conference, October 1994, San Francisco.
Hampapur, A.; Jain, R.; & Weymouth, T. E. (1995). Production model based digital video segmentation. *Journal of Multimedia Tools and Applications, 1*(1).
Jain, R. (1992). Unpublished presentation at an NSF workshop on Visual Information Management Systems, Redwood, California, February 1992.
Lee, Y. Y., & Woods, J. (1994). Video post production with compressed images. *SMPTE Journal, 103*(February), 76-84.
Mehrotra, R., & Gary, J. E. (1995). Similar-shape retrieval in shape data management. *IEEE Computer Magazine, 28*(9), 57-62.
Meng, J., & Chang, S.-F. (1996a). *Tools for compressed-domain video indexing and editing.* Un-published paper presented at the SPIE Conference on Storage and Retrieval for Image and Video Database, San Jose, California, February 1996.
Meng, J., & Chang, S. -F. (1996b). *Buffer control techniques for compressed video editing.* Unpub-lished paper presented at the IEEE International Conference on Circuits and Systems, ISCAS '96.
Meng, J.; Juan, Y.; & Chang, S. -F. (1995). *Scene change detection in an MPEG compressed video sequence* (SPIE Symposium on Electronic Imaging—Digital Video Compression: Algo-rithms and Technologies, San Jose, California, February 1995).
Niblack, W.; Barber, R.; Equitz, W.; Flickner, M.; Glasman, E.; Petkovic, D.; Yanker, P.; Faloutsos, C.; & Taubin, G. (1993). *The QBIC project: Querying images by content using color, texture and shape.* Unpublished paper presented at the SPIE 1993 International Sympo-sium on Electronic Imaging: Science and Technology, Conference 1908, Storage and Retrieval for Image and Video Databases, February 1993) (also in IBM Research Re-port RJ 9203=20 [81511], February 1, 1993, Computer Science).

Pentland, A.; Picard, R. W.; & Sclaroff, S. (In press). Photobook: Tools for content-based manipulation of image databases. *International Journal of Computer Vision.*

Picard, R. W. (1995). *Light-years from Lena: Video and image libraries of the future.* Unpublished paper presented at the IEEE International Conference on Image Processing, Washington, DC, October 1995.

Sawhney, H. S.; Ayer, S.; & Gorkani, M. (1995). *Model-based 2D and 3D dominant motion estimation for mosaicking and video representation.* Unpublished paper presented at the Proceedings of the Fifth International Conference, Computer Vision, 1995.

Smith, B. C., & Rowe, L. (1993). A new family of algorithms for manipulating compressed images. *IEEE Computer Graphics and Applications, 13*(5), 34-42.

Smith, J. R., & Chang, S. -F. (1994). *Quad-tree segmentation for texture-based image query.* Unpublished paper presented at the Proceedings of the ACM second Multimedia Conference, San Francisco, October 1994.

Smith, J. R., & Chang, S. -F. (1996a). Automated image retrieval using color and texture. *IEEE Transactions on Pattern Analysis and Machine Intelligence* (Special Issue on Digital Libraries—Representation and Retrieval, November 1996) (also Columbia University-CTR Technical Report # 414-95-20).

Smith, J. R., & Chang, S. -F. (1996b). *Tools and techniques for color image retrieval.* In *Symposium on electronic imaging: Science and technology—storage & retrieval for image and video databases IV,* vol. 2670. San Jose, CA, February.

Smith, J. R., & Chang, S. -F. (1996c). Querying by color regions using the VisualSEEk content-based visual query system. In *Intelligent multimedia information retrieval.* IJCAI.

Srihari, R. K. (1995). Automatic indexing and content-based retrieval of captioned images. *IEEE Computer Magazine, 28*(9), 49-56.

Stone, H. S., & Li, C.-S. (in press). Image matching by means of intensity and texture matching in the Fourier domain. In *Proceedings of the SPIE Conference on Image and Video Databases* (San Jose, California, January 1996).

Vaidyananthan, P. P. (1993). Orthonormal and biorthonormal filter banks as convolvors, and convolution coding gain. *IEEE Transactions on Signal Processing, 41*(June).

Wang, H., & Chang, S.-F. (1996). *Adaptive image matching in the subband domain.* Unpublished paper presented at the conference on SPIE/IEEE Visual Communications and Image Processing '96, Orlando, Florida, March 1996 (also CU/CTR Technical Report #422-95-28).

Yeo, B. -L., & Liu, B. (1995). *A unified approach to temporal segmentation of motion JPEG and MPEG compressed video.* Paper presented at the IEEE International Conference on Multimedia Computing and Systems, May 1995.

Zhang, H.; Kankanhalli, A.; & Smoliar, S. W. (1993). Automatic parsing of full-motion video. *ACM-Springer Multimedia Systems, 1*(1), 10-28.

Zhong, D.; Zhang, H. J.; & Chang, S. -F. (1996). Clustering methods for video browsing and annotation. Storage and retrieval for still image and video databases IV, IS&T/SPIE's electronic imaging. *Science & Technology, 96*(2670), San Jose, California, February 1996.

TOM HUANG, SHARAD MEHROTRA, & KANNAN RAMCHANDRAN

Multimedia Analysis and Retrieval System (MARS) Project*

To address the emerging needs of applications that require access to, and retrieval of, multimedia objects, we have started a Multimedia Analysis and Retrieval System (MARS) project at the University of Illinois. The project brings together researchers interested in the fields of computer vision, compression, information management, and database systems with the singular goal of developing an effective multimedia database management system. As a first step toward the project, we have designed and implemented an image retrieval system. This discussion describes the novel approaches toward image segmentation, representation, browsing, and retrieval supported by the developed system. Also described are the directions of future research we are pursuing as part of the MARS project.

INTRODUCTION

Advances in high performance computing, communication, and storage technologies, as well as emerging large-scale multimedia applications, has made multimedia data management one of the most challenging and important directions of research in computer science. Such systems will support visual data as "first-class" objects that are capable of being stored and retrieved based on their rich internal contents. Applications of multimedia databases include, among others:

- government and commercial uses of remote sensing images, satellite images, air photos, etc.;
- digital libraries, including digital catalogs, product brochures, training and education, broadcast and entertainment, etc.;
- medical databases, such as X-rays, MRI, etc.;
- special-purpose databases, e.g., face/fingerprint databases for security, business directories, maps, etc.

While current technology allows generation, scanning, transmission, and storage of large numbers of digital images, video and audio, existing

* This work was supported in part by the NSF/DARPA/NASA Digital Library Initiative Program under Cooperative Agreement 94-11318, in part by the U.S. Army Research Laboratory under Cooperative Agreement No. DAAL01-96-2-0003, in part by NASA under the Cooperative Agreement No. NASANAG 1-613, and in part by the University of Illinois Research Board.

practices of indexing, access, and retrieval of visual data are still very primitive. Most current systems rely on manual extraction of content information from images. Such information is stored using text annotations and indexing, and retrieval is then performed using these annotations. Although useful in some domains, such techniques are severely limited since manual indexing is inherently not scalable and, furthermore, textual descriptors are inadequate for describing many important features based on what users wish to retrieve as far as visual data (e.g., color, texture, shape, and layout). Also, textual descriptions are ineffective in supporting unanticipated user queries.

Development of multimedia database management systems requires an integrated research effort in the fields of image analysis, computer vision, information retrieval, and database management. Traditionally, these research areas have been studied in isolation with little or no interaction among the respective research communities. Image analysis and computer vision researchers have developed effective algorithms for image representation and segmentation. However, on the one hand, incorporation of these algorithms into the data management system in order to support effective retrieval is largely an open problem. On the other hand, research on information retrieval has focused on developing effective retrieval techniques to search for information relevant to users' queries. Effectiveness is measured using the precision of the information retrieved (i.e., how relevant is the retrieved information to the user?) and the recall (i.e., how much of the relevant information present in the database was retrieved?) (Salton & McGill, 1983). Efficient processing of user queries, as well as support for concurrent operations which are important for scalability, has been relatively ignored. Furthermore, research has primarily focused on textual data. Finally, database management research has concentrated on efficiency of storage and retrieval as well as on support for concurrent users and distributed processing. However, the techniques have been developed in the context of simple record-oriented data, and little has been done to extend the techniques to either textual, image, or multimedia data.

To address the challenges in building an effective multimedia database system, we have started the Multimedia Analysis and Retrieval System (MARS) project. MARS brings together a research team with interest in image analysis, coding, information retrieval, and database management. As part of the MARS project, we are addressing many research challenges including automatic segmentation and feature extraction, image representation and compression techniques suitable for browsing and retrieval, indexing and content-based retrieval, efficient query processing, support for concurrent operations, and techniques for seamless integration of the multimedia databases into the organization's information infrastructure. As a first step, we have developed a prototype image retrieval system (referred to as MARS/IRS) that supports content-based retrieval over a test bed consisting of a set of images of paintings and photographs provided by the Getty foundation. This paper describes the design and implementation of MARS/IRS including novel techniques for segmentation, representation, browsing, and retrieval. We also discuss directions of future research we are pursuing as part of the MARS project.

Many of the research topics being pursued in the MARS projects are also being addressed by other research teams both in the industry and in academia. One project related in scope is the Query by Image Content (QBIC) system being developed at IBM Almaden Research Center (Faloutsos et al., 1993; Flickner et al., 1995). The QBIC system supports queries based on color, texture, sketch, and layout of images. Another important related project is the ADVENT system developed at Columbia University (Smith & Chang, 1994, 1995, 1996; Wang, 1995; Chang, in these proceedings). Their main research focus is color/texture region extraction in both the uncompressed and the compressed domains. The color set concept is used in their color region extraction approach to make it faster and more robust. Its texture region extraction is based on the features (means and variances) extracted from Wavelet sub-bands. Instead of decompressing the existing compressed images to obtain the texture features, they perform texture feature extraction in the compressed domain, such as Discrete Cosine Transformation (DCT) and Discrete Wavelet Transformation (DWT). Other projects related to ours include Photobook at MIT (Pentland et al., 1995), Alexandria at UCSB (Manjunath & Ma, 1995), as well as the DLI projects at Stanford, Berkeley (as related by Forsyth in these proceedings), CMU, and MU (Schatz & Chen, 1996) which are working on low level feature extraction (image and video), feature representation, concept mapping, and database architecture.

MARS IMAGE RETRIEVAL SYSTEM

MARS/IRS is a simple prototype image retrieval system that supports similarity and content-based retrieval of images based on the properties of color, texture, shape, and layout. The distinguishing features of the current implementation include a novel approach toward segmentation, shape representation, support for complex content-based queries, as well as compression techniques to support effective browsing of images. In this section, we describe the current implementation of MARS/IRS.

System Architecture

The major components of MARS/IRS are shown in figure 1 and are discussed below.

- **User interface:** written using Java applets and accessible over the World Wide Web using the Netscape browser. The user interface allows users to graphically pose content-based and similarity queries over images. Using the interface, a user can specify queries to retrieve images based on a single property or a combination of properties. For example, a user can retrieve images similar in color to an input query image. A more complex query is to retrieve images that are similar in color to an input image I_1 and contain a shape similar to a specified shape in image I_2. The interface also allows users to combine image properties as well as text annotations (e.g., name of the creator, title of a painting, etc.) in specifying queries. The user interface is accessible over the WWW at PURL (<http://quirk.ifp.uiuc.edu:2020/mars/mars.html>).

- **Image Indexer:** The image indexer takes as input an image as well as its text annotation. With the help of the image analyzer, it extracts image properties (e.g., color, texture, shape). Furthermore, it extracts certain salient textual properties (e.g., name of the artist, subject of the painting, etc.) and stores these properties into the feature database.

- **Image Analyzer:** The image analyzer extracts salient image properties like the global color and texture as well as the shape. The global color is represented using a color histogram over the hue saturation value (HSV) space. At each image pixel, three texture features—coarseness, contrast, and directionality—are computed and the set of feature vectors forms a 3-D global texture histogram. Furthermore, images are segmented and the shape features of the objects in the image are represented using a modified Fourier Descriptor of the object boundary.

- **Feature Database:** An image in the feature database is represented using its image as well as textual properties. An image consists of global color histogram; a texture histogram; shape features; textual features like name of artist, subject of painting, etc. as well as color and texture layout properties. The feature database is currently implemented using POSTGRES (Stonebraker & Kemnitz, 1991). Furthermore, users can associate a full-text description with the images.

- **Query Processor:** The query processor is written on top of POSTGRES in C. It takes the query specified at the user interface, evaluates the query using the feature database, and returns to the user images that are best matches to the input query. The query language supported allows users to pose complex queries that are composed using image as well as textual properties. First, the query processor ranks the images based on individual properties. It then combines the ranking on individual properties to determine the overall ranking of the images based on the complex query. Techniques are developed to efficiently identify the best N matches without requiring that every image be ranked based on each property.

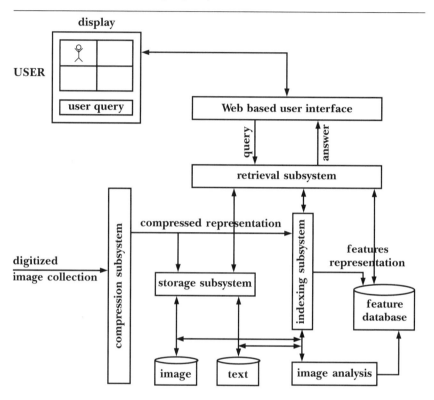

Figure 1. The MARS system componenets.

As mentioned previously, currently MARS/IRS uses as a test bed a set of images of paintings and photographs of artifacts made available to us by the Getty Museum Foundation (Museum Educational Site Licensing [MSL] Project [see Trant in these proceedings]).

Image Representation

In MARS/IRS, an image I consists of a set of global properties as well as a set of objects $\{O^I_1, O^I_2, ..., O^I_n\}$. Global properties are either:

- fixed descriptors like the artist's name, title, and museum to which the image belongs;
- free-text description of the image; or
- low-level image properties like color, texture, and layout.

Objects within an image are identified using automatic segmentation (described later in this section) and associated with each object are *local* properties which could include description of shape, average color, texture, centroid, area, as well as textual annotations. This section describes the representation of the low-level image features used in modeling an image.

Color

While color features could be represented in many color spaces, we use the hue saturation value color space since it approximates a perceptually uniform color space, making it easier for the user to specify colors. The global color histogram of an image is computed and stored. A *histogram intersection* method is used to compare the overall color content of an image with the colors specified in the user query. With respect to changes in image background colors, the histogram intersection similarity measure is more robust than the Euclidean histogram distance or matrix-weighted histogram distance. Using the histogram intersection method, a user may retrieve images in a database that contain a specific color or set of colors. For example, a user may retrieve all images that contain red and green but no blue.

Color Layout

While the color histogram is useful for queries on the relative amount of each color in an image; it is not useful for queries on the spatial location of colors. For example, it is not possible to retrieve all images that contain a red region above and to the right of a large blue region based solely on the color histogram. Such queries can be answered correctly only if an image can be accurately segmented into regions of different color, which is difficult to achieve. But for queries relating to simple spatial relationships between colors, a relatively nonideal segmentation may still be sufficient.

To represent spatial arrangement of colors in an image, we do a simple k-means clustering on the hue saturation value (HSV) histogram of an image to produce a rough segmentation. For each region in the segmentation, we store the following information for color indexing: centroid, area, eccentricity, average color, and maximum bounding rectangle. Images will be searched by comparing the relative locations and colors of the indexed regions to see if they matched the color layout query.

Texture

Texture is another important feature of images, and researchers have done a great deal of work in this area. We have implemented texture measures based on coarseness, contrast, and directionality, which are generally considered to be fairly good measures for texture.[1] At each image pixel we compute these three texture features from the pixel's local neighborhood. The set of feature vectors from all image pixels forms the 3-D global texture histogram. We compute these measures for each image and use a weighted Euclidean distance function as the matching criteria. The method described by Hideyuki Tamura (used by QBIC) uses three scalar measures and does not consider the relationship between texture components. Our method includes this texture information and thus returns better matches (i.e., the textures are perceptually more similar).

Shape

Although shape is a very important feature that a human can easily extract from an image, reliable automatic extraction and representation of shapes is a challenging open problem in computer vision.

Some simple shape features are the perimeter, area, number of holes, eccentricity, symmetry, etc. Although these features are easy to compute, they usually return too many false positives to be useful for content-based retrieval, thus they are excluded from our discussion. Advanced methods that can represent more complex shapes fall into two categories. The first category is region-based methods. These methods are essentially the Moment-Invariants Methods (MIM). The disadvantage of the MIM is its high computational cost (features are computed using the entire region including interior pixels) and low discriminatory power. The descriptors also tend to return too many false positives.

Boundary-based methods are the second category, which include the Turning Angle Method (TAM) and Fourier Descriptors (FD). These methods provide a much more complete description of shape than MIM; however, they suffer the disadvantage of being dependent on the starting point of the shape contour, and they can recover parameters (rotation, scale, starting point) only by solving a nonlinear optimization problem, which is not feasible in a real-time content-based retrieval system. Furthermore, to the extent of our knowledge, no research has been done on how to deal with the *spatial discretization* problem when using these methods.

We proposed the Modified Fourier Descriptor (MFD) (Rui et al., 1996b), which satisfies the four conditions:

1. Robustness to transformation—the representation must be invariant to translation, rotation, and scaling of shapes, as well as the starting point used in defining the boundary sequence.

2. Robustness to noise—shape boundaries often contain local irregularities due to image noise. More importantly, spatial discretization introduces distortion along the entire boundary. The representation must be robust to these types of noise.

3. Feature extraction efficiency—feature vectors should be computed efficiently.

4. Feature matching efficiency—since matching is done online, the distance metric must require a very small computational cost.

Image Segmentation

Our image segmentation is based on clustering and grouping in spatial-color-texture space. For a typical natural image, there is a high number of different colors and textures. C-means clustering is one way to reduce the complexity while retaining salient color and texture features.

1. randomly pick c starting points in the color-texture space as the initial means;

2. cluster each point as belonging to the nearest neighbor mean;

3. compute the new mean for each cluster; and

4. repeat 2 and 3 until all the clusters converge (i.e., when the number of pixels and mean value of each cluster does not change).

After this procedure, we have c clusters, each of which may correspond to a set of image pixels. We define *cluster* as a natural group which has similar features of interest. The image pixels corresponding to a particular cluster may or may not be spatially contiguous. We define a region as one of the spatially connected regions corresponding to a cluster.

The c-means clustering generally produces regions of various sizes; some of the regions are very small (containing only a few pixels). We consider these regions as speckle noise and set a minimum region size threshold to filter out these small regions. The deleted regions are merged with the largest neighboring region. After c-means clustering, we have c clusters, each corresponding to several spatial regions. The next step is to extract the desired object from the regions.

One way to do this is to define a threshold in color-texture space. If a region's color-texture feature is above the threshold, then this region is considered as the object; otherwise, it is considered as the background. One obvious disadvantage of this thresholding method is that the threshold is image-dependent. We propose an attraction-based grouping method (ABGM) to overcome this disadvantage (Rui et al., 1996a). The method is motivated by the way the human visual system might do the grouping.

As defined in physics,

$$F_{12} = G \frac{M_1 M_2}{d^2}$$

reflects how large the attraction is between the two masses M_1 and M_2 when they are of distance d. In ABGM, we use the similar concept, but now M_1 and M_2 are the size of the two regions, and d is the Euclidean distance between the two regions in 6-D spatial-color-texture space. The ABGM method is described as follows:

1. choose attractor region A_is from the clustered regions according to the knowledge of the application at hand;
2. randomly choose an unlabeled region R_j. Find the attractions F_{ij} between A_i and R_j;
3. associate region R_j with the attractor A_i that has the largest attraction to R_j;
4. repeat steps 2 and 3 until all the regions are labeled; and
5. form the output segmentation by choosing the attractor of interest and its associated regions.

Note that if the attractor is bigger or closer (in 6-D space) to an unlabeled region, its attraction will be larger, and thus the unlabeled region will be labeled to this attractor with higher probability. This is what a human visual system might do in the labeling process.

USER INTERFACE AND QUERY LANGUAGE

The user interface of MARS/IRS allows users to browse images sequentially (or in a random order), as well as to graphically pose content-based queries over the database of images. Queries supported are a Boolean combination of query terms. The semantics of the query is to retrieve images ranked on the degree to which the image satisfies the input query. A query term is either *simple* or *complex*. A simple term corresponds to textual annotations or image properties like color and texture. For example, a query:

```
containing_color(color identifier)  ^
similar_texture_to_image(image  id=4000)
```

is a Boolean combination of the following two query terms combined using a conjunction operator:

- `containing_color(color identifier)`, and
- `similar_texture_to_image(image  id=4000)`.

The first term refers to images that contain a given color (possibly chosen from a color pallet). The second refers to images whose texture matches the texture of the image with the identifier 4000. The system will retrieve images containing the specified color that also have a texture similar to the image 4000.

The user interface supports many ways in which users can specify query terms. Colors can be chosen from a color pallet or from the images that are currently being displayed in the MARS/IRS display window. To specify a color using an image, a user first loads the image from the display into the work space (by clicking on the image). The user can then choose either the global color of the loaded image as a query term (in which case the query term specifies retrieval of images whose global color histogram is similar to that of the loaded image), or alternatively, the user can choose the average color of some object[2] within the image as a query term by clicking on the object (the objects within an image are highlighted when the image is loaded into the work space for this purpose). Mechanisms similar to those used for specifying color query can be used for specifying texture query terms as well. Furthermore, MARS/IRS supports mechanisms for both specifying color layout query terms as well as selecting a color layout similar to the layout of a given image.

In contrast to the simple query terms, a complex query term is of the form:

```
contains_object(object description query)
```

The complex query term refers to images that contain an object that matches the object description query. The object description query may itself be a Boolean combination of image-based, as well as textual, features associated with the objects. The user interface also supports graphical mechanisms for composing object description queries.

The query mechanism supported by MARS/IRS provides a versatile tool for content-based retrieval. Using Boolean operators, users can form very complex queries. One special complex query is the *similarity query* when a user wishes to retrieve all the images similar to a given input image. Such a query is interpreted to mean images similar to the input image based on *all* the features and objects associated with the input image (obviously, such queries are reasonably inefficient). We are currently exploring information retrieval techniques including the query refinement mechanism of relevance feedback (Salton & McGill, 1983) to meaningfully answer similarity queries effectively and efficiently.

Query Processing

A query processor takes a query and retrieves the best N images that satisfy the query. Associated with the query is a *query tree*. Leaf nodes of the tree correspond to simple query terms based on a single property—e.g., global color similar to that of an input image I_1. Internal nodes in the tree correspond to Boolean operators—**and, or**, and **not**—as well as to complex query terms corresponding to objects contained in the image. The query tree is then evaluated as a pipeline from the leaf to the root. The leaf node n_j returns a ranked list of I, $sim(I,Q_{nj})$ to its parent, where I is an image and $sim(I,Q_{n_j})$ is a measure of match between the image I and the query represented by the leaf node n_j. For example, a leaf node n_j corresponding to the query term representing the global color of an image I' returns a ranked list of $I, sim(I,Q_{n_j})$, where $sim(I,Q_{n_j})$ is the measure of the intersection of color histograms corresponding to images I and I'.

The internal nodes n_p receive such ranked lists from each child and then combine to compute a ranked list of $I, sim(I,Qn_p)$, where $sim(I,Qn_p)$ is a measure of similarity between the image I and the query represented by the internal node n_p. This list is then input to the higher nodes in the pipeline which use it to compute their best matches. To rank the images according to the query represented by parent nodes, first the similarity measures associated with child nodes are *normalized*. Normalized similarity measures of different child nodes are then used to rank the images based on the degree of match to the query represented by the parent node. In our current implementation, a simple approach to normalization and ranking of images is adopted. Let an internal node n_p consist of child nodes n_1, n_2, ..., n_m. The normalized similarity of an image I to the query corresponding to the child node n_j (represented by $sim(I, n_j)$) is taken to be the inverse of the rank of I based on its similarity to the query represented by node n_j (notice that the range of the normalized similarity lies between 0 and 1). The similarity of the image I to the query represented by node n_p is computed as follows:

$$sim(I, Qn_p) = min(sim(I, Qn_1), sim(I, Qn_2),..., sim(I, Qn_m)), where\ Qn_p = Qn_1\ Qn2 ... Qn_m)$$

$$sim(I, Qn_p) = max(sim(I, Qn_1), sim(I, Qn_2),..., sim(I, Qn_m)), where\ Qn_p = Qn_1\ Qn2 ... Qn_m)$$

An advantage of such a simple normalization and ranking algorithm is that it can be implemented very efficiently and does not require that every image be ranked based on each property in order to compute the best N matches. However, the resulting retrieval is not very effective. We are currently exploring usage of more complex retrieval models (e.g., vector space models, inference network retrieval model) used in information retrieval to improve retrieval effectiveness. Effective and efficient retrieval techniques for feature-based queries is one of our primary research concerns in the near future.

Representation and Compression for Fast Browsing Using Wavelets

Due to the obvious volume of data being stored and processed in the database, it is important to address efficient ways to represent and compress these data. A key goal here is not just to achieve a substantial compression ratio in order to reduce the amount of storage needed but, even more important, to do so in a framework that supports some of the important database tasks like browsing and object-based retrieval—i.e., to have a representation data structure that lends itself to these tasks without needing to completely decompress the data. Toward this end, we propose a novel representation and compression data structure that is based on wavelets. Wavelets represent a mathematical tool based on multiresolution analysis that permits a natural decomposition of a signal or image into a hierarchy of increasing resolutions, thereby making them very suitable candidates for browsing applications.

Since their introduction, wavelets have become increasingly popular within the image coding community as an effective decorrelating transform to be used in the de facto standard architecture of loss coders, consisting of a linear transform followed by a quantization stage, and final entropy coding of the quantized symbol stream. Although initially the performance of wavelet based coders was only marginally better than that of previous existing subband coders, with the introduction of Shapiro's embedded zerotree wavelet (EZW) coder that is based on the zerotree data structure, an entire new avenue of research was started, with coders exploiting, in different forms, the fact that, even after decorrelation, significant structure remains in the subbands. Careful studies of the statistics of image subbands led to many improvements over the standard zerotree algorithm; however, this increased efficiency in coding often came at the expense of high computational complexity.

There are a number of ways to go about the complexity problem. One possibility, very appealing for the Image Databases application because of the simplicity with which transform domain data are represented, is that of fixing the quantization strategy to something reasonable (e.g., choose a single uniform quantizer for all subbands) and optimizing the entropy coder instead. Probably one of the simplest techniques of lossless data compression is that of run lengths. Zero run lengths have been very successfully applied a few years ago to the JPEG standard; surprisingly, none of the existing high performance wavelet-based coders make use of these. To test how useful one such representation can be for our purposes, we took two typical test images and computed the entropy of such a representation:

Image	Lena		Barbara	
Distortion (PSNR)	33.58	36.67	27.32	30.94
Entropy (bpp)	0.2501	0.5042	0.2467	0.4968
Distortion (PSNR)	33.17	36.28	26.77	30.53
Zerotrees (bpp)	0.2500	0.5000	0.2500	0.5000

It is clear from these numbers that any decent entropy coding scheme will do a good job at compressing this symbol stream, since by taking such a straightforward approach we are obtaining performance improvements over the standard zerotrees (it is conceivable that some work along these lines will yield further improvements). Besides, if low complexity implementations are sought, there are computationally more efficient entropy coders than the adaptive arithmetic coder. We are currently exploring this approach. Preliminary versions of a coder based on these ideas show that performance comparable to that achieved by much more complex schemes can be accomplished while taking less than five seconds to run on a PC-like machine. Our encoder/decoder requires only one floating point multiplication/division per pixel, does not require an arithmetic coder (only static Huffman coding, no run-time adaptation), and is entirely based on table lookup operations with tables computed at the encoder and encoded in the bitstream, thus avoiding hard-to-justify choices of prestored parameters. Yet, under such stringent complexity constraints, its coding performance on typical test images is superior to that of the state-of-the-art zerotree wavelet-based algorithm, and less than 1dB lower than that of the absolute best coders published in the literature, while drastically outperforming them in terms of speed.

This substantial speedup basically enables the incorporation of high performance wavelet based image coding techniques into applications which, like in the Image Databases case, no hardware implementations are possible. Furthermore, our coder supports a key requirement of the databases application—i.e., progressive mode transmission. This feature is important for browsing since low resolution images are encoded at the beginning of the compressed bitstream; if network delays occur, the user can view partial reconstructions of his query, and if it turns out that the retrieved image is not the one he was looking for, then transmission can be aborted before the whole image is received, thus making the interactive process much faster.

FUTURE RESEARCH

The MARS project was started to address the growing need for developing an effective multimedia database management system. Such an effort requires an integrated approach encompassing the fields of image analysis and coding, computer vision, information management, and database systems. As a first step toward MARS, we have developed an image retrieval system which incorporates some novel approaches to image segmentation, object representation, image coding, and query processing. However, the prototype system built is only in its infancy and further investigation is required before we come close to our goals of developing an effective multimedia database management system. Below we discuss future research directions within the MARS project.

Coding for Retrieval

Work in the coding aspects will focus on making evaluations of content-based queries on images possible directly on the compressed domain without having to fully decompress the image. The coding methods being explored for this application make use of a feature unique to the wavelet transform—i.e., the structure in the transform domain is related to the spatial structure in the image. Unlike in other transforms, this makes it feasible to obtain easy access to shape representations directly in the wavelet domain. Research will be done to determine to what extent this is feasible and/or practical. It has been observed empirically that object structure can be clearly recognized in the wavelet domain. However, heavy use will need to be made of the semantic content of the scene being coded to make the task of identifying shapes feasible.

Automated Image Feature Extraction

Automated feature extraction is one of the most important requirements for a scalable multimedia database system. We will focus our attention primarily on automated texture feature extraction. Methods dealing with texture extraction fall into two main categories. The first one is a statistics-based method, such as the Markov Random Field model, the Co-occurrent Matrix, Fractal Model, etc. The second one is the transform-based method, including Discrete Fourier Transform (DFT), Gabor Filter, DWT models, etc. The statistics-based methods are normally computationally expensive, and the accuracy is lower than that of transform-based methods. Therefore, the transform-based methods are preferred.

Among the transform-based methods, DFT cannot achieve localization in the transformed domain and the Gabor Filter involves a complex number computation whereas the DWT is both localized in the transformed domain and easy to compute. Almost all of the existing DWT models use quad-tree decomposition in the spatial domain (pyramid and tree structures in the transformed domain). An obvious disadvantage of quad-tree-based methods is that the segmentation that they can perform must be of square shape (Egger et al., 1996; Gever & Kajcovski, 1994). However, the majority of the natural images contain texture regions of arbitrary shapes. It is almost impossible to find a square texture region inside a natural image. Besides, rotation-invariance is also an almost ignored research issue (Haley & Manjunath, 1995). We will explore a DWT model which can achieve the following goals:

* automated feature extraction;
* a texture region of arbitrary shape;
* a texture feature that is rotation-invariant.

Efficient Feature Indexing

A primary retrieval technique in multimedia databases is to use features extracted from the images. Hence, efficient indexing and retrieval of the features is very crucial for scalability of the system. The feature space normally is very high dimensional and, therefore, usage of conventional multidimensional and spatial indexing methods (e.g., R-trees, quad trees, grid files) is not feasible for feature indexing. Existing multidimensional index methods are only useful when the number of dimensions are reasonably small. For example, the R-tree based methods, which are among the most robust multidimensional indexing mechanisms, work well only for multidimensional spaces with dimensionality around 20. Other methods do not even scale to 20 dimensions. An approach used by the QBIC to overcome the dimensionality curse of the feature space is to transform the high dimensional feature space to a lower dimensional space using, for example, a K-L transform. An R^* tree is then used for indexing and retrieval in a lower dimensional space. The retrieval over the index provides a superset of the answers which can then be further refined in the higher dimensional space. While the approach is attractive and the QBIC authors report good retrieval efficiency over small image databases, it is not clear whether it will scale to large databases and complex feature spaces that are very highly multidimensional. In such situations, the high number of false hits in the lower dimensional space might make the approach unusable. We will explore extensions to the QBIC approach and/or alternate methods to overcoming the dimensionality curse. One important direction of research is methods for selecting optimal ways to map a high dimensional feature space to a lower dimensional space based on the nature of commonly occurring queries and the nature of the feature vectors.

Effective Retrieval Models

As discussed earlier, the retrieval model used to implement complex Boolean queries in our current implementation is very simple. The choice of the retrieval model has been dictated by issues of efficiency, simplicity, and quick prototyping. We are now examining more complex retrieval models developed in the information retrieval literature for supporting Boolean queries over the image feature database. Among the models being examined is the inference network model used by the INQUERY system (Callan et al., 1992). We will also explore how index structures can be used to support the developed retrieval model efficiently.

Integration with SQL

An important consideration in the design of the multimedia database system is its integration with the organization's existing databases. This requires integration of the query language developed for the multimedia database (which allows content-based and similarity retrieval) with SQL (a popular database query language). Such an integration will allow users to develop complex applications in which images as well as other multimedia data can be considered simply as another data type and the applications have a mechanism for retrieving information based on both visual as well as traditional nonvisual properties of data in the same query. Another related concept that we will explore is the correlation of concepts from one media to another.

Support for Concurrent Access

Scalable design requires that concurrent operations (indexing new images, retrievals, updates) be supported over the multimedia database. Supporting concurrent operations over the feature database is challenging since it contains multidimensional data and uses multidimensional access structures (e.g., R-trees) for efficient retrieval. Concurrent access of multidimensional access methods is an important open research problem. A common requirement for concurrent access in database systems is to provide phantom protection to achieve degree three consistency or repeatable read (RR) (Gray & Reuter, 1993). Key-range locking employed in B-tree, a mature dynamic indexing mechanism in a single attribute database system, is a well-known and robust solution. The major issue is that this scheme depends on the linear order of keys. However, in R-tree—a dynamic index structure used in multidimensional space—the linear order of keys does not exist. As a result, new mechanisms to overcome the phantom problem for multidimensional data need to be developed. One promising direction is to use two versions of R-tree where all operations can concurrently run in the new version's R-tree after they set the locks on the proper entry in the old version's R-tree. The old version R-tree is essentially used as a partitioning of the space into lockable granules. The old version can either be used to provide static partitioning of the multidimensional space, which will result in a simpler solution but will result in lower concurrency, or could be updated by a periodic version switch resulting in a dynamically changing space partitioning. This technique will support higher concurrency but will be significantly more complex.

Supporting Concept Queries

In a large number of applications of multimedia retrieval systems, users seldom use low-level image features (i.e., shape, color, texture) directly to query the database. Instead, the user interacts with the system using high-level concepts (e.g., a beach, forest, yellow flowers, a sunset) in specifying a particular image content. These concept queries, in turn, need to be translated into queries over the low-level features so as to be answered using the feature database. Such a translation results in a complex query over the low-level feature space.

Providing capability to support concept queries over the feature database is one of the prime reasons we chose to implement support for complex Boolean queries in MARS/IRS. However, in the current implementation, the MARS/IRS system does not provide any help to the user in mapping a high-level concept query into an equivalent query over the low-level feature space. We are currently investigating user interface extensions that can (partially) automate such a translation. In the approach being investigated, the system uses relevance feedback from users to learn concepts.

ACKNOWLEDGMENT

The authors would like to acknowledge Yong Rui's help in writing this paper.

NOTES

[1] Psychophysical studies suggest that the human visual system uses these three measures as primary features for texture discrimination.

[2] Identified using the segmentation method described in the section on Image Segmentation.

REFERENCES

Callan, J. P.; Croft, W. B.; & Harding, S. M. (1992). The INQUERY retrieval system. In A. M. Tjoa & I. Ramos (Eds.), *Proceedings of the Third International Conference on Database and Expert Systems Applications* (Valencia, Spain) (pp. 78-83). New York: Springer-Verlag.

Egger, O.; Ebrahimi, T.; & Kunt, M. (1996). Arbitrarily-shaped wavelet packets for zerotree coding. In *IEEE international conference on accoustics, speech & signal processing: Volume 4: ICASSP Proceedings* (Atlanta, Georgia, May 7-10, 1996). Piscataway, NJ: IEEE.

Faloutsos, C.; Flicker, M.; Niblack, W.; Petkovic, D.; Equitz, W.; & Barber, R. (1993). *Efficient and effective querying by image content* (IBM Research Report RJ 9453 [83074]).

Flickner, M. et al. (1995). Query by image and video content: The QBIC System. *IEEE Computer, 28*(9), 23-32.

Gevers, T., & Kajcovski, V. K. (1994). Image segmentation by directed region subdivision. Unpublished presentation at the *Proceedings of the International Conference on Image Processing* (Austin, Texas, November 13-16, 1994). Los Alamitos, CA: IEEE Computer Society Press.

Gray, J., & Reuter, A. (1993). *Transaction processing: Concepts and techniques.* San Mateo, CA: Morgan Kaufmann.

Haley, G. M., & Manjunath, B. S. (1995). Rotation-invariant texture classification using modified gabor filters. In *Proceedings of the International Conference on Image Processing* (Washington, DC, October 23-26, 1995) (pp. 262-265). Los Alamitos, CA: IEEE Computer Society Press.

Manjunath, B. S., & Ma, W. Y. (1995). Texture features for browsing and retrieval of image data, CIPR TR-95-06, July.

Pentland, A.; Picard, R. W.; & Sclaroff, S. (1995). Photobook: Tools for content-based manipulation of image databases. In W. Niblack & R. Jain (Eds.), *Storage and retrieval for image and video databases II, vol. 2185*: SPIE Proceedings (San Jose, California, February 7-8, 1994) (pp. 34-47). Bellingham, WA: SPIE.

Rui, Y.; She, A. C.; & Huang, T. S. (1996a). Automated region segmentation using attraction-based grouping in spatial-color-texture space (to appear in the Proceedings of

116

the ICIP.

Rui, Y.; She, A. C.; & Huang, T. S. (1996b). *Modified Fourier descriptor for shape representation — A practical approach*. Unpublished presenation to the First International Workshop on Image Databases and Multi Media Search. Amsterdam, The Netherlands.

Salton, G., & McGill, M. J. (1983). *Introduction to modern information retrieval*. McGraw Hill Computer Science Series). New York: McGraw-Hill.

Schatz, B., & Chen, H. (1996). Special issue on digital library initiative. *IEEE Computer, 29*(5).

Smith, J. R., & Chang, S.-F. (1994). Tools and techniques for color image retrieval. In I. K. Sethi & R. Jain (Eds.), *Storage & Retrieval for Image and Video Databases IV, Vol. 2670: SPIE Proceedings* (San Jose, California, February 1-2, 1996). Bellingham, WA: SPIE.

Smith J. R., & Chang, S.-F. (1995). Single color extraction and image query. In *Proceedings of the international conference on image processing: Volume 3* (Washington, DC, October 23-26, 1995) (pp. 528-531). Los Alamitos, CA: IEEE Computer Society Press.

Smith J. R., & Chang, S-F. (1996). Automated binary texture feature sets for images retrieval. In *Proceedings of the international conference on image processing*. Los Alamitos, CA: IEEE Computer Society Press.

Stonebraker, M., & Kemnitz, G. (1991). The POSTGRES Next-Generation Database Management System. *Communications of the ACM, 34*(10), 78-92.

Wang, H. (1995). *Compressed-domain image search and applications*. Columbia University Technical Report.

117

DAVID A. FORSYTH, JITENDRA MALIK, THOMAS K. LEUNG, CHRIS BREGLER, CHAD CARSON, HAYIT GREENSPAN, & MARGARET M. FLECK

Finding Pictures of Objects in Large Collections of Images

Retrieving images from very large collections using image content as a key is becoming an important problem. Users prefer to ask for pictures using notions of content that are strongly oriented to the presence of objects, which are quite abstractly defined. Computer programs that implement these queries automatically are desirable but are hard to build because conventional object recognition techniques from computer vision cannot recognize very general objects in very general contexts.

This paper describes an approach to object recognition structured around a sequence of increasingly specialized grouping activities that assemble coherent regions of image that can be shown to satisfy increasingly stringent constraints. The constraints that are satisfied provide a form of object classification in quite general contexts.

This view of recognition is distinguished by far richer involvement of early visual primitives, including color and texture; the ability to deal with rather general objects in uncontrolled configurations and contexts; and a satisfactory notion of classification. These properties are illustrated with three case studies: one demonstrates the use of descriptions that fuse color and spatial properties; one shows how trees can be described by fusing texture and geometric properties; and one shows how this view of recognition yields a program that can tell, quite accurately, whether a picture contains naked people or not.

INTRODUCTION

Very large collections of images are becoming common, and users have a clear preference for accessing images in these databases based on the objects that are present in them. Creating indexes for these collections by hand is unlikely to be successful because these databases can be gigantic. Furthermore, it can be very difficult to impose order on these collections. For example, the California Department of Water Resources' collection contains approximately half-a-million images. Another example is the collection of images available on the Internet, which is notoriously large and disorderly. This lack of structure makes it hard to rely on textual annotations in indexing. More practical alternatives are computer programs that could automatically assess image content (Sclaroff, 1995).

Another reason that manual indexing is difficult is that it can be hard to predict later content queries—for example, local political figures may reach national importance long after an image has been indexed. In a very large collection, the subsequent reindexing process becomes onerous.

Classic object recognition techniques from computer vision cannot help with this problem. Recent techniques can identify specific objects drawn from a small (on the order of 100 items) collection, but no present technique is effective at distinguishing, for example, people from cows, a problem usually known as classification. This discussion presents case studies illustrating an approach to determine image content that is capable of object classification. The approach is based on constructing rich image descriptions that fuse color, texture, and shape information to determine the identity of objects in the image.

MATERIALS AND OBJECTS—"STUFF" VERSUS "THINGS"

Many notions of image content have been used to organize collections of images (e.g., see Layne, 1994). Relevant here are notions centered on objects; the distinction between materials—"stuff"—and objects—"things"—is particularly important. A material (e.g., skin) is defined by a homogeneous or repetitive pattern of fine-scale properties but has no specific or distinctive spatial extent or shape. An object (e.g., a ring) has a specific size and shape. This distinction (in computer vision, Ted Adelson has emphasized the role of filtering techniques in early vision for measuring stuff properties) and a similar distinction for actions is well-known in linguistics and philosophy (dating back at least to Whorf [1941]) where they are used to predict differences in the behavior of nouns and verbs (e.g., Taylor, 1977; Tenney, 1987; Fleck, 1996).

To a first approximation, 3D materials appear as distinctive colors and textures in 2D images, whereas objects appear as regions with distinctive shapes. Therefore, one might attempt (following, for example, Adelson) to identify materials using low-level image properties and identify objects by analyzing the shape of, and the relationships between, 2D regions. Indeed, materials with particularly distinctive color or texture (e.g., sky) can be successfully recognized with little or no shape analysis, and objects with particularly distinctive shapes (e.g., telephones) can be recognized using only shape information.

In general, however, too much information is lost in the projection onto the 2D image for strategies that ignore useful information to be successful. The typical material, and so the typical color and texture, of an object is often helpful in separating the object from other image regions and in recognizing it. Equally, the shapes into which it is typically formed can be useful cues in recognizing a material. For example, a number of other materials have the same color and texture as human skin at typical image resolutions. Distinguishing these materials from skin requires using the fact that human skin typically occurs in human form.

OBJECT RECOGNITION

Current object recognition systems represent models either as a collection of geometric measurements—typically a CAD or CAD-like model—or as a collection of images of an object. This information is then compared with image information to obtain a match. Comparisons can be scored by using a feature correspondence either to back-project object features into an image or to determine a new view of the object and overlay that on the image. Appropriate feature relationships can be obtained by various forms of search (e.g., Huttenlocher & Ullman, 1986; Grimson & Lozano-Perez, 1987; Lowe, 1987). Alternatively, one can define equivalence classes of features, each large enough to have distinctive properties (invariants) preserved under the imaging transformation. These invariants can then be used as an index for a model library (examples of various combinations of geometry, imaging transformations, and indexing strategies include Lamdan et al., 1988; Weiss, 1988; Forsyth et al., 1991; Rothwell et al., 1992; Stein & Medioni, 1992; Taubin & Cooper, 1992; Liu et al., 1993; Kriegman & Ponce, 1994).

Each case described so far models object geometry exactly. Systems that recognize an object by matching a view to a collection of images of an object proceed in one of two ways. In the first approach, correspondence between image features and features on the model object is either given a priori or is established by search. An estimate of the appearance in the image of that object is then constructed from the correspondences. The hypothesis that the object is present is then verified using the estimate of appearance (as in Ullman & Basri, 1991). An alternative approach computes a feature vector from a compressed version of the image and uses a minimum distance classifier to match this feature vector to feature vectors computed from images of objects in a range of positions under various lighting conditions (as in Murase & Nayar, 1995).

All of the approaches described rely heavily on specific detailed geometry, known (or easily determined) correspondences, and either the existence of a single object on a uniform known background (as in the case of Murase & Nayar, 1995) or the prospect of relatively clear segmentation. None is competent to perform abstract classification; this emphasis appears to be related to the underlying notion of model rather than to the relative difficulty of the classification versus identification. Notable exceptions appear in Nevatia and Binford (1977), Brooks (1981), Connell

(1987), and Zerroug and Nevatia (1994), which attempt to code relationships between various forms of volumetric primitive, where the description is in terms of the nature of the primitives involved and of their geometric relationship.

CONTENT-BASED RETRIEVAL FROM IMAGE DATABASES

Algorithms for retrieving information from image databases have concentrated on material-oriented queries and have implemented these queries primarily using low-level image properties such as color and texture. Object-oriented queries search for images that contain particular objects; such queries can be seen either as constructs on material queries (Picard & Minka, 1995) as essentially textual matters (Price et al., 1992) or as the proper domain of object recognition. A third query mode looks for images that are near iconic matches of a given image (e.g., Jacobs et al., 1995). This matching strategy cannot find images based on the objects present because it is sensitive to such details as the position of the objects in the image, the composition of the background, and the configuration of the objects—e.g., it could not match a front and a side view of a horse.

The best-known image database system is QBIC (Niblack et al., 1993) which allows an operator to specify various properties of a desired image. The system then displays a selection of potential matches to those criteria, sorted by a score of the appropriateness of the match. The operator can adjust the scoring function. Region segmentation is largely manual, but the most recent versions of QBIC (Ashley et al., 1995) contain simple automated segmentation facilities. The representations constructed are a hierarchy of oriented rectangles of fixed internal color and a set of tiles on a fixed grid, which are described by internal color and texture properties. However, neither representation allows reasoning about the shape of individual regions, about the relative positioning of regions of given colors, or about the cogency of geometric co-ocurrence information, and so there is little reason to believe that either representation can support object queries.

Photobook (Pentland et al., 1993) largely shares QBIC's model of an image as a collage of flat homogenous frontally presented regions but incorporates more sophisticated representations of texture and a degree of automatic segmentation. A version of Photobook incorporates a simple notion of object queries using plane object matching by an energy minimization strategy (Pentland et al., 1993, p. 10). However, the approach does not adequately address the range of variation in object shape and appears to require images that depict single objects on a uniform background. Further examples of systems that identify materials using low-level image properties include Virage (home page at <http://

www.virage.com> and elsewhere in this volume), Candid (home page at <http://www.c3.lanl.gov/~kelly/CANDID/main.shtml> and Kelly et al., 1995), and Chabot (Ogle & Stonebraker, 1995). None of these systems code spatial organization in a way that supports object queries.

Variations on Photobook (Picard & Minka, 1995; Minka, 1995) use a form of supervised learning known in the information retrieval community as "relevance feedback" to adjust segmentation and classification parameters for various forms of textured region. When a user is available to tune queries, supervised learning algorithms can clearly improve performance given appropriate object and image representations. In the most useful applications of our algorithms, however, users are unlikely to want to tune queries. Those who object to pictures of naked people are unlikely to want to spend time looking at such pictures to help tune a learning algorithm, though one might speculate that seekers could sell tuning services to avoiders.

More significantly, the representations used in these supervised learning algorithms do not code spatial relationships. Thus, these algorithms are unlikely to be able to construct a broad range of effective object queries. While relevance feedback can be effective at adjusting a metric by which image relevance is scored, it is hard to believe that user-supervised learning would be the technique of choice for establishing such intricate constructs as the variations in appearance associated with different views of a body plan.

A GROUPING-BASED FRAMEWORK FOR OBJECT RECOGNITION

Our approach to object recognition is to construct a sequence of sucessively abstracted descriptors, at an increasingly high level, through a hierarchy of grouping processes. At the lowest level, grouping is based on spatiotemporal coherence of local image descriptors—color, texture, disparity, motion—with contours and junctions extracted simultaneously to organize these groupings. There is an implicit assumption in this process that coherence of these image descriptors is correlated with the associated scene entities being part of the same surface in the scene. At the next stage, the assumptions that need to be invoked are more global (in terms of size of image region) as well as more class specific. For example, a group that is skin-colored, has an extended bilateral image symmetry, and has near parallel sides should imply a search for another such group nearby because it is likely to be a limb.

This approach leads to a notion of classification where object class is increasingly constrained as the recognition process proceeds. Classes need not be defined as purely geometric categories. For instance, in a scene expected to contain faces, prior knowledge of the spatial configuration of eyes, mouth, etc. can be used to group what might otherwise be regarded as separate entities. As a result, the grouper's activities become increasingly specialized as the object's identity emerges; these constraints are evoked by the completion of earlier stages in grouping. The particular attractions of this view are:

- that the primary activity is classification rather than identification;
- that if grouping fails at some point, it is still possible to make statements about an object's identity;
- that it presents a coherent view of top-down information flow that is richer than a crude search; and
- that the model base now consists of information that is oriented primarily to vision (i.e., hints about grouping activities) rather than to CAD or graphics.

Slogans characterizing this approach are: grouping proceeds from the local to the global and grouping proceeeds from invoking generic assumptions to more specific ones. The most similar ideas in computer vision are those of a body of collaborators usually seen as centered around Binford and Nevatia (see, for example Nevatia & Binford, 1977; Brooks, 1981; Connell, 1987; Zerroug & Nevatia, 1994), and the work of Zisserman et al. (1995). Where we differ is in:

1. attributing much less importance to the recovery of generalized cylinders as the unifying theme for the recognition process; and

2. offering a richer view of early vision, which must offer more than contours extracted by an edge detector (an approach that patently fails when one considers objects like sweaters, brick walls, or trees).

A central notion in grouping is that of coherence, which is hard to define well but captures the idea that regions should (in some sense) "look" similar internally. Examples of coherent regions include regions of fixed color, tartan regions, and regions that are the projection of a vase. We see three major issues:

1. *Segmenting images into coherent regions based on integrated region and contour descriptors:* An important stage in identifying objects is deciding which image regions come from particular objects. This is simple when objects are made of stuff of a single fixed color. Most objects, however, are covered with textured stuff, where the spatial relationships between colored patches are an important part of any description of the stuff. The content-based retrieval literature cited above contains a wide variety of examples of the usefulness of quite simple descriptions in describing images and objects. Color histograms are a particularly popular example; however, color histograms lack spatial

cues and so must misidentify, for example, the English and the French flags. In what follows (see the Case Study 1 section), we show two important cases: in the first, measurements of the size and number of small areas of color yield information about stuff regions—such as fields of flowers—that cannot be obtained from color histograms; in the second, the observation that a region of stuff is due to the periodic repetition of a simple tile yields information about the original tile and the repetition process. Such periodic textures are common in real pictures, and the spatial structure of the texture is important in describing them.

2. *Fusing color, texture, and shape information to describe primitives:* Once regions that are composed of internally coherent stuff have been identified, 2D and 3D shape properties of the regions need to be incorporated into the region description. In many cases, objects either belong to constrained classes of 3D shapes—for example, many trees can be modeled as surfaces of revolution—or consist of assemblies of such classes—for example, people and many animals can be modeled as assemblies of cylinders. It is often possible to tell from region properties alone whether the region is likely to have come from a constrained class of shapes (e.g., see Zisserman et al., 1995); knowing the class of shape from which a region came allows other inferences. As we show in one of the following sections (see section on Case Study 2), knowing that a tree can be modeled as a surface of revolution simplifies marking the boundary of the tree and makes it possible to compute an axis and a description of the tree.

3. *Classifying objects based on primitive descriptions and relationships between primitives:* Once regions have been described as primitives, the relationships between primitives become important. For example, finding people or animals in images is essentially a process of finding regions corresponding to segments and then assembling those segments into limbs and girdles. This process involves exploring incidence relationships and is constrained by the kinematics of humans and animals. We have demonstrated the power of this constraint-based representation by building a system that can tell quite reliably whether an image contains naked people or not, which is briefly outlined in the later section describing Case Study 3.

CASE STUDY 1:
COLOR AND TEXTURE PROPERTIES OF REGIONS

In the foreseeable future, it will be hard to provide users with a complete set of object concepts with which to query collections of images. To cover this omission, users can be provided with a query language that manipulates combinations of the early visual properties that describe stuff regions. If these cues are properly chosen and can be automatically extracted, quite successful query mechanisms result. Their usefulness most probably follows because they represent a sensible choice of cues from the perspective of object recognition.

Color histograms have proven a useful stuff query but are poor at, for example, distinguishing between fields of flowers and a single large flower, because they lack information as to how the color is distributed spatially. The size and spatial distribution of areas of color is a natural stuff description—and hence, query—which is particularly useful for outdoor scenes in the case of hues ranging from red to yellow. Individual areas are hard to segment and measure, but a useful approximation can be obtained by:

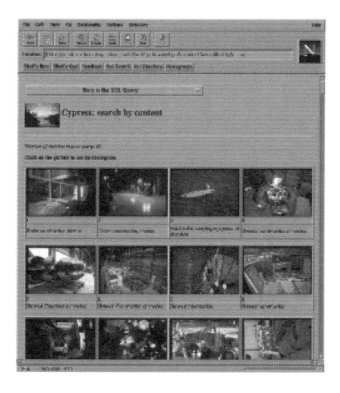

Figure 1. Querying the Cypress database for images that contain a large proportion of yellow pixels produces a collection of responses that is eclectic in content; there is little connection between the response to this query and particular objects. While these queries can be useful, particularly when combined with text information, they are not really concept or "thing" queries.

- forming R-G and B-Y opponent channels;
- coarsely requantizing these channels for various hues to form hue maps, where an orange hue map would reflect which pixels fall within a range of hues around orange;
- forming a Gaussian pyramid (after Burt & Adelson, 1983) for each hue map;
- thresholding the difference between pyramids at neighboring scales and summing to reflect the distribution of edge energy.

Finally, if an image has high energy at a coarse scale in, for example, the orange hue map, this is taken to mean it contains a large orange area;

Figure 2. Querying the Cypress database for images that contain a large number of small yellow areas and a horizon yields scenic views of fields of flowers. The horizon is obtained by searching in from each boundary of the image for a blue region, extending to the boundary, that does not curve very sharply. In this case, the combination of spatial and color queries yields a query that encapsulates content surprisingly well. While the correlation between object type and query is fortuitous and relevant only in the context of the particular database, it is clear that the combination of spatial and chromatic information in the query yields a more powerful content query than color alone. In particular, the language of areas is a powerful and useful early cue to content.

comparison with the color histogram makes it possible to distinguish between few and many small areas. While this approximation is coarse, it provides extremely useful information about content. As figures 1 and 2 show, queries composed of a combination of this information with textual cues, or with an estimate of a horizon, correlate extremely strongly with content in the present Cypress database (this query engine is available on the World Wide Web at <http://elib.cs.berkeley.edu>).

A second important spatial ordering of color is the periodic repetition of a basic tile (see figure 3). Such regions can be a representation which describes the individual basic element and then represents the spatial relationships between these elements. Spatial relationships are represented by a graph where nodes correspond to individual elements and arcs join spatially neighboring elements. With each arc r_{ij} is associated an affine map A_{ij} that best transforms the image patch $I(x_j)$ to $I(x_i)$. This affine transform implicitly defines a correspondence between points on the image patches at x_i and x_j.

Figure 3. A textile image. The original image is shown on the left, and the center image shows the initial patches found. The crosses are the locations of units grouped together. The image on the right shows the segmented region is displayed. Notice that the rectangle includes two units in the actual pattern. This is due to the inherent ambiguity in defining a repeating unit— two tiles together still repeat to form a pattern.

Regions of periodic texture can be detected and described by:

- detecting "interesting" elements in the image;
- matching elements with their neighbors and estimating the affine transform between them;
- growing the element to form a more distinctive unit; and
- grouping the elements.

The approach is analogous to tracking in video sequences; an element is "tracked" to spatially neighboring locations in one image rather than from frame to frame. Interesting elements are detected by breaking an image into overlapping windows and computing the second moment matrix (as in Forstner, 1993; Garding & Lindeberg, 1994), which indicates whether there is much spatial variation in a window and whether that variation is intrinsically one- or two-dimensional. By summing along the dominant direction, "flow" regions—such as vertical stripes on a shirt—can be distinguished from edges. Once regions have been classified, they can be matched to regions of the same type.

An affine transform is estimated to bring potential matches into registration, and the matches are scored by an estimate of the relative difference in intensity of the registered patches. The output of this procedure is a list of elements which form units for repeating structures in the image. Associated with each element is the neighboring patches which match well with the element together with the affine transform relating them. These affine transforms contain shape cues as well as grouping cues (Malik & Rosenholtz, 1994).

The final step is to group the elements by a region-growing technique. For each of the eight windows neighboring an element, the patch which matches the element best and the affine transform between them is computed. Two patches are grouped by comparing the error between an element and its neighboring patch with the variation in the element. Of course, as the growth procedure propogates outward, the size and shape of the basic element in the image will change because of the slanting of the surface.

CASE STUDY 2:
FUSING TEXTURE AND GEOMETRY TO REPRESENT TREES

Recognizing individual trees makes no sense; instead it is necessary to define a representation with the following properties:

- it should not change significantly over the likely views of the tree;
- it should make visual similarities and visual differences between trees apparent. In particular, it should be possible to classify trees into intuitively meaningful types using this representation; and

- it should be possible to determine that a tree is present in an image, segment it, and recover the representation without knowing what tree is present.

Trees can then be classified according to whether the representations are similar or not (see figure 4).

Branch length and orientation appear to be significant components of such a representation. Since trees are typically viewed frontally, with their trunks aligned with the image edges and at a sufficient distance for a scaled affine viewing model to be satisfactory, it is tempting to model a tree as a plane texture. There are two reasons not to do so: considering a tree as a surface of revolution provides grouping cues, and there is a reasonable chance of estimating parameters of the distribution of branches in 3D. Instead, we model a tree as a volume with a rotational symmetry with branches and leaves embedded in it. Because of the viewing conditions, the image of a tree corresponding to this model will have a bilateral

Figure 4. The viewing assumptions mean that trees have vertical axes and a reflectional symmetry about the axis. This symmetry can be employed to determine the axis by voting on its horizontal translation using locally symmetric pairs of orientation responses. **Left**: The symmetry axis superimposed on a typical image, showing also the regions that vote for the symmetry axis depicted. **Right**: In this image, there are several false axes generated by symmetric arrangements of trees; these could be pruned by noticing that the orientation response close to the axis is small.

symmetry about a vertical axis, a special case of the planar harmonic homology of Mukherjee et al. (1995). This axis provides part of a coordinate system in which the representation can be computed. The other is provided by the outline of the tree (see figure 5), which establishes scale and translation along the axis and scale perpendicular to the axis. A representation computed in this coordinate system will be viewpoint stable for the viewpoints described.

Assuming that the axis and outline have been marked, the orientation representation is obtained by forming the response of filters tuned to a range of orientations. These response strengths are summed along the axis at each orientation and for a range of steps in distance perpendicular to the axis relative to width. The representation resulting from this process (which is illustrated in figure 6) consists of a map of summed strength of response relative to orientation and distance from the axis. As the figure shows, this representation makes a range of important differences between trees explicit. Trees that have a strongly preferred branch orientation (such as pine trees) show a strong narrow peak in the representation at the appropriate orientation; trees, such as monkey puzzle trees, which have a relatively broad range of orientations of branches, show broader peaks in the representation. Furthermore, the

Figure 5. The outline can be constructed by taking a canonical horizontal cross-section and scaling other cross-sections to find the width that yields a cross-section that is most similar. **Left:** An outline and axis superimposed on a typical image. **Center:** The cross-sections that make up the outline superimposed on an image of the tree. **Right:** The strategy fails for trees that are poorly represented by orientations alone, as in this case, as the comparisons between horizontal slices are inaccurate. Representing this tree accurately requires using filters that respond to areas as well; such a representation would also generate an improved segmentation.

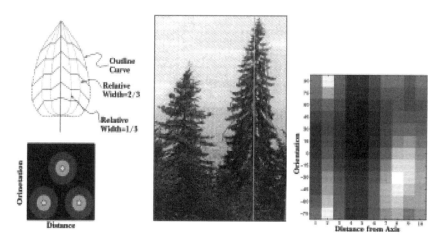

Figure 6. The orientation representation is obtained by computing the strength of response at various orientations with respect to the axis, at a range of perpendicular distances to the axis. These distances are measured relative to the width of the outline at that point and so are viewpoint stable. Responses at a particular orientation and a particular distance are summed along the height of the outline. The figure on the left illustrates the process; the representation has three clear peaks corresponding to the three branch orientations taken by the illustrative tree. The image on the extreme right shows the representation extracted for the tree in the center image. In our display of the orientation representation, brighter pixels correspond to stronger responses; the horizontal direction is distance perpendicular to the tree axis relative to the width of the tree at the relevant point, with points on the tree axis at the extreme left; the vertical direction is orientation (which wraps around). In the given case, there is a sharp peak in response close to the axis and oriented vertically, which indicates that the trunk of the tree is largely visible. A second peak oriented at about 30° and some distance out indicates a preferred direction for the tree branches.

representation distinguishes effectively between trees that are relatively translucent—such as the monkey puzzle—and those that are relatively opaque.

Finding the Axis and the Outline of a Tree

As the discussion of the representation shows, an axis and outline are important in forming the representation. Both can be found by exploiting the viewing assumptions, known constraints on the geometry of volumetric primitives, and the assumed textural coherence of the branches. The axis, which by the assumptions on viewing, is vertical and is found using a Hough transform, where pairs of strong orientation responses that display a reflectional symmetry (i.e., angles to the vertical are symmetric, and the vertical coordinates are similar) generate votes for a vertical axis. Local maxima of the accumulator array, which obtain more than a specified minimum number of votes, are accepted as axes. Symmetric arrangements of trees generate false axes, which can be pruned by observing that regions near the axes, while symmetric, do not have strong orientation responses.

Once found, the axis serves as an organizing principle for a search for the outline of the tree. In particular, the viewing conditions, combined with an assumption of spatial homogeneity (this assumption is not always true, but is useful), imply that horizontal "slices" of tree are scaled versions of the same statistical process. In turn, this means that the outline of the tree can be generated from a single good cross-section region by a process of a search up the axis. The good section is found by searching out from the axis, at a variety of heights, to find a cross-section where a sharp change in orientation properties signals that the boundary of the tree is found.

CASE STUDY 3:
FUSING COLOR, TEXTURE, AND GEOMETRY TO FIND PEOPLE AND ANIMALS

A variety of systems have been developed specifically for recognizing people or human faces. There are several domain-specific constraints in recognizing humans and animals: humans and (many) animals are made out of parts whose shape is relatively simple; there are few ways to assemble these parts; the kinematics of the assembly ensures that many configurations of these parts are impossible, and, when one can measure motion, the dynamics of these parts are limited, too. Most previous work on finding people emphasizes motion, but face-finding from static images is an established problem. The main features on a human face appear in much the same form in most images, enabling techniques based on principal component analysis or neural networks proposed by, for example, Pentland et al. (1994), Sung and Poggio (1994), Rowley et al. (1996), and Burel and Carel (1994). Face-finding based on affine covariant geometric constraints is presented by Leung et al. (1995).

However, segmentation remains a problem; clothed people are hard to segment because clothing is often marked with complex colored patterns, and most animals are textured in a way that is intended to confound segmentation. Attempting to classify images based on whether they contain naked people or not provides a useful special case that emphasizes the structural representation over segmentation, because naked people display a very limited range of colors and are untextured. Our system for telling whether an image contains naked people:

- first locates images containing large areas of skin-colored region;
- then, within these areas, finds elongated regions and groups them into possible human limbs and connected groups of limbs.

Images containing sufficiently large skin-colored groups of possible limbs are reported as potentially containing naked people. No pose estimation, back-projection, or verification is performed.

Marking skin involves stuff processing; skin regions lack texture and have a limited range of hues and saturations. To render processing invariant to changes in overall light level, images are transformed into a log-opponent representation, and smoothed texture and color planes are extracted. To compute texture amplitude, the intensity image is smoothed with a median filter; the result is subtracted from the original image, and the absolute values of these differences are run through a second median filter. The texture amplitude and the smoothed R-G and B-Y values are used to mark as probably skin all pixels whose texture amplitude is no larger than a threshold, and whose hue and saturation lie in a fixed region. The skin regions are cleaned up and enlarged slightly to accommodate possible desaturated regions adjacent to the marked regions. If the marked regions cover at least 30 percent of the image area, the image will be referred for geometric processing.

The input to the geometric grouping algorithm is a set of images in which the skin filter has marked areas identified as human skin. Sheffield's implementation of Canny's (1986) edge detector, with relatively high smoothing and contrast thresholds, is applied to these skin areas to obtain a set of connected edge curves. Pairs of edge points with a near-parallel local symmetry (as in Brady & Asada, 1984) and no other edges

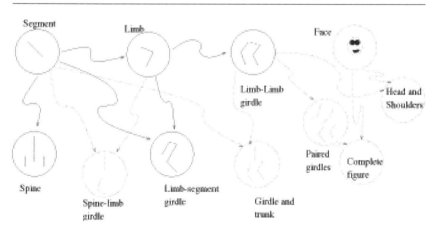

Figure 7. The grouping rules (arrows) specify how to assemble simple groups (e.g., body segments) into complex groups (e.g., limb-segment girdles). These rules incorporate constraints on the relative positions of 2D features, induced by geometric and kinematic constraints on 3D body parts. Dashed lines indicate grouping rules that are not yet implemented. Notice that this representation of human structure emphasizes grouping and assembly but can be comprehensive.

between them are found by a straightforward algorithm. Sets of points forming regions with roughly straight axes (termed "ribbons" by Brooks, 1981) are found using a Hough transformation.

Grouping proceeds by first identifying potential segment outlines, where a segment outline is a ribbon with a straight axis and relatively small variation in average width (see figure 7). Pairs of ribbons whose ends lie close together, and whose cross-sections are similar in length, are grouped to make limbs. The grouper then proceeds to assemble limbs and segments into putative girdles. It has grouping procedures for two classes of girdle—one formed by two limbs and one formed by one limb and a segment. The latter case is important when one limb segment is hidden by occlusion or by cropping. The constraints associated with these girdles are derived from the case of the hip girdle and use the same form of interval-based reasoning as used for assembling limbs. It is not possible to reliably determine which of two segments forming a limb is the thigh: the only cue is a small difference in average width, and this is unreliable when either segment may be cropped or foreshortened.

system configuration	response ratio	test response	control response	test images marked	control images marked	recall	precision
skin filter	7.0	79.3%	11.3%	448	485	79%	48%
A	10.7	6.7%	0.6%	38	27	7%	58%
B	12.0	26.2%	2.2%	148	94	26%	61%
C	11.8	26.4%	2.2%	149	96	26%	61%
D	9.7	38.6%	4.0%	218	170	39%	56%
E	9.7	38.6%	4.0%	218	171	39%	56%
F (primary)	10.1	42.7%	4.2%	241	182	43%	57%
G	8.5	54.9%	6.5%	310	278	55%	53%
H	8.4	55.9%	6.7%	316	286	56%	52%

Table 1. Overall classification performance of the system, in various configurations, to 4,289 control images and 565 test images. Configuration F is the primary configuration of the grouper, fixed before the experiment was run, which reports a naked person present if either a girdle, a limb-segment girdle, or a spine group is present, but not if a limb group is present. Other configurations represent various permutations of these reporting conditions—e.g., configuration A reports a person present only if girdles are present. There are fewer than fifteen cases because some cases give exactly the same response.

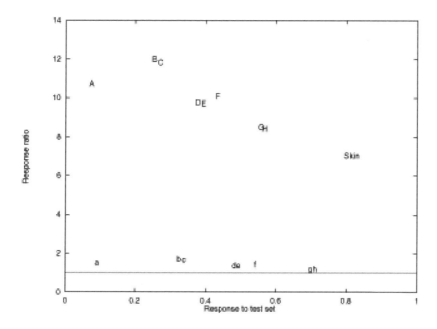

Figure 8. The response ratio (percent incoming test images marked/percent incoming control images marked), plotted against the percentage of test images marked, for various configurations of the naked people finder. Labels "A" through "H" indicate the performance of the entire system of skin filter and geometrical grouper together, where "F" is the primary configuration of the grouper. The label "skin" shows the performance of the skin filter alone. The labels "a" through "h" indicate the response ratio for the corresponding configurations of the grouper, where "f" is again the primary configuration of the grouper; because this number is always greater than one, the grouper always increases the selectivity of the overall system. The cases differ by the type of group required to assert that a naked person is present. The horizontal line shows response ratio one, which would be achieved by chance. While the grouper's selectivity is less than that of the skin filter, it improves the selectivity of the system considerably. There is an important trend here; the response ratio increases and the recall decreases as the geometric complexity of the groups required to identify a person increases. This suggests: (1) that the presence of a sufficiently complex geometric group is an excellent guide to the presence of an object, (2) that our representation used in the present implementation omits a number of important geometric structures. **Key:** A: limb-limb girdles; B: limb-segment girdles; C: limb-limb girdles or limb-segment girdles; D: spines; E: limb-limb girdles or spines; F: (two cases) limb-segment girdles or spines and limb-limb girdles, limb-segment girdles or spines; G, H each represent four cases, where a human is declared present if a limb group or some other group is found.

135

Spine-thigh groups are formed from two segments serving as upper thighs and a third which serves as a trunk. The thigh segments must have similar average widths, and it must be possible to construct a line segment between their ends to represent a pelvis in the manner described above. The trunk segment must have an average width similar to twice the average widths of the thigh segments. Finally, the whole configuration of trunk and thighs must satisfy geometric constraints that follow from the kinematics of humans. The grouper asserts that human figures are present if it can assemble either a spine-thigh group or a girdle group.

CONCLUSION

Object models quite different from those commonly used in computer vision offer the prospect of effective recognition systems that can work in quite general environments. In this approach, an object is modeled as a loosely coordinated collection of detection and grouping rules. The object is recognized if a suitable group can be built. Grouping rules incorporate both surface properties (color and texture) and shape information. This type of model gracefully handles objects whose precise geometry is extremely variable, where the identification of the object depends heavily on nongeometrical cues (e.g., color), and on the interrelationships between parts.

In this view of an object model and of the recognition process, model information is available to aid segmentation at about the right stages in the segmentation process in about the right form. As a result, these models present an effective answer to the usual critique of bottom up vision— i.e., that segmentation is too hard in that framework. In this view of the recognition process, the emphasis is on proceeding from general statements ("skin color") to particular statements ("a girdle"). As each decision is made, more specialized (and thereby more effective) grouping activities are enabled. Such a model is likely to be ineffective at particular distinctions ("John" versus "Fred") but effective at the kind of broad classification required by this application—an activity that has been, to date, very largely ignored by the object recognition community.

Much work is required to fully elaborate and test this model of modeling and recognition, but there is reason to believe that it will extend to cover a wide range of objects, including at least animals assembled according to the same basic body plan as humans. Our view of models gracefully handles objects whose precise geometry is extremely variable, where the identification of the object depends heavily on nongeometrical cues (e.g., color), and on the interrelationships between parts. While the present model is handcrafted and is by no means complete, there is good reason to believe that an algorithm could construct a model of this form, automatically or semi-automatically, from a 3D object model or from a range of example images.

ACKNOWLEDGMENTS

We thank Joe Mundy for suggesting that the response of a grouper may indicate the presence of an object. Aspects of this research were supported by the National Science Foundation under grants IRI-9209728, IRI-9420716, IRI-9501493; an NSF Young Investigator award; an NSF Digital Library award, IRI-9411334; an instrumentation award, CDA-9121985; and by a Berkeley Fellowship.

REFERENCES

Ashley, J; Barber, R.; Flickner, M. D.; Hafner, J. L.; Lee, D.; Niblack, W.; & Petkovich, D. (1995). Automatic and semiautomatic methods for image annotation and retrieval in QBIC. In W. Niblack & R. Jain (Eds.), *Storage and retrieval for image and video databases III: Volume 2420: SPIE Proceedings* (San Jose, California, February 9-10, 1995) (pp. 24-35). Bellingham, WA: SPIE.

Brady, J. M., & Asada, H. (1984). Smoothed local symmetries and their implementation. *International Journal of Robotics Research, 3*(3), 36-61.

Brooks, R. A. (1981). Symbolic reasoning among 3-D models and 2-D images. *Artificial Intelligence, 17*(1-3), 285-348.

Burel, G., & Carel, D. (1994). Detecting and localization of face on digital images. *Pattern Recognition Letter, 15*(10), 963-967.

Burt, P. J., & Adelson, E. H. (1983). The Laplacian Pyramid as a compact image code. *IEEE Transactions on Communications.* Com-31(4), 532-540.

Canny, J. F. (1986). A computational approach to edge detection. *IEEE Transactions on Pattern Analysis Machine Intelligence, 8*(6), 679-698.

Connell, J. H., & Brady, J. M. (1987). Generating and generalizing models of visual objects. *Artificial Intelligence, 31*(2), 159-183.

Fleck, M. (1996). The topology of boundaries. *Artificial Intelligence, 80*(1), 1-27.

Förstner, W. (1993). Image matching. In R. Haralick & L. Shapiro (Eds.), *Computer and robot vision* (vol. 2). Reading, MA: Addison-Wesley.

Forsyth, D. A.; Mundy, J. L.; Zisserman, A. P.; Heller, A.; Coehlo, C.; & Rothwell, C. A. (1991). Invariant descriptors for 3D recognition and pose. *IEEE Transactions on Pattern Analysis and Machine Intelligence, 13*(10), 971-991.

Gårding, J., & Lindeberg, T. (1994). Direct estimation of local surface shape in a fixating binocular vision system. In *Third European conference on computer vision—ECCV '94: Vol. 1: Proceedings* (Stockholm, Sweden, May 2-6, 1994) (pp. 365-376). Stockholm, Sweden: ECCV.

Grimson, W. E. L., & Lozano-Pérez, T. (1987). Localising overlapping parts by searching the interpretation tree. *IEEE Transactions on Pattern Analysis and Machine Intelligence, 9*(4), 469-482.

Huttenlocher, D. P., & Ullman, S. (1986). Object recognition using alignment. In *First international conference on computer vision: Vol. 1: Proceedings* (London, June 8-11, 1987) (pp. 102-111). Washington, DC: IEEE Computer Society Press.

Jacobs, C. E.; Finkelstein, A.; & Salesin, D. H. (1995). Fast multiresolution image querying. In R. Cook (Ed.), *SIGGRAPH-95 conference proceedings* (August 6-11, 1995) (pp. 277-285). New York: ACM SIGGRAPH.

Kelly, P. M.; Cannon, M.; Hush, D. R. (1995). Query by image example: The comparison algorithm for navigating digital image databases (CANDID) approach. In W. Niblack & R. Jain (Eds.), *Storage and retrieval for image and video databases III: Vol. 2420: SPIE Proceedings* (San Jose, California, February 9-10, 1995) (pp. 238-249). Bellingham, WA: SPIE.

Kriegman, D., & Ponce, J. (1994). Five distinctive representations for recognition of curved surfaces using outlines and markings. In M. Hebert, J. Ponce, T. Boult, & A. Gross (Eds.), *Object representation in computer vision: International NSF-ARPA workshop proceedings* (New York, December 5-7, 1994) (Lecture Notes in Computer Science: 994, pp. 89-100). Berlin: Springer-Verlag.

Lamdan, Y.; Schwartz, J. T.; & Wolfson, H. J. (1988). Object recognition by affine invariant matching. In *IEEE Computer Society Conference on Computer Vision and Pattern recognition (CVPR '88) Proceedings* (Ann Arbor, Michigan, University of Michigan) (pp. 335-344). Washington, DC: IEEE Computer Society Press.

Layne, S. S. (1994). Some issues in the indexing of images. *Journal of the American Society of Information Science, 45*(8), 583-588.

Leung, T. K.; Burl, M. C.; & Perona, P. (1995). Finding faces in cluttered scenes using random labelled graph matching. In *Proceedings of the Fifth international conference on computer vision* (Cambridge, Massachusetts, June 2-23, 1995) (pp. 637-644). Los Alamitos, CA: IEEE Computer Society Press.

Liu, J.; Mundy, J. L.; Forsyth, D. A.; Zisserman, A. P.; & Rothwell, C. A. (1993). Efficient recognition of rotationally symmetric surfaces and straight homogenous generalized cylinders. *IEEE Computer Society conference on computer vision and pattern recognition (CVPR '93) Proceedings* (New York, June 15-18, 1993). Los Alamitos, CA: IEEE Computer Society Press.

Lowe, D. G. (1987). The viewpoint consistency constraint. *International Journal of Computer Vision, 1*(1), 57-72.

Malik, J., & Rosenholtz, R. (1994). Recovering surface curvature and orientation from texture distortions: A least squares algorithm and sensitivity analysis. In J. -O. Eckland (Ed.), *Third European conference on computer vision (ECCV '94) Proceedings* (Stockholm, Sweden, May 2-6, 1994) (Lecture Notes in Computer Science: 800, pp. 353-364). Berlin: Springer-Verlag.

Minka, T. (1995). *An image database browser that learns from user interaction.* Unpublished article by Massachusetts Institute of Technology media lab report # TR 365.

Mukherjee, D. P.; Zisserman, A.; & Brady, J. M. (1995). Shape from symmetry—detecting and exploiting symmetry in affine images. *Philosophical Transactions of the Royal Society of London* [Series A: Physical Sciences and Engineering], 351(1695), 77-106.

Murase, H., & Nayar, S. K. (1995). Visual learning and recognition of 3D objects from appearance. *International Journal of Computer Vision, 14*(1), 5-24.

Nevatia, R., & Binford, T. O. (1977). Description and recognition of curved objects. *Artificial Intelligence, 8,* 77-98.

Niblack, W.; Barber, R.; Equitz, W.; Flickner, M.; Glasman, E.; Petkovic, D.; & Yanker, P. (1993). The QBIC Project: Querying images by content using colour, texture and shape. In W. Niblack (Ed.), *Storage and retrieval for image and video databases: Vol. 1908: SPIE Proceedings* (San Jose, California, February 2-3, 1993) (pp. 173-187). Bellingham, WA: SPIE.

Ogle, V. E., & Stonebraker, M. (1995). Chabot: Retrieval from a relational database of images. *IEEE Computer, 28*(9), 40-48.

Pentland, A.; Picard, R. W.; & Sclaroff, S. (1993). P*hotobook: Content-based manipulation of image databases.* Unpublished MIT Media Lab Perceptual Computing TR No. 255.

Pentland, A.; Moghaddam, B.; & Starner, T. (1994). View-based and modular eigenspaces for face recognition. In *Proceedings of the IEEE Computer Society Conference on computer vision and pattern recognition* (CVPR '94, Seattle, Washington, June 21-23, 1994) (pp. 84-91). Los Alamitos, CA: IEEE Computer Society Press.

Picard, R. W., & Minka, T. (1995). Vision texture for annotation. *Journal of Multimedia Systems, 3*(1), 3-14.

Polana, R., & Nelon, R. (1993). Detecting activities. In *Proceedings of the IEEE Computer Society Conference on computer vision and pattern recognition* (CVPR '93, New York, June 15-18, 1993) (pp. 2-13). Los Alamitos, CA: IEEE Computer Society Press.

Price, R.; Chua, T.-S.; & Al-Hawamdeh, S. (1992). Applying relevance feedback to a photo-archival system. *Journal of Information Science, 18*(3), 203-215.

Rothwell, C. A.; Zisserman, A.; Mundy, J. L.; & Forsyth, D. A. (1992). Efficient model library access by projectively invariant indexing functions. In A. Rosenfeld (Chair), *Proceedings of the IEEE Computer Society conference on computer vision and pattern recognition* (CVPR '92, Champaign, Illinois, June 15-18, 1992) (pp. 109-114). Los Alamitos, CA: IEEE Computer Society Press.

Rowley, H.; Baluja, S.; & Kanade, T. (In press). Human face detection in visual scenes. *Neural Information Processing Systems, 8.*

Sclaroff, S. (1995). *World wide web image search engines* [White paper for NSF Workshop on Visual Information Management, June 1995]. Unpublished manuscript by Boston University Computer Science Department (Report #TR95-016).

Stein, F., & Medioni, G. (1992). Structural indexing: Efficient 3D object recognition. *IEEE Transactions on Pattern Analysis and Machine Intelligence, 14*(2), 125-145.

Sung, K. K., & Poggio, T. (1994). *Example-based learning from view-based human face detection.* Unpublished MIT Artificial Intelligence Lab Memo No. 1521.

Taubin, G., & Cooper, D. B. (1992). Object recognition based on moment (or alegebraic) invariants. In J. L. Mundy & A. P. Zisserman (Eds.), *Geometric invariance in computer vision.* Cambridge, MA: MIT Press.

Taylor, B. (1977). Tense and continuity. *Linguistics and Philosophy, 1,* 199-220.

Tenny, C. L. (1987). *Grammaticalizing aspect and affectedness.* Unpublished doctoral dissertation, Department of Linguistics and Philosophy, Massachusetts Institute of Technology.

Ullman, S., & Basri, R. (1991). Recognition by linear combination of models. *IEEE Transactions on Pattern Analysis and Machine Intelligence, 13*(10), 992-1006.

Weiss, I. (1988). Projective invariants of shapes. *Proceedings of the DARPA Image Understanding Workshop* (pp. 1125-1134). San Francisco, CA: Morgan Kaufmann Publishers.

Whorf, B. L. (1941). The relation of habitual thought and behavior to language. In L. Spier, A. Hallowell, & S. Newman (Eds.), *Language, culture, and personality, essays in memory of Edward Sapir.* Unpublished paper of the Sapir Memorial Publication Fund, Menasha, WI.

Zerroug, M., & Nevatia, R. (1994). From an intensity image to 3D segmented descriptions. In *Proceedings of the 12th international conference on pattern recognition* (Jerusalem, October 9-13, 1994) (pp. 108-113). Los Alamitos, CA: IEEE Computer Society.

Zisserman, A.; Mundy, J. L.; Forsyth, D. A.; Liu, J. S.; Pillow, N.; Rothwell, C. A.; & Utcke, S. (1995). Class-based grouping in perspective images. In *Proceedings of the fifth international conference on computer vision.* (Cambridge, Massachusetts, MIT, June 20-23, 1995) (pp. 183-188). Los Alamitos, CA: IEEE Computer Society Press.

ROHINI K. SRIHARI

Using Speech Input for Image Interpretation, Annotation, and Retrieval*

This research explores the interaction of textual and photographic information in an integrated text/image database environment. Specifically, three different applications involving the exploitation of linguistic context in vision are presented. Linguistic context is qualitative in nature and is obtained dynamically. By understanding text accompanying images or video, we are able to extract information useful in retrieving the picture and directing an image interpretation system to identify relevant objects (e.g., faces) in the picture. The latter constitutes a powerful technique for automatically indexing images.

A multistage system, PICTION, which uses captions to identify human faces in an accompanying photograph, has been developed. We discuss the use of PICTION's output in content-based retrieval of images to satisfy focus of attention in queries. The design and implementation of a system called Show&Tell—*a multimedia system for semi-automated image annotation—is discussed. This system, which combines advances in speech recognition, natural language processing (NLP), and image understanding (IU), is designed to assist in image annotation and to enhance image retrieval capabilities. An extension of this work to video annotation and retrieval is also presented.*

INTRODUCTION

This discussion explores the interaction of textual and photographic information in an integrated text/image database environment. In designing a pictorial database system, some of the major issues to be addressed are the amount and type of processing required when inserting new pictures into the database and efficient retrieval schemes for query processing. Searching captions for keywords and names will not necessarily yield the correct information, as objects mentioned in the caption are not always in the picture, and often objects in the picture are not explicitly mentioned in the caption. Performing a visual search for objects of interest (e.g., faces) at query time would be computationally too expensive, not to mention time-consuming. It is clear that selective processing of the text and picture at data entry time is required.

Whereas most techniques for automatic content-based retrieval of images and video have focused exclusively on statistical classification

* This work was supported in part by ARPA Contract 93-F148900-000.

techniques, the approach presented here is based on object recognition. By exploiting multimodal content accompanying an image or video, object recognition (which otherwise would be considered a futile approach) is enabled. By integrating robust statistical techniques with object-recognition techniques (where possible), one obtains true semantic content-based retrieval.

The need for exploiting domain-specific and scene-specific context in vision has been acknowledged; Strat and Fischler (1991) discuss such an approach. The core research here has centered on the use of linguistic context in image understanding. There are several issues which make this problem interesting and challenging on both the image understanding and natural language processing fronts. First, information obtained from language is qualitative. Since most vision algorithms rely on quantitative information (e.g., geometric site models), considerable effort has been expended in designing (or redesigning) vision algorithms to exploit qualitative context. Second, the task of extracting useful information from language and converting it to a suitable representation for use by an image understanding system has also been investigated. Finally, the design of a robust system combining image understanding and natural language processing within the framework of a convenient multimedia user interface has posed the greatest challenge.

Significant progress has been made in the design of a system which exploits linguistic context in the task of image interpretation. A theoretical model for using natural language text as collateral information in image understanding has been formulated; collateral information has been represented as a set of *constraints*. Preliminary natural language processing techniques for extracting collateral information from text have been formulated. A control stucture has been designed which efficiently exploits the above constraints in the process of image interpretation.

Finally, this research has led to three prototype systems: (1) PICTION (Srihari et al., 1994; Srihari, 1995c; Srihari & Burhans, 1994) which, when given a captioned newspaper photograph, identifies human faces in the photograph; (2) *Show&Tell*, a semi-automated system for image annotation and retrieval; and (3) *MMVAR*, a Multimedia system for Video Annotation and Retrieval. It should be noted that the last system is still under construction. This discussion presents an overview of all three systems with an emphasis on their use in content-based retrieval.

PICTION: A CAPTION-BASED FACE IDENTIFICATION SYSTEM

PICTION (Srihari, 1995c) is a system that identifies human faces in newspaper photographs based on information contained in the associated caption. More specifically, when given a text file corresponding to a newspaper caption and a digitized version of the associated photograph, the system is able to locate, label, and give information about people mentioned in the caption. PICTION is noteworthy since it provides a computationally less expensive alternative to traditional methods of face recognition in situations where pictures are accompanied by descriptive text. Traditional methods employ model-matching techniques and thus require that face models be present for all people to be identified by the system; our system does not require this. Furthermore, most current face recognition systems (Chellappa et al., 1995) use "mugshots" (posed pictures) of people as input; due to standardized location and homogeneous scale, detection of facial features is facilitated. Recognizing faces which have been automatically segmented out of an image is a much more difficult problem.

A significant amount of work in face location and gender discrimination has been developed and employed in the above mentioned system. PICTION has served as the basis for research in content-based retrieval from image databases (Srihari, 1995a)—retrieval is based on information from the image (face identification) as well as information gleaned from the caption.

We now discuss our work on content-based retrieval of images which takes into account both the information content from the caption as well as the information content from the picture. There are four distinct sources of information which we have identified in computing the similarity between a query and a captioned image. These are:

- text-based objective term similarity (exact match);
- text-based content term similarity (inexact match);
- image-based objective term similarity (exact match); and
- image similarity (inexact match).

Text-based objective terms include manually assigned keywords or other *keys* which have been assigned values using manual techniques. Examples of such keys are: (1) names of people in the picture, (2) who (or what) is actually depicted in the picture (not necessarily the names of the people as in item 1), (3) the event type, (4) the location, (5) the time, (6) the general mood of the picture (happy, somber, serious, etc.). More recently, Chakravarthy (1994) discusses methods of automatically assigning values to such keys. Although it is possible to derive values for some predefined keys, other robust methods of measuring content-term similarity between a query and captioned image should also be considered. The availability of large-scale lexical resources such as machine-readable dictionaries and WordNet enable such methods. For example, for each content word W_q in the query, one could count the number of words in a caption with the same context by following pointers from W_q; each pointer represents a different type of relationship. The scores are weighted by the distance (path length) from the original word. Other methods of capturing context include computing dictionary definition overlap.

Any positive object/people identification made by PICTION is represented in the database by the image coordinates. Similarly, any characteristic information that has been visually verified (e.g., gender or color of hair) is also noted. Image-based information useful in determining the presence of an individual can be quantified based on: (1) whether the face was identified; (2) the size, orientation, etc. of the face; and (3) the method used to identify faces. The last measure of similarity concerns purely image-based techniques which have been discussed extensively in the image processing literature. Examples of such measures include texture similarity.

Based on the above measures of similarity, we can compute a combined similarity measure between a query and a captioned image as:

$$Sim(CapImage, Query) = \hat{\alpha}\ \{text\ objective\_term\ similarity\}$$
$$+\beta\ \{text\ content\_term\ similarity\}$$
$$+\gamma\ \{image\ objective\_term\ similarity\}$$
$$+\delta\ \{image\ similarity\}$$

We are in the process of empirically attempting the values for $\hat{\alpha}$, β, γ, and δ. Intuitively, we can see that higher emphasis should be placed on the exact match components, especially the image-based exact match component. In the next section, we describe the dynamic assignment of weights in order to satisfy the focus of attention in users queries. The order of presentation of images to the user will depend on the value of the above metric.

Dynamic Satisfaction of Emphasis in Image Retrieval

We have performed experiments where text and image information are dynamically combined to best satisfy a query. In such cases, a user specifies not only the context of the picture he is seeking but also indicates whether the emphasis should be on image contents or text content. An example of this is illustrated in Figure 1. This illustrates the top two "hits" on the following queries: (1) *find pictures of military personnel with Clinton*, (2) *find pictures of Clinton with military personnel*, and (3) *find pictures of Clinton*. In the first query, the emphasis is more on satisfying the context of "military personnel." In the second, the emphasis is more on Clinton, and in the final query, there is no context provided; therefore in the last query, the user presumably is only seeking good pictures of Clinton. We have already described methods of computing contextual similarity based on the text. To measure how well the picture contents satisfy the query, we have considered the following factors: (1) whether the required

Left: President Clinton, right, talks with Colin Powell, left, during a ceremony at the White House marking the return of soldiers from Somalia on May 4.
Right: Four aircraft performing daredevil stunts on U.S. Armed Forces Day open house. President Bill Clinton took part in the celebrations and gave away awards to the best Cadets from the U.S. military and armed forces.

Left: President Clinton, right, talks with Colin Powell, left, during a ceremony at the White House marking the return of soldiers from Somalia on May 4.
Right: President Bill Clinton and Vice-President Al Gore walk back to the White House after they welcomed back U.S. troops returning from Somalia at the White House.

Left: President Bill Clinton gives a speech to a group of eleventh graders at Lincoln High School on his visit there April 2.
Right: President Bill Clinton, center, responds to questions put forth by interrogators.

Figure 1. Top 2 (left, right) responses to the following three queries. Row 1: Find pictures of military personnel with Clinton; Row 2: Find Pictures of Clinton with military personnel; Row 3: Find pictures of Clinton.

face was actually identified (by PICTION), (2) the size and orientation of the face, and (3) the centrality of the face in the image. The last factor is given a very low weight compared to the first two.

As the results illustrate, the first query is weighted more toward similarity of text context; notice that the second hit does not even contain any people, let alone Clinton. The words "Armed Forces" (which are part of a larger title) caused a strong contextual match; we are attempting to refine our measures of context to overcome such problems. The second query results in pictures with Clinton for the most part; the picture with the airplanes is ranked very low. The last query produces the best pictures of Clinton with disregard for context.

Although this is only a preliminary foray into a truly integrated text/image content-based retrieval system, it illustrates the additional discriminatory capabilities obtained by combining the two sources of information.

PICTION has its limitations since: (1) captions can get arbitrarily complex in terms of extracting reliable information, (2) face location and characterization tools are not sufficiently robust to be used in a completely automated system, and (3) there are limitations encountered in attempts to derive 3D information from a static 2D image; a classic example is the processing of spatial relations such as *behind*. Our recent efforts have concentrated on developing an interactive system for multimedia image annotation.

SHOW&TELL: A MULTIMEDIA SYSTEM FOR SEMI-AUTOMATED IMAGE ANNOTATION

Show&Tell is a system which combines speech recognition, natural language processing, and image understanding. The goal of this image annotation project is to take advantage of advances in speech technology and natural language (NL)/image understanding (IU) research to make the preparation of image-related collateral more efficient.

We have developed a prototype system consisting of two phases. The first phase (illustrated in figures 1a and 1b) consists of automatic interpretation/indexing of images. It begins by using mouse input to detect roads and subsequently partition the image based on road networks. Next, an analyst views the image and describes it in spoken language, pointing from time to time to indicate objects or regions in the image. A state-of-the-art speech recognition system is employed in transcribing the input and synchronizing the speech with the mouse input. The resulting narrative is processed by a natural language understanding component which generates visual constraints on the image. This in turn, is used by an image interpretation system in detecting and labeling areas, roads, and buildings in the image. Finally, a facility to attach additional collateral to objects which have been identified has been provided. The output of the system is thus an NL collateral description and an annotated image. The annotated image consists of: (1) a semantic representation of the text, and (2) locations of objects or regions identified in the image. Information is represented such that spatial reasoning, temporal reasoning, and other contextual reasoning is enabled.

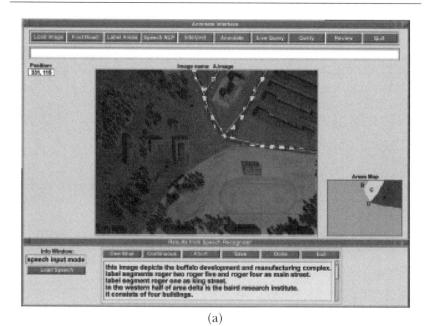

(a)

(b)

Figure 2. (a) result of road detection; (b) results of image interpretation

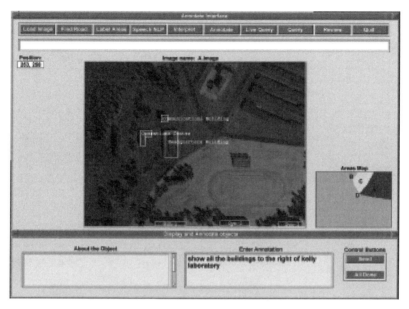

Figure 3. Results of querying.

In the second phase, we provide point and click querying synchronized with speech on the annotated images. For example, the query *Show all man-made structures to the west of this <click> forest* would cause the appropriate areas in the image to be highlighted; each of these could be further queried for corresponding textual information. This is illustrated in figure 2.

There are several assumptions we are making in specifying the task and our proposed solution. From the perspective of an image analyst, this approach constitutes a healthy compromise between: (1) tedious manual annotation, even when tools such as *snakes* are provided, and (2) completely automated (image-based) interpretation. Since the task involves *co-referencing* image areas with textual descriptions, our system uses the text for dual purposes: co-referencing as well as for assisting image interpretation.

The second assumption concerns the use of preconstructed geometric site models. These have been used effectively in the RADIUS community for registering new images of a known site and subsequently for change detection. The initial version of *Show&Tell* does not use site models since the objective was investigation of linguistic context alone. The version in development takes a different approach by utilizing site models.

Finally, at this point we assume that an approximate shape representation for objects is sufficient for reasoning purposes. We represent objects

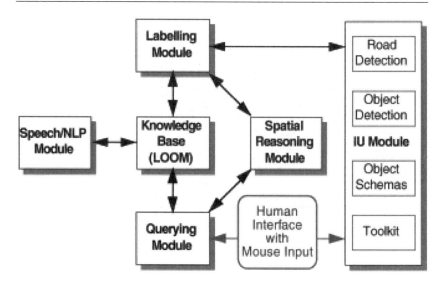

Figure 4. Functional architecture of *Show & Tell* System.

such as buildings or areas by simple bounding boxes with orientation; polylines are used for roads, rivers. Our system does allow for more exact representations for display purposes.

Figure 4 illustrates the functional architecture of *Show&Tell*. Techniques from several subdisciplines of artificial intelligence have been assimilated into this system, including computer vision, natural language understanding, spatial reasoning, knowledge representation, and information retrieval. The system is implemented in C and LISP and uses LOOM (ISI/USC) for knowledge representation; BBN's HARK speech recognition software is employed. It has been tested using images from the RADIUS model board series; these aerial images depict buildings, roads, foliage, power plants, etc. The system is now described in detail.

Knowledge Representation

We are currently using a description logic language, LOOM (ISX Corporation), to construct an object-oriented model of our world. Multiple levels of representation are employed for objects in our world. Apart from the standard composition and specialization relations between entities, we also define a *concrete* relation to relate entities at different levels of abstraction (Niemann et al., 1990). Consider the entity *building* for example; a three-level representation is used for this: (1) building *concept* where functional information is stored, (2) building *objects* which represent instances of buildings in an image, and (3) polygons which represent the shape (geometry) of a building object. This representation scheme permits visual and conceptual information to be stored in a distinct, yet shareable, manner.

Pre-Processing: Semi-Automated Road Detection

Roads form natural partitions in aerial scenes. They serve as useful landmarks upon which the analyst may base his/her description of the image. In our algorithm, it is assumed that the analyst provides an initial seed for the detection. Every connected network requires a separate seed. The algorithm is based on controlled continuity splines (Kess et al., 1987) and entropy minimization (Geman, 1994).

Speech and Language Processing

The speech annotation facility is comprised of two parts: (1) speech processing, resulting in transcribed ASCII text; and (2) natural language processing of the ASCII text. The limitations of the speech recognizer, combined with the requirement for real-time language processing strongly influenced the design of this interface.

Figure 5 illustrates a sample speech annotation used in processing the image in figure 1. In designing the speech annotation facility, there were several issues that had to be addressed. These included:

- Constraining the vocabulary and syntax of the utterances to ensure robust speech recognition; the active vocabulary is limited to 2,000 words.

- Avoiding starting utterances with words such as *this, the;* such words promote ambiguities resulting in poor recognition performance.

- Synchronizing the speech input with mouse input (e.g., *this is Kelly Laboratory*). Currently, we assume only one mouse click per utterance; the constrained syntax allows unambiguous synchronization.

- Providing an editing tool to permit correction of speech transcription errors.

In this first prototype of *Show&Tell*, the text (resulting from speech recognition) was processed as a complete narrative unit (i.e., "batch mode") rather than a sentence at a time. The justification for this is that it leads to more efficient search strategies; if all information is known a priori, the system can select an interpretation strategy which best exploits the information. Such a scenario is also reasonable if speech annotations are to be recorded and processed off-line. Finally, collateral information residing in site folders typically consists of narratives; thus any progress made in processing such narratives has broad applicability.

Processing narratives has intrinsic difficulties. People may refer to the same entity in several ways—e.g., *Baldy Tower, the tall building, the skyscraper.* Anaphoric references *it* and *them* are ubiquitous in narratives and

```
This image depicts the buffalo development and manufacturing
    complex.
Label segments roger two roger four and roger five as main
    street.
Label segment roger three as king street.
In the western half of area delta is the baird research institute.
It consists of four buildings.
Of these the leftmost is a long rectangular building.
Label this as the kelly laboratory.
This is used for developing and testing new products.
Label the l-shaped building as the operations center.
Label the large two storied building as the headquarters building.
This is where most of the administrative offices are located.
Label the small square building as the communications building.
```

Figure 5. Sample speech annotation for image in figure 2a.

require maintaining previous history. An important element in language processing is the construction of domain-specific ontologies. For example, it is important to know that a gym is a building and is associated with athletic facilities. Construction of large-scale ontologies such as this remains an open problem. With the proliferation of machine-readable lexical resources, working ontologies may be constructed which are sufficient for restricted domains.

Understanding spatial language in context (e.g., *the buildings on the river*) can get arbitrarily complex. To ensure robustness, we curtail idiomatic use of prepositions. Identifying and classifying proper noun sequences is a problem which also needs to be addressed. It is recognized that natural language understanding is itself a complex area. Since we are using language to simplify the task of vision, constraints have been imposed on the syntax and semantics of utterances to simplify processing. Although the IA cannot use unrestricted "natural language," there is sufficient flexibility to render it a convenient interface.

The output of language processing is a set of constraints on the image. These can be: (1) spatial, (2) characteristic (i.e., describe properties of an object or area), or (3) contextual. Constraints may be associated with single objects or a collection of objects (e.g., *the set of ten buildings*). The set of LOOM assertions output falls into two categories: (1) area, building, and aggregate concepts, etc.; and (2) relations between concepts indicating spatial and other relationships.

Using Scene-Specific Context for Image Interpretation

Recently, there has been a lot of academic interest in the *Integration of Natural Language and Vision* (INLV) (McKevitt, 1994; Srihari, 1995b). One of the objectives of this research effort is to use the interpretation of data in one modality to drive the interpretation of data in the other. We highlight the fact that collateral-based vision exploits a reliable hypothesis of scene contents. We obtain this hypothesis from sources other than bottom-up vision to aid the vision processing. However in the INLV community, there is sufficient interest in using bottom-up vision to generate natural language descriptions of scenes; to use vision techniques in natural language understanding; and to model deep representation and semantics of language and perception. We choose a far more conservative goal of examining how image interpretation can benefit from collateral information.

The use of collateral information is extended in this domain by: (1) devising a uniform representation for domain- and picture-specific constraints, (2) employing spatial reasoning to use partial interpretation results in guiding the application of the vision processing tools, and (3) generalize the problem representation in an object-oriented manner to deal with multiple object types (not just faces).

The idea of using partial interpretation results to localize the search for related objects has been used in several vision systems. Earlier, we classified constraints as contextual, spatial, and characteristic. When the control algorithm employs any of these constraints to disambiguate candidates, we call them *verification* constraints and when it employs them to locate candidates for an object, we term them *locative* constraints. We assume cost and reliability measures for our object locators and attribute verifiers are available. The control algorithm loops over three stages: (1) decision stage, (2) labeling stage, and (3) propogation stage.

The input to the interpretation module consists of a constraint graph. The nodes represent objects such as buildings, roads, logical areas, and aggregates of these. The arcs denote the spatial and characteristic constraints on these objects. A *working* constraint graph is created incrementally by adding nodes chosen by the decision module. Partial labeling is attempted, and the results are used for spatial prediction (Chopra & Srihari, 1995).

Annotation and Querying

Figures 2 and 3 illustrate the annotation and querying functions provided in *Show&Tell*. These are the facilities which eventually are most valuable to an IA—all the processing described to this point enables these functions. Using the annotation tool, an IA may point to an object (which has already been segmented) and type in any further information which may be relevant. Such information would be available for querying at a later point.

Querying is with respect to a single image or (eventually) across an image database. Currently, we have focused on spatial and ontological queries—e.g., *Show all buildings to the right of Kelly Laboratory* or *Show all athletic facilities*. Future plans include temporal query processing as well as a speech interface.

Rohini K. Srihari

MMVAR: A MULTIMODAL SYSTEM FOR VIDEO ANNOTATION AND RETRIEVAL

The objective of this project is to create a multimodal system for video annotation and retrieval. Although the system is general enough to be applicable for any video, it is most suited for video such as intelligence surveillance; such video is characterized by long panoramic sequences (aerial or ground-level) of natural scenes, activities involving people and vehicles, building complexes, etc. The objective is to automatically derive a semantic segmentation of the video such that it can be efficiently queried based on its contents. Since automatic statistical segmentation techniques based on video alone are not useful for retrieval purposes, the speech annotation is used as a guideline for determining logical discontinuities in the video. Features such as long pauses in annotation and the presence of keywords are combined with video-level segmentation in order to arrive at a semantic segmentation of the video. Statistical natural language processing techniques are subsequently invoked which attempt to classfiy the resulting shots based on topic.

The goal is to produce a robust scalable system demonstrable by late August 1996. This will serve as a sound infrastructure for further research in combining linguistic and visual information for intelligent content-based retrieval.

The system we are working on has the following functionality: (1) populating (entering new video into) the database, (2) annotation of existing video using a speech interface, and (3) retrieval of video based on exact and inexact (full text) techniques. All this is being provided in a single graphical user interface.

Populating Database

This feature permits new video to be entered into the video database. We allow either digital video to be entered or a video capture facility to be used. Video is segmented using statistical segmentation techniques and stored in the database as video objects. These constitute the atomic units of the database.

Video Annotation

This feature permits the creation of nonvideo objects by augmenting video with audio, text, graphical overlays, etc. Users employ a speech recording device to attach video annotation to a video. This is subsequently processed offline by a speech recognition algorithm. The output is video synchronized with corresponding audio, text, and any graphical overlays input by the user. The following features are permitted:

- multiple annotations per video;
- ability to pause video and continue speech annotation;

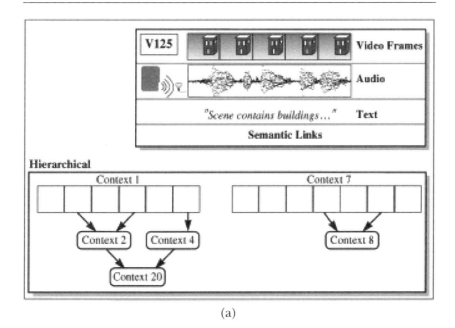

(a)

Query: Find me information on **military plane crashes ...**
[disasters, transportation, airplanes, military]

Video Database	Semantic Knowledge Base	
V124	disasters	.90
	transportation	.80
Text *"Site of a plane wreck..."*	airplanes	.85
Semantic: **obj248**		
V128	airplane	1.00
	transportation	.95
Text *"Plane taking off..."*		
V682	transportation	.95
	disasters	.90
Text *"Car crash..."*		

(b)

Figure 6. (a) hierarchical classification of video objects; (b) combining information sources in retrieval.

- ability to do single frame annotation using speech and graphical overlays (e.g., drawing circles, squares, etc.). For example, a user could circle an area and say "this area appears to have been damaged by a bomb blast." Eventually such input will be useful in tracking objects, precise retrieval, etc., but in the first phase this input is not being used; and
- ability to use speech and text in conjunction.

Information Retrieval

The objective is to retrieve relevant shots using techniques beyond simple keyword match. We attempt to capture the context of a natural-language query, and subsequently, retrieve those shots whose annotations best match the given context.

This research draws on progress made in the document retrieval domain, namely the idea of full-text search (Salton, 1988). In this, the context of a document is represented by a vector of weighted index terms. Documents may be clustered in vector space, thereby allowing more efficient matching techniques; a hierarchical search through centroids of clusters may be used to quickly find documents matching the query of the context thereby avoiding sequential search.

This method needs adaptation if it is to be used with text annotations corresponding to video shots. The primary problem is the sparseness of data (i.e., words) which makes computation of the context vector difficult. To overcome this, we use *WordNet* as well as word concordances to generate a neighborhood of words related to a given word; *WordNet* includes relationships such as synonymy, hypernomy, hyponomy, etc. Using statistical procedures, it is possible to compute the co-occurence probabilities of the given word with each of these words. This enables a larger set of weighted index terms to be computed, thereby permitting classification techniques such as the above to be used. Thus it is possible to retrieve a shot with the annotation "vehicles can be seen crossing the causeway...." as a result of the query "find shots with cars on bridges."

Vision Module

Target tracking refers to the process that in each frame of a video sequence, the target is segmented automatically and highlighted until it disappears in the sequence. We assume that the target is manually segmented out at the first frame of tracking. Then this target will be automatically tracked down in all the following frames. Owing to the nature of this problem, its solution has great application interest in intelligence surveillance and monitoring.

Due to the camera focal change (e.g., zoom in/out), camera motion, and/or the target motion, the 2D images of the target in different frames may have different shapes and intensity/color values. An automatic tracking algorithm should be able to handle these changes in different frames. This requires an appropriate model for description of the motion of the 3D target. Development of this motion model is nontrivial, because this model needs to balance the time requirement for video-rate processing and the complexity for parameterization of 3D motion. Any target tracking algorithm should be fast enough to catch the video rate when in display. On the other hand, many conventional 3D motion models involve nonlinear search, which is impractical in this application domain. Development of an algorithm with an appropriate model to satisfy the two constraints is our goal for this task.

SUMMARY

Since true semantic indexing is achievable only by understanding the scene contents, the approach presented here has focused on an object-recognition approach to content-based retrieval. Problems posed by traditional approaches to object recognition are overcome by incorporating multimodal content accompanying images/video. In particular, the use of linguistic context in image understanding has been exploited. Both automated (PICTION) and semi-automated applications (*Show&Tell*, MMVAR) have been presented.

Much work remains in making this technique completely viable; in particular, the development of robust image understanding algorithms which can exploit multimodal (and interactive) context is required. The work presented here is only a start. Issues relating to scalability and computational effort must also be examined. Finally, techniques for integrating multimodal indexes must be developed. These indexes may be generated by: (1) statistical pattern recognition techniques (e.g., color, texture), (2) object recognition techniques (e.g., face locators), or (3) text processing algorithms, to name a few. Such integration will ultimately provide the balance between computational feasibility and the need for semantic retrieval.

REFERENCES

Chakravarthy, A. (1994). Representing information need with semantic relations. In *Proceedings of COLING-94*, 1994. Kyoto, Japan.

Chellappa, R.; Wilson, C. L.; & Sirohey, S. (1995). Human and machine recognition of faces: A survey. *Proceedings of the IEEE, 83*(5), 704-740.

Chopra, R., & Srihari, R. (1995). Control structures for incorporating picture-specific context in image interpretation. In *Proceedings of IJCAI-95* (pp. 50-55). San Mateo, CA: Morgan Kaufmann.

Geman, D. (1994). The entropy strategy for shape recognition. In *IEEE-IMS Workshop on information theory and statistics* (October 27-29, 1994). Alexandria, VA:

ISX Corporation. (1991). *LOOM users guide, Version 1.4*. Available from: <http://www.isi.edu/isd/LOOH/documentation/loom.docs.html>.

Kass, M.; Witkin, A.; & Terzopoulos, D. (1987). Snakes: Active contour models. In *Proceedings of the First International Conference on Computer Vision* (pp. 259-268).

McKevitt, P. (Ed.). (1994). *Workshop on the integration of natural language and vision, AAAI-94* (Proceedings of the 12th national Conference on Artificial Intelligence). Seattle, WA: AAAI Press.

Niemann, H.; Sagerer, G. F.; Schroder, S.; & Kummert, F. (1990). Ernest: A semantic network system for pattern understanding. *IEEE Transactions on Pattern Analysis and Machine Intelligence, 12*(9), 883-905.

Salton, G. (1988). *Automatic text processing.* Addison-Wesley.

Srihari, R. K., & Burhans, D. T. (1994). Visual semantics: Extracting visual information from text accompanying pictures. In *Proceedings of AAAI-94* (pp. 793-798). Seattle, WA:

Srihari, R. K.; Chopra, R.; Burhans, D.; Venkataraman, M.; & Govindaraju, V. (1994). Use of collateral text in image interpretation. In *Proceedings of the ARPA workshop on image understanding* (pp. 897-908). Monterey, CA:

Srihari, R. K. (1995a). Automatic indexing and content-based retrieval of captioned images. *IEEE Computer, 28*(9), 49-56.

Srihari, R. K. (Ed.). (1995b). *Computational models for integrating language and vision* (Proceedings of the AAAI-1195 Fall Symposium). Menlo Park, CA: AAAI Press.

Srihari, R. K. (1995c). Use of captions and other collateral text in understanding photographs. *Artificial Intelligence Review* (special issue on Integrating Language and Vision), *8*(5), 409-430.

Strat, T. M., & Fischler, M. A. (1991). Context-based vision: Recognizing objects using information from both 2-D and 3-D imagery. *IEEE Transactions on PAMI, 13*(10), 1050-1065.

MEG BELLINGER

Digital Imaging:
Issues for Preservation and Access

This discussion outlines some of the issues that must be considered before digital imaging of paper-based research material should be adopted as a preservation method. In addition, the quality of the digital image in terms of resolution and pixel depth, as well as issues of authenticity, verification, and bibliographic integrity will be discussed. In this context, issues associated with preserving or archiving digital formats will be considered as well as current initiatives in place to address the preservation of digital media.

INTRODUCTION

The precise number of ongoing projects in institutions to convert paper-based library and archival research materials into digital format is unsurveyed. Yet the exponential growth of a wide diversity of materials readily available through computer networks is redefining previous notions of collection development, management, and resource sharing. Even as the vision of the digital library becomes increasingly more of a reality, as yet, digital imaging cannot and should not be considered to be synonymous with preservation.

What must be clearly understood is that the preservation of paper-based materials through digitization and the preservation of digital media are related issues but warrant separate discussion. Digital imaging projects that are described as efforts to preserve the endangered original must answer questions of whether the digital image will faithfully reproduce the original and how continued access to the digital format can be ensured.

Preservation of paper-based materials entails either the stabilization of the original artifact and the subsequent control of its environment, the creation of a surrogate to reduce use of the original and thereby perpetuate its existence, or, when the original is unstable, the transfer of the intellectual content to another more stable medium to ensure availability in the new medium.

For the past two decades, high volume preservation efforts and funding have been focused on reformatting or copying information from unstable originals to media with proven and verifiable standards for longevity. For paper-based materials, this has meant primarily preservation microfilming. Standards for quality reproduction of the content of the original and for ensuring the technical quality and longevity of preservation microfilm are clearly defined, universally accepted, and rigorous. However, even minimum standards for digital imaging for preservation quality have not been defined.

In order for something to be preserved through reformatting, there must be assurance that the quality of the reproduction is adequate to reproduce the intellectual content of the original and that the media to which information is transferred is stable and accessible now and in the future. The diversity of materials in libraries and archives requires a customization of appropriate approaches to optimize the particular attributes of the original. The chosen reformatting method for preservation has traditionally been dependent upon the ability to reproduce adequately those qualities of the original to an acceptable level of reproduction.

QUALITY

Whereas a microfilm of an original is an analog copy, a digital image of a document is a representation of the original rendered through pixels and bit-depth. What pixel depth and resolution is good enough for preservation purposes? When producing a digital image, the ability to produce, transfer, and store a high resolution image is a major factor affecting cost because of available equipment, time of actual scan, and file size.

At the most basic level, the representational capability of digital imaging is a factor of two attributes: (1) the number of dots, or pixels in the image, and (2) the pixel depth or range of values each pixel has. Higher resolution scanners are available including drum scanners which are capable of rendering a high optical resolution of up to 8000 dpi. For the most part, however, their use is limited to the high-end segment of the commercial market, especially for medical and graphic arts applications. The expense of creating and editing, as well as storage and transmission, is not practical for preserving large research collections.

The hardware and software that have been developed in order to accommodate high volume image production and management have evolved from the forms-management industry. Most direct flatbed and sheetfed scanners currently have the capability of rendering a bilevel image at an average of 200 to 400 dots per inch.

Digital cameras promise an effective throughput comparable to preservation microfilming and a digital resolution of up to 270 dpi for an 8.5" x 11" document. Commercially available high production microfilm scanning equipment can render an effective resolution of up to 600 dpi for an 8.5" x 11" sized original, but even as a bitonal image, the resulting uncompressed file is over 4MB. As an 8-bit grayscale file, a 600 dpi scan of an 8.5"x11" document is nearly 34MB. Even for new systems with extensive RAM and powerful coprocessing, these files are difficult to manage in a production environment.

As a point of comparison, a laser printer produces a page with a resolution of 300 dpi; an average typeset book has a dpi of 1200 (Robinson, 1993, p. 11). A 300 dpi resolution bilevel image will render a typeface of 6 points mostly readable on a computer screen. It will ordinarily print well (though not to publication standards). A 600 dpi resolution will render a typeface of 4 points legibly. It will display well even at several degrees of magnification on a higher-resolution monitor, and it will print to publication standard (Robinson, 1993, p. 6). This "high quality" level represents the best reproduction now available using commercially available standard hardware and software for high throughput scanning.

In order to achieve resolution at least as high as the average preservation microfilm, an image must be scanned at 600 dpi (the same resolution as microfilm) (Robinson, 1993, p. 25). Even the highest resolution bilevel image (bit depth = 1) will not represent an adequate facsimile of the original if that original has a high level of tonality. Most standard document scanning and processing hardware and software is developed to render uniformly sized single white sheets of paper with black print. Scanners capable of grayscale imaging are widely available, yet the software development for production-level post-scan processing lags behind significantly, making 8-bit scanning as yet only a high-end solution.

A 600 dpi bilevel image of an original text page may be legible on screen and, when printed out, may be used to represent the original text and line art. However, any nontextual information will likely be lost if the tonal value of the information is such that the bilevel scanning cannot adequately render it into black or white pixels. In this situation, the recording device must choose between rendering a tonal value in the original as either black or white. When faced with an intermediate tonal value (a pencil mark, a stain), the information will be recorded as black and white. In an example of black text on white paper where there are faint markings or staining, an attempt to render the text legibly may result in the loss of the markings, and the stain may be recorded as black. Text or line art with badly faded inks or with poor contrast because of the deterioration of the paper quality will be compromised in bitonal scanning. Graphic materials and handwritten documents will not be well represented by a bilevel image unless there is a consistently high level of contrast coupled with a low tonal range.

A distinction can and should be made between transmissive and archival quality. A digital image, for example, may be good enough for many scholarly purposes, yet this does not make it good enough to replace the original. If the goal of a digitization project is access alone, then current microcomputer screen resolution and network bandwidth limitations suggest that images have a pixel dimension of less than 640 x 480 to prevent the need for scrolling and a depth of 8 bits or less. However, this resolution is often not sufficient to retain important characteristics of the original document. It is often necessary to create the highest resolution image possible for reproduction and then produce lower resolution derivatives from the original for viewing. The resolution of the transmission image is determined by the delivery technology.

Compromises in quality are acceptable when the purpose of imaging is a matter of access only and preservation of information of the original has been assured through conservation or preservation reformatting. However, when the intent of digitization is the reproduction or replacement of the original, the highest possible resolution and tonality must be applied.

The resolution selected for imaging library materials, however, is limited by the availability of technology to cost-effectively reproduce text at high resolutions and the practical transfer and storage issues associated with large file sizes. An uncompressed 300 dpi bilevel image of a tabloid sized newspaper page is approximately 2MB. The same page scanned at 300 dpi in 8-bit will result in an uncompressed image of 16MB. Of course, compression will vastly reduce these file sizes, but even so, in the aggregate, one weekly retrospective newspaper published for 100 years and averaging sixteen pages an issue will result in bilevel files of 166.4 gigabytes and 8-bit files of 1400 gigabytes.

QUALITY AS A FACTOR OF AUTHENTICITY AND VALIDATION

Digital images are not as yet considered legally valid. In his article "Long-Term Intellectual Preservation," Peter Graham (1994) points out that the greatest asset of digital information—i.e., the ease with which an identical copy can be made—is also its greatest liability. Digital images can easily be altered either accidentally or intentionally. File corruption can occur accidentally through data transfer, compression, or copying. A myriad of image editing programs exist today by which one can intentionally alter unprotected image files and, through overwriting, remove any trace of the earlier digital copy.

As digital files are processed to remove speckling and unintentional artifacts introduced by scanning, intentional artifacts such as significant marginalia and markings may also be removed. Photoediting techniques such as cloning, masking, and pasting can add or alter information.

In addition, what is structurally whole and linear in paper and microfilm is rendered into separate files/entities in digitization. This means new works can be "published" through reorganizing image files and also means that parts of the original text may be inadvertently deleted.

When a digital image is intended as a replacement of the original, decisions must be made on the level of image quality enhancements that may compromise the informational content of the original. In addition, capabilities to digitally mark or authenticate digital images must be developed, as well as practices for the use of metadata that include information about structural content and integrity.

PRESERVATION OF THE MEDIUM

In addition to questions of quality to ensure that the intellectual content of the original is represented in the digital image, the questions remain about preserving the systems in which images are stored, viewed, and transmitted. The current pace of technological change is staggering. Backward compatibility from software and media generations are only promised by some technology providers. Media selected for the transfer and preservation of information must, by definition, provide greater stability and longevity than the original medium.

Preservation microfilming produces one master and subsequent generations for copying or for use. Each generation represents some loss of fidelity. Properly produced and stored, silver halide microfilm has a life expectancy of 500 years.

Digital images may be copied repeatedly without loss of fidelity as long as the media upon which it is stored remains stable and the equipment and software required to open and copy the image is available. Estimates published in the "Storage Technology Assessment Report" by the National Media Lab in 1994 put the life expectancy of optical media (CD-ROM, magneto Optico, and WORM) at anywhere from 5 to 100 years, depending upon manufacture and storage conditions. Magnetic tape is given a life expectancy of two to thirty years (National Media Lab, 1994).

Given the extreme span of these estimates, as Jeff Rothenburg (1995) stated in his article, "Insuring the Longevity of Digital Documents": "It is only slightly facetious to say that digital information lasts forever—or 5 years, whichever comes first" (p. 42). Rothenburg's concern goes beyond the question of the longevity of media to the very hardware, processes, and software used to write the digital information to the media and to store and retrieve it.

Estimates vary, but rates of hardware and software obsolescence can be anywhere from two to five years (Research Libraries Group, 1995, p. 3). Data refreshment and migration have been posed as solutions to the problems of technological obsolescence. Refreshment is the act of copying from one medium to another; however, given the life expectancy of optical and magnetic media cited above, and the astonishing rate of technological obsolescence, migration is considered the more robust method to ensure the preservation of digital information. Migration is the movement of information content from obsolete systems to current hardware and software systems so that information remains accessible and usable.

In the Task Force report, migration is defined:

> as a set of organized tasks designed to achieve the periodic transfer of digital materials from one hardware/software configuration to another, or from one generation of computer technology to a subsequent generation. The purpose of the migration is to retain the ability to display, retrieve, manipulate, and use digital information in the face of constantly changing technology. Migration includes refreshing as a means of digital preservation but differs from it in the sense that it is not always possible to make an exact digital copy or replica of a database or other information object, inasmuch as hardware and software change and still maintain the compatibility of the object with a new generation of technology. (Research Libraries Group, 1995, p. 4)

The responsibility, fiscal commitment, and managerial control required to move terabytes of data on a two- to five-year cycle are daunting. Nevertheless, these are the most significant issues to be resolved before one can assume that the information is preserved.

WHAT MUST BE DONE

Digitization is a reality, but we must not allow ourselves the illusion that digital imaging is preserving until we develop shared understandings, best practices, and have the technology and infrastructure in place to assert that our digital products meet the stated goal—i.e., whether of access or preservation but ideally of both.

DEFINE GOALS

The traditional definitions of preservation no longer hold in the digital image context. A major function of preservation in the paper-based world has been to ensure longevity through managing the artifact. By necessity this has been a reactive effort. Whereas universities and libraries have been repositories of information, they are now largely the creators of image collections. This translates to greater opportunity, as well as greater responsibility, for ensuring that preservation concerns are addressed as part of the process.

Imaging does not equate to longevity, and it is the proactive position of the preservation community on issues of quality that can ensure that the stated intent of preservation is a reality. Collection development or creation policies must guard the intellectual content of digital images and ensure that the infrastructure is in place to manage and preserve the collections once created.

DEFINE THE UNIVERSE AND UNDERSTAND IT

How many imaging projects and image collections are there? What is the content and scope of these projects? What are the selection, reproduction, and distribution protocols in place for these collections?

We need to develop and maintain a comprehensive juried list of digital imaging projects. The extraordinary speed with which advances are being made means that we cannot take five years to develop standards that become obsolete within months. However, we can develop best practices based on shared information.

The capability of producing high resolution digital images is only limited by the availability of current technology and the funds to apply it to preservation programs. The high throughput scanners render low resolution images and will not accommodate many of the formats that are in immediate need of reformatting. Digital cameras are promising but as yet limited for high production applications. Before choices are made to digitize, the limitations of the technology and the cost trade-offs must be clearly investigated and understood.

Without question, digital imaging technology is revolutionizing access to research materials. The pace of the technology's adoption is not likely to be contained by warnings and caveats. To truly optimize the use of the technology, a clear understanding of both the promise *and* the limitations of the technology must exist. Only through complete understanding can we hope to achieve the goals that we conceive for library imaging projects.

REFERENCES

Graham, P. (1994). *Long-term intellectual preservation: Digital imaging technology for preservation* (Proceedings from an RLG Symposium). Mountain View, CA: Research Libraries Group.

National Media Lab. (1994). *Storage technology assessment report* (Version: Final 1.1). St. Paul, MN: National Media Lab.

Research Libraries Group. Commission on Preservation and Access. (1995). *Preserving digital information* (Draft Report of the Task Force on Archiving of Digital Information. Version 1.0, August 4, 1995). Washington, DC: RLG and the Commission.

Robinson, P. (1993). *The digitization of primary textual sources* (Office for Humanities Communication Publication, no. 4). Oxford, England: Oxford University Computing Services.

Rothenberg, J. (1995). Ensuring the longevity of digital documents. *Scientific American, 272*(January), 42-47.

DONALD E. LUMAN

Preserving the Past: The Development of a Digital Historical Aerial Photography Archive

The University of Illinois Map and Geography Library maintains a collection of approximately 60,000 individual prints of historical aerial photography that were acquired during the years 1936-1941, for which there are no remaining negatives. Because of high use by library patrons, the collection is deteriorating and a method of preservation is needed. A pilot study was conducted to evaluate the feasibility and appropriateness of digital conversion using high-quality, high-precision scanning. Results indicate that scans produced from the original paper prints exhibit no loss of feature detail, is cost effective on a frame-by-frame basis, and therefore a program of digital conversion should be considered.

INTRODUCTION

Resource-based agencies in Illinois utilize a variety of data sources to derive information concerning the condition and extent of the state's natural and anthropogenic ecosystems, and vertical aerial photography is a singularly unique data source that provides an ungeneralized view of both past and present landscapes. The University of Illinois' Map and Geography Library maintains a repository of more than 160,000 vertical aerial photographs of Illinois counties that were acquired from the late 1930s through 1988, the largest single collection of vertical aerial photography in Illinois. Contained within this collection is statewide historical aerial photography acquired from 1936 to 1941, the most complete U.S. Department of Agriculture coverage known to exist in Illinois. The use of the aerial photography collection at the Map and Geography Library averages 2,000 photos per month, and this usage is resulting in damage and degradation of irreplaceable photography for the period of 1936-1941 for which no known negatives arc available. Furthermore, while it is still possible to purchase copies of the post-1950 aerial photography from the U.S. Department of Agriculture, this results in a costly time delay for the user.

THE PROBLEM

There is a significant rate of attrition for the Map and Geography Library's aerial photography collection. The greatest cause of attrition is loss, but deterioration and damage are also significant factors. While the post-1950 photography is replaced at the rate of one county per year, pre-1950 aerial photography cannot be readily replaced.

Ideally, the original source for prints for pre-1950 aerial photography are silver nitrate film negatives. Approximately 60,000 of the Map and Geography Library's aerial photographs fit into this category. Unfortunately, original negatives no longer exist for the oldest photography (e.g., 1936-1941), these having been destroyed because, as they became unstable, the heat of hydration caused the nitrate-based film to become gelatinous and combust. Beginning in 1983, the U.S. Navy and the National Archives made a roll-to-roll same-scale conversion of nitrate-based negatives for most states using Kodak 2422 Aerographic Duplicating Film. However, in order to reduce costs of reproduction, aerial photography for some states (including Illinois) were duplicated using a 70mm (2.75 inch) film format. In Illinois, users have complained that reproductions from the 70mm duplicates are poor, and therefore the existing prints for Illinois' earliest aerial photography are the only remaining high-quality source—and this collection is rapidly deteriorating.

THE SOLUTION

Two strategies are being employed at the University of Illinois to preserve the aerial photography collection: (1) prolong the life of the existing photos through simple preservation techniques, and (2) reproduce the oldest historical aerial photography in a digital format. In order to prolong the life of the existing prints, the Map and Geography Library has experimented with several methods of preservation: (1) encapsulating photography in a mylar envelope, (2) reprography of the original prints, and (3) policies that minimize the handling of the prints but allow accessibility. Aerial photography is no longer permitted to leave the premises, and a modest amount of photointerpretation equipment is available. Photographic reproduction of the pre-1950 aerial photography is currently not an option due to the lack of available storage space. Despite these straightforward measures, deterioration of the oldest aerial photography is continuing.

A second strategy that has been investigated involves high quality/ high resolution scanning of the pre-1950 aerial photography, or at least the oldest aerial photography. This form of reproduction accomplishes two objectives: (1) feature detail is faithfully and permanently preserved, and (2) there is no need for a second archive of photographic prints. In addition to preserving aerial photography, the scanned imagery can be edited to improve contrast and repair damage caused by fading and improper processing of the original photos. For example, original prints that have faded because of over fifty years of exposure to natural and artificial light sources can be enhanced by contrast stretching.

A pilot study was conducted by the author using a Crossfield drum scanning system provided by Scantech Color Systems, Inc., Champaign, Illinois. By experimenting with several scanning rates using examples of pre-1950 aerial photography, an optimal sampling rate was determined based upon factors including photo scale, print quality, and paper type. While the optimum sampling rate can vary from photograph to photograph, this rate generally ranges between 31 and 42 micrometers per picture element (pixel). The relationship between these two sampling rates can be more easily understood by relating each to the resulting ground resolution. Using a sample photograph at a nominal scale of 1:20,000 (1 inch = approximately 1,667 feet) that has a contact size of 7 x 9 inches, a sampling rate of 31 micrometers per pixel results in a digital file of approximately 55 megabytes with a ground resolution equivalent to 2.8 feet per pixel. Similarly, a sampling rate of 42 micrometers per pixel produces a digital file of approximately 32 megabytes with a ground resolution equivalent to 3.8 feet per pixel. Careful examination of the original aerial photographs with the scanned imagery revealed that no additional feature detail was added at the higher sampling rate (e.g., 31 micrometers/pixel), and in fact blurring of some surface features was evident. In addition, almost a 60 percent savings in terms of storage space is afforded by the lower sampling rate of 42 micrometers per pixel, and this factor becomes significant when planning for the scanning of county-wide historical aerial photography that can involve over 200 individual photographs.

GEOGRAPHIC INFORMATION SYSTEMS APPLICATIONS

Once historical aerial photographs have been scanned, they can be related to other GIS data sources. This can be demonstrated through a practical application. A few individual frames of historical aerial photography acquired in 1939 for a portion of McHenry County, Illinois, were scanned using the 42 micrometer/pixel sampling rate described above. In addition, the U.S. Geological Survey DOQ (digital orthophoto quadrangle) for McHenry County was acquired. The DOQ is a 1-meter ground resolution image encompassing a geographic area of 3.75 minutes of both latitude and longitude at a source scale of 1:12,000 (1 inch=1,000 feet), and the image data are cast onto the Universal Transverse Mercator projection (NAD 83). DOQs have been mathematically corrected so that distortions from the terrain, camera lens, and from the perspective view have been removed. For McHenry County, the primary source of the DOQ was 1988 NAPP I photography.

Since the DOQs are already geometrically corrected, it is a straight-forward mathematical process to transform the scanned historical photographs to conform to the corresponding DOQs. This is facilitated by the

Figure 1. Vertical area photograph situated over McHenry, Illinois, acquired July 16, 1939. After scanning, the image was geometrically corrected to conform to the corresponding digital orthophoto quadrangle.

Figure 2. Digital orthophoto acquired over the McHenry, Illinois area on April 19, 1988.

fact that the sampling rate used for the scanning of the historical aerial photography results in a ground resolution of approximately 3.8 feet (approximately 1.16 meters), which is very similar to that of the 1-meter DOQ. After a sufficient number of corresponding ground control points are located on both images, the resulting resampled and rescaled historical imagery can be overlain on the corresponding orthophoto. Change analysis can be employed to delineate the location and extent of landscape conversions that have occurred between the two acquisition dates.

Figure 1 is a geometrically corrected, historical aerial photograph that was originally acquired over McHenry, Illinois, on July 16, 1939, at a scale of approximately 1:11,250 (1 inch=approximately 940 feet). Figure 2 is the corresponding USGS DOQ for the same geographic area acquired on April 19, 1988. Visual inspection of Figures 1 and 2 shows that a remarkable amount of change has occurred during the forty-nine year time interval between the two dates of photography. Most noticeable is the conversion of rural farmland and wooded land to residential and commercial land use that has developed south and west of the original built-up area of McHenry. At the lower right margin of Figure 1 and adjacent to the Fox River is a large, palustrine deep marsh (PEMf) characterized by two separated areas of open water (dark, nearly black-toned areas) and interspersed with emergent vegetation (variegated gray-toned areas). By 1988, the majority of this high-quality marsh had been converted to a diked/impounded riverine open water wetland (R2OWh). Such conversions of palustrine wetland habitat are common in northeastern Illinois, and the use of scanned historical aerial photography in conjunction with digital orthophotography dramatizes such landscape changes.

The pilot project also investigated the need to rectify the scanned historical photography in the same manner as the DOQs in order to remove distortions induced by terrain, camera lens, etc. The historical aerial photography shown in Figure 1 was not rectified and only geometrically corrected to register with the associated DOQ imagery, and this approach is quite adequate for many applications where precise ground location is not necessary. For example, the average horizontal error in registration between Figures 1 and 2 is on the order of a few meters. Examples of scanned historical photography, along with the corresponding USGS DOQ and 1:24,000-scale USGS DEM (digital elevational model) data, were prepared for two selected geographic areas in St. Clair and Jo Daviess Counties that express moderate local relief. These data were provided to a commercial firm (Intera Corporation of Ontario, Canada) for the purpose of determining the potential cost of producing historical digital orthophotography. Intera Corporation, which is an approved vendor for the production of USGS DOQs, provided their services at no cost.

Briefly stated, it was ascertained that the production of digital orthophotography developed from historical aerial photography is probably cost prohibitive. Among the factors contributing to this conclusion are the following:

1. Ideally, the rectification procedure requires that camera lens calibration data be provided. Such information includes the camera make/model, lens type/number, focal length, etc. Prior to 1943, U.S. governmental agencies did not formalize camera calibration procedures, and therefore this information is not generally available for the oldest historical aerial photography acquired by the U.S. Department of Agriculture (Brad Johnson, U.S. Geological Survey, personal communication, January 26, 1995). If such data were available for older aerial photography, these would logically reside with the civilian companies that acquired the photography. However, many of these companies either do not exist any longer, have purged these older calibration reports, or have changed addresses and thus are difficult to locate.

2. For both the aerial photography used in Figure 1 as well as the sample data provided to Intera Corporation, nearly fifty years had transpired between the acquisition dates of the scanned historical aerial photography and the DOQs developed from recent NAPP I and NAPP II aerial photography. As a result of the numerous landscape changes that have occurred (e.g., widening of roads, rural to urban/built-up land use conversions, vegetation succession, etc.), collecting a sufficient number of similar ground control points on both dates of imagery for the geometric correction procedure proved to be very time consuming.

3. In one example, a data set incorporating three scanned historical aerial photographs (two end-lapped photographs with one side-lapped photograph), Intera Corporation furnished the rectified historical aerial photography back to the authors for the purpose of ascertaining mosaickability. It was subsequently discovered that remaining distortions were sufficient to preclude the creation of a controlled mosaic, and that only semi-controlled mosaicking was possible. The resolution of the remaining distortions was deemed cost-prohibitive.

CONCLUSION

The results of an intensive pilot project has demonstrated that high-quality precision scanning of historical aerial photography is a viable archiving alternative. At the cost of approximately $30.00 per frame, this is also an affordable alternative for limited geographic areas. However, even the scanning of the pre-1950 collection of statewide aerial photography encompassing some 60,000 frames is presently cost-prohibitive. It is suggested that cost-sharing initiatives with state and local governmental agencies may be a practical method of distributing the cost. During the period of the pilot project, the University of Illinois Library and one county governmental agency cost-shared to quantize the oldest set of county-wide USDA aerial photography.

Once developed through a joint funding or other funding agreements, the U.S. Geological Survey DOQ product is an inexpensive ($32.00 for each county-based CD ROM) and potentially valuable resource for site-level GIS applications. At the date of this writing, DOQ production for approximately seventeen Illinois counties is either completed or in process. In contrast, the development of digital orthophotography from historical aerial photography appears to be cost-prohibitive at the present time. However, for a large portion of Illinois and on a site-by-site basis, the authors suggest that a simple geometric correction of the scanned photography is sufficient for most GIS applications where the inclusion of historical landscape information may be useful.

Additional information regarding the availability and scanning of historical aerial photography can be acquired by contacting either Donald Luman (217/244-2179) or Christopher Stohr (217/244-2186) at the Illinois State Geological Survey, 615 East Peabody Drive, Champaign, IL 61820. The availability of USGS DOQs as well as all other USGS digital products can be easily reviewed using the Internet USGS World Wide Web home page (http://info.er.usgs.gov/) or by using anonymous ftp (ftp nmdpow9.er.usgs.gov).

Contributors

MEG BELLINGER is the President of Preservation Resources, a division of OCLC. For the last several years, Ms. Bellinger has been leading the development of OCLC's digital scanning capabilities since joining the organization in 1993. Prior to joining Preservation Resources, she was Vice President of Editorial and Development at Research Publications International, part of the Thomson Organization. Ms. Bellinger has been an invited lecturer at a number of national library and archival venues and has spoken on the topic of the conversion of retrospective research materials to digital media. She received her MLS in 1984 and has been active in the library preservation community since 1988.

HOWARD BESSER is Visiting Associate Professor at the University of California Berkeley School of Information Management & Systems, where he teaches, does research, and is the Principal Investigator for a grant examining a multi-institution digital library project. From 1994 to 1996 he was on the faculty of the University of Michigan's School of Information where he headed a committee developing a curriculum in multimedia and digital publishing. Dr. Besser has served in an advisory capacity to numerous libraries, museums, and cultural heritage institutions. He currently serves on the Management Committee of the Museum Educational Site Licensing Project. He has served as co-chair of the American Library Association's Technology & the Arts Interest Group.

SHIH-FU CHANG is an Assistant Professor at the Department of Electrical Engineering and the Center for Telecommunications Research of Columbia University. He received his Ph.D. degree in Electrical Engineering and Computer Sciences from the University of California at Berkeley in 1993. Professor Chang is currently co-leading the development of the Video on Demand testbed at the Image and Advanced TV Laboratory of Columbia University. He is also actively involved in Columbia's Digital Library project and a new center on Image Technology for New Media. His research interests focus on visual information systems, image/video coding, and visual communications. His group has developed prototype systems for content-based image/video retrieval, compressed-domain video indexing and manipulation, and MPEG real-time video server. His research has been supported by awards from the National Science Foundation and IBM, and he serves on the editorial boards and program committees of several international conferences and journals.

DAVID A. FORSYTH is Associate Professor of Computer Science at the University of California at Berkeley. He holds a bachelor of science and a master of science degree in Electrical Engineering from the University of the Witwatersrand, Johannesburg, and a doctorate in Philosophy from Balliol College, Oxford. He is currently associate professor of computer science at the University of California at Berkeley.

P. BRYAN HEIDORN is an instructor and researcher at the Graduate School of Library and Information Science at the University of Illinois at Urbana-Champaign where he joined the faculty in 1995. Mr. Heidorn's research interests include natural language processing, spatial cognitive modeling, and image storage and retrieval. His current work involves natural language understanding for the generation of metric models for images synthesis and retrieval. He teaches in the areas of information system automation and information retrieval. Mr. Heidorn is an active member of the American Society of Information Science and the American Society for Computing Machinery.

THOMAS S. HUANG is William L. Everitt Distinguished Professor in the Department of Electrical and Computer Engineering, University of Illinois at Urbana-Champaign (UIUC) and Research Professor at the Coordinated Science Laboratory and the Beckman Institute for Advanced Science and Technology at the University of Illinois. He is the Chair of the Human Computer Intelligent Interaction major research theme at the Beckman Institute. Before joining UIUC, he served on the faculties of MIT and Purdue University. His research interests lie in the broad area of information processing especially in the acquisition, representation, analysis, manipulation, and visualization of multidimensional signals and data. He has published eleven books and more than 300 journal and conference papers on digital filtering, digital holography, image/video compression, image enhancement, image databases, and vision/speech-based human computer interface.

RAMESH JAIN is currently a Professor of Electrical and Computer Engineering, and Computer Science and Engineering at University of California at San Diego (UCSD). Before joining UCSD, he was a Professor of Electrical Engineering and Computer Science, and the founding Director of the Artificial Intelligence Laboratory at the University of Michigan,

Ann Arbor. He has also been affiliated with Stanford University, IBM Almaden Research Labs, General Motors Research Labs, Wayne State University, University of Texas at Austin, University of Hamburg, West Germany, and Indian Institute of Technology, Kharagpur, India. His current research interests are in multimedia information systems, interactive video, image databases, machine vision, and intelligent systems. He was the founder and the Chairman of Imageware, Inc., an Ann Arbor-based company dedicated to revolutionize software interfaces for emerging sensortechnologies. He is the founding chairman of Virage, a San Diego-based company developing systems for Visual Information Retrieval.

DONALD E. LUMAN is a Senior Geologist at the Department of Natural Resources, Illinois State Geological Survey. In 1993, Dr. Luman was an Associate Professor of Geography at Northern Illinois University and has twenty years of teaching experience. His research focuses on the application of remote sensing technologies to landscape characteristics and was a recipient of the 1996 Award for Best Scientific Paper in Remote Sensing by the American Society of Photogrammetry and Remote Sensing. Dr. Luman also taught several workshops involving remote sensing applications in the United States, Kenya, Thailand, and China.

LOIS F. LUNIN is the editor of *Perspectives*, a journal within the *Journal of the American Society for Information Science*. She is also the author or co-author of three books, numerous chapters, and more than 150 articles on information systems design, databases, electronic images, multimedia, and the Internet, and a contributing editor to several publications including *Information Today*. She has held faculty positions in several major medical schools including the Johns Hopkins University School of Medicine and the Cornell University Medical College, has served as a consultant to government agencies, foundations, the Pan American Health Organization, medical and dental schools, and has lectured on five continents on information and its communication.

RAJIV MEHROTRA is currently an Associate Professor in the Department of Mathematics and Computer Science of the University of Missouri-St. Louis. His current research interests include content-based visual information modeling and retrieval, multimedia information management, image processing, and computer vision. He is co-editing (with W.I. Grosky and R.C. Jain) a book entitled "A Handbook of Multimedia Information Systems" to be published by Prentice Hall. Dr. Mehrotra has either written or edited a number of publications in the area of multimedia information systems. He is a senior member of IEEE and a member of ACM.

SHARAD MEHROTRA is an Assistant Professor in the Department of Computer Science, University of Illinois at Urbana-Champaign since 1994. Before joining the University of Illinois, he worked as a scientist for Matsushita Information Technology Laboratory, Princeton from 1993 to 1994. His research interests include database management, distributed systems, and information retrieval. Mr. Mehrotra has authored over twenty journal and conference papers in transaction processing, multidatabase systems, text indexing systems, and distributed information systems.

KANNAN RAMCHANDRAN has been an Assistant Professor in the Electrical and Computer Engineering Department, and a Research Assistant Professor in the Beckman Institute at the University of Illinois at Urbana-Champaign since 1993, when he received his doctorate in Electrical Engineering from Columbia University. He was a Member of the Technical Staff at AT&T Bell Labs, New Jersey, from 1984 to 1990. His research interests include image and video compression, multirate signal processing and wavelets, telecommunications, and image communications. He has over forty journal and conference publications in these areas and holds three patents.

BETH SANDORE is the Coordinator for Imaging Projects and Associate Professor in the University of Illinois Library at Urbana-Champaign. She recently co-authored with F. W. Lancaster *Technology and Management in Library and Information Services*. She has published a number of articles in the areas of systems development and evaluation in libraries and currently chairs the Evaluation Working Group of the Museum Educational Site Licensing Project.

ROHINI K. SRIHARI received her Ph.D. in Computer Science from the State University of New York at Buffalo in 1992. At present she is a Research Scientist at the Center of Excellence for Document Analysis and Recognition (CEDAR) at the State University of New York at Buffalo. Her current research centers on integrating text and image information in content-based retrieval systems. This is an extension of her earlier work on the use of collateral text (e.g., captions) in image understanding. Ms. Srihari is directing projects funded by NSF and DARPA in this area.

JENNIFER TRANT is Partner and Principal Consultant at Archives & Museum Informatics, Pittsburgh, Pennsylvania, where she advises clients regarding the management of information about cultural heritage. Her areas of expertise include strategic information management, use of network technologies for access to cultural heritage information, computerized museum collection documentation (in both text and image form), and international standards development initiatives. Ms. Trant's past clients include the Getty Institute, for whom she established and directed the Museum Educational Site Licensing Project. She publishes regularly on issues relating to the "virtual museum" and edits *Archives and Museum Informatics: Cultural Heritage Informatics Quarterly* published by Kluwer Academic Publishers.

INDEX

2D images, 65-66

2D regions in images, 122; describing and comparing, 65-66

3D objects: describing and comparing, 66-68; object-related queries, 80;

AAMD (Association of Art Museum Directors), 41 n.13

Adelson, Ted, 122

ABGM (Attraction-based grouping methods), 110-111

Absolute location of image features, 95

Abstraction. *See* Levels of content abstraction

Academic community. *See* LIS communities

Academic Press Image Directory Service, 37

Access to collection contents: access points in records, 45; concurrent access issues in system design, 118; determining frequency of access, 45; video content access problems, 85, 86

Accuracy of digital images. *See* Authentication of images; Integrity of images

Administering rights and use restrictions. *See* Rights and use restrictions

ADVENT system, 105

Aerial photography archives, 169-175

AHIP (Getty Art History Information Project); image quality studies, 23; MESL project, 29

Alexandria project, 105

Alphanumeric data. See Text records

Altering images. See Integrity of images; Tools

American Society of Media Photographers (ASMP), 37

AMICO (Art Museum Image Consortium), 41 n.13

Analysis of images. See Content-based retrieval; Extracting data from images; Feature-based retrieval

Andrew W. Mellon Foundation, 39

Animals, identifying in images, 135-139

Annotation of content. *See also* Text records; annotating images with speech and gesture, 148-154; annotating video with speech, 155-158; iconic annotation languages, 52; ImageQuery system tools, 14;

natural language collateral information, 144; stream-based annotation of video, 52

Annual Clinic on Library Applications of Data Processing, 1

Architecture of systems; client-server architecture, 13, 15-17, 99; CVEPS system, 97-99; flexibility and expandability, 26, 47, 104, 117, 118; ImageQuery system, 15-17; MARS system, 105-107; MESL deployment system, 38; *Show&Tell* system, 151; video content retrieval databases, 86; VisualSEEk system, 94

Archiving. *See* Digital preservation projects

Area calculations (MARS project), 108, 109

Arithmetic coders in image compression, 115

Art Museum Image Consortium (AMICO), 41 n.13

Ashmore, Lara, 26

ASMP (American Society of Media Photographers), 37

Association of Art Museum Directors (AAMD), 41 n.13

Attraction-based grouping methods (ABGM) in image segmentation, 110-111

Audio annotation: annotating images with speech and gesture, 148-154; annotating video with speech, 155-158

Authentication of images: authentication notes in metadata information, 21-22, 53-54; demand for quality multimedia content, 34; LIS community role in future, 20; rights holders needs for protection, 36; scanning quality issues, 164-165

Authoring tools for video, 97-98, 99

Automatic and semi-automatic indexing. *See also* Extracting data from images; Manual indexing; annotating images with speech and gesture, 148-154; annotating video, 155-158; color indexing, 93, 108; color set indexing, 92; impact on system scalability, 117; in document conversion bid, 50; MARS system image indexer, 106; needs assessment for new systems, 46; overview, 4-9; secondary indexing structures, 64; spatial data indexing, 79; video indexing issues, 96; VisualSEEk system, 93

Axes in tree image identification, 132-135

Back projection in color extraction, 91

Backward compatibility of files, 165

Bandwidth: high level interactions, 73; needs assessment of network requirements, 46-47

Basing queries on sample images. See Query by pictorial example (QPE)

BBN Hark speech recognition, 151

Bellinger, Meg, 9, 161-167

Benefits of digital imaging systems, 44-45

Besser, Howard: history of image databases, 2-3, 11-28; need for international standards, 47-48; network needs for systems, 46-47

Bids for document conversion, 50

Bit streams, reducing information to, 72

Bit-mapped graphics, 33

Body segments, identifying, 136

Boolean queries, 14, 111, 112

Bottom-up vision in scene description, 154

Boundary-based shape extraction, 65-66, 109

Branches in tree image identification, 132

Bregler, Chris, 7-8, 121-142

Brokerage pricing model, 37

Browsing: as basic query type, 75, 79; fuzzy queries, 75; in MARS system, 111; in video retrieval, 96-97, 98; increasing browsing speed with wavelets, 113-115

Building systems from scratch, 46

California Department of Water Resources collection, 121

Camera lens calibration data, 174

Camera operations in video: detecting, 97-98; retrieval issues caused by, 157-158

Candid system, 125

Canny's edge detector, 136

Captions on pictures, searching, 143, 144-148

Capture process information: cropping and image adjustment data, 21, 54; light source, 21; scale of image to scanned source, 21, 173; scan date and personnel, 21, 53, 78; scanner make, 21, 53

Capturing images: aerial photographs, 170-171; defining resolutions needed by users, 23-24, 162-164; service bureau scanning bids, 49-50

Carson, Chad, 7-8, 121-142

C.A.S.I.S. (Centre for Advanced Study of Information Systems, Inc.), 52

Cataloging images, terminology issues in, 24

CBVQ (content-based visual query). See Content-based retrieval

CCC (Copyright Clearance Center), 37

CCITT Group III compression standard, 13

CD-ROM life expectancy, 165

Centre de Hautes Etudes Internationales D'Informatique Documentaire, 52

Centre for Advanced Study of Information Systems, Inc., 52

Centroids (MARS), 108

Chang, Shih-Fu, 5-6, 89-102

Chromatic information. See Color extraction

C.I.D. (Centre de Hautes Etudes Internationales D'Informatique Documentaire), 52

CIMI (Computerized Interchange of Museum Information), 19

Classifying objects: based on primitives, 127; people or animal identification, 135-139; tree identification, 131-135

CLens software, 26

Client-server architecture. See also Architecture of systems

CVEPS system, 99; development of, 13; ImageQuery system, 15-17

Clothing, problems extracting images of, 135

Clustering in image segmentation, 110

C-means clustering in image segmentation, 110

Coalition for Networked Information, 21

Coarseness measure in texture, 108
Coders in image compression, 114-115
Coherence in grouping process, 126
Collateral information. See Annotation of content
Collection development: need for policies, 166-167; redefined by digital access, 161
Collections of images. *See also names of specific systems or projects*; commercial vendor collections, 19; demand for content, 34; determining frequency of access, 45; determining storage capacity needs, 46; disorderly Internet collections, 121; history of image databases, 11-13; pricing models for collection use, 36-37; types of content, 72-73
Color extraction: as feature-retrieval property, 81, 92; color sets, 91, 105; extraction techniques, 105; for regions of images, 127-131; hue maps, 129; in grouping-process object retrieval, 125; in image segmentation, 110-111; in primitive descriptions, 127; indexing color in images, 93; retrieving images by sample color, 112, 124, 127-131; spatial relationships of color in images, 108
Color histograms: as lacking spatial cues, 126; extracting in MARS system, 106, 108; histogram matching, 82
Color monitors: display device issues, 12-13; monitor requirements, 48
Columbia University's ADVENT system, 105
Commercial vendor collections, 19
Commission on Preservation and Access, 20
Complex queries in MARS system, 111-112
Compressed Video Editing and Parsing System. *See* CVEPS system
Compression: based on wavelets, 113-115; compressed-domain feature extraction, 91, 96; lossless data compression, 114, 116; video bit rates, 100; video retrieval, 96
Computed features (VIMSYS), 78
Computer processor imaging requirements, 12
Computer vision technologies grouping process, 126; image segmentation issues, 81; interaction with databases, 59; objects vs. materials, 122; reliance on geome-tric site models, 144
Computerized Interchange of Museum Information (CIMI), 19
Concept querying, 118-119
Concurrent access issues in system design, 118
Consortium pricing model, 37
Containment queries, 80
Content-based retrieval: combining approaches, 90, 92-93, 146; content defined, 90; developments in, 25, 52-53; feature-based retrieval projects. See Feature-based retrieval; keyword-based retrieval, 83, 89, 90, 143; loss of information in, 67-68; measuring effectiveness, 104; modeling data in databases, 60-63; multimedia content retrieval, 72, 103-104, 148-158; object recognition, 122-127, 131-139; overview, 59-60; query by pictorial example. See Query by pictorial example (QPE); semantic content-based retrieval, 76-77, 89, 144, 146; shape similarity-based retrieval. *See* Shape similarity-based retrieval; spatial image retrieval. *See* Spatial information and relationships; system components for, 90; types of queries and responses, 63-64, 89
Contrast: contrast stretching in scanning, 170; in display systems, 48; measuring in texture, 108; problems in scanning, 163
Controlled community splines, 152
Convergence in display systems, 48
Converting documents to digital format: preservation issues, 161; service bureau bids and advantages, 49-50; silver nitrate file negatives, 170
Co-occurrent matrix model in texture extraction, 116
Copies of published reproductions, 32
Copying original works, 31-33
Copyright Clearance Center (CCC), 37
Copyrights. *See also* Rights and use re-

strictions; copyrightable images, 40 n.4, 53-54; types of image reproductions, 32

Corbis Media, 19, 37

Co-referencing images with text records, 148-154

Costs: compressed-domain approach to video retrieval, 96; digital orthophotography costs, 174; document conversion costs, 50; face recognition software costs, 145; implementation of different types of retrieval, 89; MESL cost studies, 29, 39; pricing models for collection use, 36-37; quality perception and, 23; scanning aerial photographs, 171, 174-175; system needs assessments, 47; transaction costs for determining rights, 41 n.5

Cropping data in metadata information, 21, 54

Cryptography standards, 20

Cultural heritage community. *See* LIS communities

CVEPS system: overview, 96-97; remote online editing, 99; retrieval methods, 98-99; system components, 97-99

Cypress database, 127, 128, 129, 130

Data migration, 20, 165-166

Data refreshing, 20, 165-166

Databases. *See* Digital imaging and retrieval systems; *names of specific systems or projects*

Dates of scanning: in VIMSYS model, 78; including in metadata information, 21, 53

DCT (Discrete Cosine Transformation), 105

Decomposition of images in query proccss, 93

Delivery platforms. *See* Platforms

Demand for multimedia content, 34

Derived features (VIMSYS), 78

Derived variables in image distance function, 93

Designing digital imaging systems. *See also* Architecture of systems; Platforms; cost constraints, 47, 50; data input issues: *file conversion assessment, 49-50; image sources, 21-22, 33, 45, 54; image types to be included, 45;* scanning requirements, *13, 21, 46, 53;* specifying topic domain, *45, 73;* determining legal issues, 45; hardware: *display monitors, 48-49; flexibility and expandability, 47, 117; integration with other systems, 46, 117-118; network requirements, 12, 46-47; storage capacity needs, 46, 171;* lease, purchase or build decisions, 46; overview, 2-3; planning for disasters, 51-52; preliminary design issues, 43; purpose, 44-45; software: *concurrent access issues, 118; database software needs assessment, 45; flexibility and expandability, 47, 117; indexing/retrieval features, 46, 89; integration with other systems, 46, 117-118; performance criteria, 46; specifying search and query modes, 45; standards for file formats and compression, 46, 47-50;* systems analysis, 44-50; use patterns and user analysis, 45; vendor interview ques-tions, 49

DFT (Discrete Fourier Transform model), 116

Dictionaries: machine-readable dictionaries, 145-146; MESL project text data dictionary, 38

Digital camera resolution, 162

Digital images: 2D and 3D images, 65-68, 80, 122; annotating, 14, 52, 148-158; authentication, 20, 21-22, 34, 53-54; defined, 33; demand for, 34; extracted properties or features. *See* Extracting data from images; feature or object properties, 108; file sizes, 12, 78, 162-163, 164; header information, 21, 53, 77-78; integrity, 20, 21, 54, 164-165; levels of abstraction. *See* Levels of content abstraction; life expectancy, 20, 165; low-level properties (color, texture, layout), 107, 108-109; MARS system image indexer, 106; off-color images, 55-56; preserving, 161, 165-166; problems in data retrieval techniques, 60; quality of scanning, 13, 21, 46, 53, 162-166; segmentation, 110-111; specifying sources, 21-22, 33, 45, 54; text record. *See* Text records; types of reproductions, 31-33

Digital imaging and retrieval systems.

INDEX

See also names of specific systems or projects; architecture of systems. *See* Architecture of systems; clearinghouse of image database products, 19; compression issues, 13, 91, 96, 100, 113-116; cross-database user interface (ImageQuery), 18; designing. *See* Designing digital imaging systems; disaster planning, 51-52; display devices, 12-13, 47-48; history, 11-13; juried list of projects, need for, 167; LIS community role in future, 19-20; network requirements, 12, 46-47; planning and implementation, 2-3; recent projects and developments, 18-19; research in querying and retrieval, 24-25; scalability, 26, 118; scanning systems, 13, 21, 46, 53; social and ethical concerns, 53; storage systems and requirements, 11-12; system evaluation, 39, 104; systems analysis, 44-50; user interfaces. *See* User interfaces; vendor interview questions, 49

Digital media longevity issues: data migration vs. data refreshing, 20; LIS community role, 20; longevity of digital documents, 161, 165-166

Digital orthophoto quadrangles, 171-174

Digital preservation projects: aerial photography project, 169-175; archival preservation scan quality, 162-164; overview, 9; preserving digital media, 161, 165-166; preserving paper-based materials, 161

Digital signature standards, 20

Directionality in texture, 108

Disaster planning, 51-52

Discrete Cosine Transformation method, 105

Discrete Fourier Transform model, 116

Discrete Wavelet Transformation method, 105

Disparity in grouping-process object retrieval, 125

Display devices: history and development, 12-13; specifications, 47-48

Displaying images in user interfaces, 46

Dissolve detection in video, 96

Distortion in image representation, 114

DLI projects, 105

Documenting image system information, 51-52

Documents: aerial photographs, 169-175; archival scan quality, 162-164; changing nature of documents, 71; converting to digital images, 49-50; preservation issues, 161

Domain event layers (VIMSYS), 76-77

Domain knowledge: defining important attributes, 85; domain-specific ontologies, 153; in face retrieval databases, 84; semantic query use of, 80; spatial relationships in aerial images, 151-152; specifying special domains, 45, 73; video knowledge base, 86

Domain objects (VIMSYS), 76-77

DOQs (digital orthophoto quadrangles), 171-174

Dot pitch in monitor requirements, 48; dpi resolutions, 163

Drawing shapes for queries, 80, 83 fig.4, 95

Dublin Core standards, 20

DWT (Discrete Wavelet Transformation) method, 105, 116

Dynamic description of data, 61, 62

Dynamic discovery in database architecture, 15

Eccentricity of color (MARS), 108

Eccentricity of shapes (MARS), 109

Edges of images: detecting, 136; edge energy, 129

Edit Decision Lists (EDL), 99

Editing scans, 164. *See also* Integrity of images

Editing video, 96-97, 99

Editions of images, 22

Effectiveness of retrieval, 104

Eigenfaces, 85

Embedded zerotree wavelet coder, 114

Encapsulation of images, 20

Entropy coding in image representation, 114

Entropy minimalization, 152

Ethernet, 12

Ethical concerns of digital imaging systems, 53-56

Euclidean histogram distance, 108

Evaluation stage of MESL project, 39

Events, querying by, 75-77, 80-81, 98

Expandability of systems. *See* Scalability of imaging projects

External image processing tools. *See* Image processing tools for users

Extracting data from images: color data *back projection in extraction, 91;* color *histograms, 82, 106, 108; color layout extraction, 108; extraction techniques, 105; for regions of images, 127-131; Gaussian pyramids in extraction, 129;* extraction defined, 25; feature data, 91, 96, 116; MARS system image analyzer, 106; object features and geometry, 123-124; shape data, 65-66, 81, 93, 109-110; spatial data, 76-77, 92-93, 95-96, 110-111; temporal data, 76-77, 80-81, 98; texture data: *automating texture extraction, 116, 127-131; basic feature extraction, 81, 82; problems extracting images of clothed people, 135;* VIMSYS model, 77-78; EZW (Embedded zerotree wavelet) coder, 114

Face retrieval databases: PICTION system, 144-148; problems in, 135; Xenomania system, 84-85

Faces of three-dimensional shapes, 67

FD (Fourier Descriptors), 109

Feature recognition in facial queries, 146

Feature-based retrieval. *See also* Extracting data from images; combining with spatial relationships, 92; defined, 90; feature extraction, 91; features in video scenes, 98; hierarchy of grouping processes, 125-127; in MARS system, 106, 107-111; in VIMSYS model, 77-78; projects and methods, 124-125; reliance on object geometry, 123-124; road detection, 152

Features of new systems, designing. *See* Designing digital imaging systems

Fees: document conversion, 50; image rights fee scales, 33; MESL pricing models, 36-37

File formats: conversion assessment, 49-50; including in header information, 21, 53; needs assessment for new systems, 46

File sizes: estimations for scanned images, 162-163; image file sizes, 12;

in VIMSYS model, 78; scanning average newspaper archive, 164

Finding agency model, 37

Fleck, Margaret M., 7-8, 121-142

Flexibility of systems, 47. *See also* Scalability of imaging projects

Flow regions in images, 131

Forsyth, David A., 7-8, 121-142

Fourier Descriptors (FD), 109

Fractal model in texture extraction, 116

Frames in video, access to, 86

Frequency of system access, determining, 45

F_u, F_d, and F_c feature set (VIMSYS), 77-78

Functions of new systems, designing. *See* Designing digital imaging systems

Fuzzy queries, 74, 75

Gabor Filter model in texture extraction, 116

Gaussian pyramids in color extraction, 129

Gender discrimination in face recognition, 145

Geographic Information Systems (GIS), 171-174

Geometry: geometric site models, 150; geometrically correcting scans, 171; in people or animal identification, 135-139; in tree identification, 131-135

Getty Art History Information Project: image quality studies, 23; MESL project, 29

Getty foundation, 105

Getty Information Institute. *See* Getty Art History Information Project

GIS systems, 171-174

Graham, Peter, 164

Graphic annotations for video segments, 155

Graphic user interfaces (GUI), 14. *See also* User interfaces

Greenspan, Hayit, 7-8, 121-142

Grid files method in image indexing, 117

Ground control points in aerial photographs, 174

Grouping process: attraction-based grouping method, 110-111; identifying people in images, 137; object-based retrieval, 125-127; region-growing techniques, 131

Groups involved in systems design, 46

Guidelines for building systems, 19

GUIs, 14. *See also* User interfaces

Handel, Mark, 26

Handwritten documents, problems in scanning, 163

Hard disk storage systems: determining capacity needs, 46; history of development, 11-12; resolution/space tradeoff, 171

Hardware obsolescence, 165

Header information in images. *See also* Metadata; in VIMSYS model, 77-78; metadata standards, 21, 53

Heidorn, P. Bryan, 1-10

Hierarchical levels of content analysis developing concept querying, 118-119; in grouping processes, 125-127; levels of abstraction in image descriptions, 62-63, 76-77; MUSEUM model, 62-63; spatial relationships in aerial images, 151-152; video scene browser, 98-99, 156; VIMSYS model, 76-77

Histograms: as lacking spatial cues, 126; color histogram matching, 82; extracting in MARS system, 106; histogram intersection method, 108

History of digital imaging, 11-13

Holders of image rights: determining rights holders, 30-33; including in metadata information, 22, 54-55; museum administration and negotiation issues, 30, 33; needs of rights holders and rights users, 35-36; rights holder's collective pricing model, 37

Holes in shapes (MARS), 109

Hough transforms in tree identification, 134

HSV space, 106

Huang, Tom, 6-7, 103-120

Hue maps in images, 129

Hue saturation value space, 106

Huffman coding in image compression, 115

IA (image analysts), 154

IBM Almaden Research Center: content-based retrieval research, 52-53; QBIC system, 81, 92, 105, 124

Iconic annotation languages, 52

Iconic matches of images, 124

Image analysts (IA), 154

Image compression. *See* Compression

Image Directory Service (Academic Press), 37

Image equivalency notes in metadata information, 21-22, 53-54

Image header information, 21, 53, 77-78

Image longevity. *See* Digital media longevity issues

Image object layers (VIMSYS), 76-77

Image processing. *See* Content-based retrieval; Extracting data from images

Image processing tools for users. *See* Tools

Image representation layers (VIMSYS), 76-77

Image understanding research, 148

ImageLib listserv and clearinghouse, 19

ImageQuery system, 14-18

Imaging systems. *See* Digital imaging and retrieval systems; *names of specific systems or projects*

Implementing systems: determining cost constraints, 47; overview, 2-3

IMPRIMATUR, 40 n.1

Incremental queries: hierarchy of grouping processes, 125-127; refinement process in content-based queries, 64, 74; user-tuned queries, 125

Indexing. *See* Automatic and semi-automatic indexing; Manual indexing

Inference network retrieval model, 117

Information science community. *See* LIS communities

INLV (Integration of Natural Language and Vision), 154

INQUERY system, 117

Integrated queries (cross-media), 76

Integrated text/image retrieval systems, 144-148

Integrating systems: new systems with existing ones, 46; with SQL applications, 117-118

Integration of Natural Language and Vision (INLV), 154
Integrity of images: alteration notes in metadata information, 21, 54; LIS community role in future, 20; scanning quality issues, 164-165
Intellectual property rights. *See* Rights and use restrictions
Intelligence surveillance applications, 157
Interest levels of users, responding to, 75
Internal nodes in query trees (MARS), 112
Internet's disorderly image collections, 121
Interviewing system vendors, 49
Intrinsic variables in image distance function, 93
ISX Corporation's LOOM, 151

Jain, Ramesh, 5, 71-88
Java-based applications, 91, 93, 106
JPEG compression standard, 13

Key-range locking in databases, 118
Keywords: adding to video, 155; as too time-consuming, 89; complementing with content-based retrieval, 90; computing distances between, 83; for newspaper photos, 145; searching picture captions for, 143; user-assigned terms, 24-25
Knowledge domains. *See* Domain knowledge
Kodak Picture Exchange (KPX), 19, 37

Labeling content: image areas with mouse gestures, 148-154; video with annotations, 155-158
Landford, A. G., 49
Language processing in *Show&Tell* system, 152-153
Layers of abstraction in data modeling. *See* Levels of content abstraction
Leaf nodes in query trees (MARS), 112
Leasing systems, 46
Legal issues. *See* Ethical concerns of digital imaging systems; Rights and use restrictions
Lens calibration data, 174
Leung, Thomas K., 7-8, 121-142
Levels of content abstraction: devel-

oping concept querying, 118-119; hierarchy of grouping processes, 125-127; in feature indexing, 117; MUSEUM model, 62-63; PinPoint system, 82; spatial relationships in aerial images, 151-152; video scene hierarchy, 98, 156; VIMSYS model, 76-77
Library community. *See* LIS communities
Life expectancy of media, 165
Light source notes in metadata information, 21
Limiting queries. *See also* Incremental queries; by domain, 80; graphically, 80; hierarchy of grouping processes, 125-127; refinement process in content-based queries, 64, 74; user-tuned queries, 125
Linking to external tools: future development of tools, 26; ImageQuery system, 16-17
LIS communities: as sharing common culture, 35; change in nature of libraries, 71; collection development and creation policies, 166-167; defined, 27 n.1; demand for multimedia content, 34; redefinition of resource sharing, 161; role in future system development, 19-20; role in standards development, 20-23
Listservs devoted to imaging, 19
Location mode queries, 79
Location of features in images, 92. *See also* Spatial information and relationships
Locative constraints (*Show&Tell*), 154
Locator service pricing model, 37
Longevity of digital documents. *See* Digital media longevity issues
LOOM (ISI/USC), 151
Lossless data compression, 114, 116
Low-resolution images, 33
Luman, Donald E., 9, 169-175
Lunin, Lois F., 3, 43-57
LZW compression standard, 13

Machine vision technologies. *See* Computer vision technologies
Machine-readable dictionaries, 145-146
Magnetic tape life expectancy, 165
Magneto Optico media life expectancy, 165

Mainframe computer system storage, 12

Malik, Jitendra, 7-8, 121-142

Managing collections, 161

Manual indexing. *See also* annotation of content; in document conversion bid, 50; in video knowledge base, 86; needs assessment for new systems, 46; reindexing images, 122; resources for, 1, 104; scalability issues, 104; time issues, 89; user-assigned keywords, 24-25; vocabulary and terminology issues, 24

Manually segmenting shape information, 81

Markings on documents, 163

Markov Random Field model in texture extraction, 116

MARS system: future research directions, 115-119; image representation and retrieval, 107-111; overview, 6-7, 105; prototype, 104-105; query processing, 112-115; system architecture, 105-107; use of wavelets, 113-115; user interface, 111-112; Web site address, 106; MARS/IRS system, 105

Massachusetts Institute of Technology: Media Streams, 52; Photobook, 52, 105, 124

Materials, object, 122-123, 127-131

Matrix-weighted histogram distance, 108

Meadows, T., 47-48

Measuring effectiveness of retrieval, 104

Media Streams (M.I.T.), 52

Mehrotra, Rajiv, 4-5, 59-69

Mehrotra, Sharad, 6-7, 103-120

Meng, Jianhao, 5-6, 89-102

MESL (Museum Educational Site Licensing Project): as testbed for for multisite environment, 19; deployment system, 38; evaluation, 39; goals, 29, 34-35; participants, 34-35, 41 n.7; pricing models, 36-37; progress to date, 37-38; site licensing agreement, 38; World Wide Web site, 41 n.12

Metadata: authentication and image equivalency data in, 21-22, 53-54; capture process information in, 21, 53; defined, 27 n.2; in VIMSYS model, 77-78; LIS communities' role in standards development, 20-23; rights and use restrictions in, 22, 54-55; technical imaging and file information in, 21, 53; using in searches, 75

MFD (Modified Fourier Descriptor), 109-110

Microfilm: life expectancy, 165; scanning equipment, 162

MIM (Moment-Invariants Methods), 109

Mini-worlds in databases, 60-63

M.I.T. (Massachusetts Institute of Technology): Media Streams, 52; Photobook, 52, 105, 124

MMVAR system: classifying video objects, 155; overview, 8-9, 155; retrieval, 157; vision module, 157-158

Modal matching in content-based retrieval, 52

Modeling data in databases, 60-63

Modified Fourier Descriptor (MFD), 7, 109-110

Modular system architecture, 15-17

Moment-Invariants Methods (MIM), 109

Monitors. *See* Display devices

Mosaicking aerial photograph scans, 174

Motion and moving objects: detecting in video, 97-98; in grouping-process object retrieval, 125; tracking in video, 157-158

Mouse input into images, 148-154

MPEG compression standard, 96

Mukherjee, D. P., 133

Multidimensional point access methods, 66

Multilevel abstraction hierarchies. *See* Levels of content abstraction

Multimedia Analysis and Retrieval System. *See* MARS system

Multimedia retrieval systems. *See also* Content-based retrieval; Video content retrieval; demand for educational multimedia content, 34; development of, 103-104

MMVAR system, 155-158; reducing information to bit streams, 72;

Show&Tell system, 148-154; Multi-media system for Video Annotation and Retrieval. *See* MMVAR system

MULti-SEmantic Unstructured data Model. *See* MUSEUM data model

MUSE Educational Media, 29

MUSEUM data model: features, 62-63 overview, 4-5; shape similarity-based retrieval, 64-68

Museum Educational Site Licensing Project. *See* MESL (Museum Educational Site Licensing Project)

Museums. *See also* LIS communities; print model of rights administration, 33, 36; rights administration issues, 30, 33

Naked people, identifying in images, 135-139

Narratives, processing, 152

National Media Lab, 165

Natural language processing: annotating images with speech and gesture, 148; annotating video, 155; in ideal system, 73-74; in video retrieval, 157; *Show&Tell* system, 152-153

Negotiating rights and use restrictions, 30, 33

Networks: imaging requirements, 12; needs assessment, 46-47

News on demand databases, 86

Newspaper photographs, 144-148

Nude people, identifying in images, 135-139

Object-based retrieval: extracting features and geometry, 123-124; hierarchy of grouping processes, 125-127; object recognition, 122-123; objects defined, 122; people or animal identification, 135-139; tree identification, 131-135

OCLC, 21

Off-color or offensive images, 55-56

On-site conversion, 50

Ontologies, domain specific, 153

Optical media life expectancy, 165

Original visual works, 32

Outlines of trees, 133-135

Panning, detecting in video, 96, 97

Paper-based materials, preserving, 161

Parsing video, 97

Patterns of system use, determining, 45

People, identifying in images, 135-139

Performance criteria for new systems, 46

Perimeters of shapes (MARS), 109

Periodic textures in images, 127, 130-131

Personnel: involved in scanning, 21; involved in systems design, 46

Per-use image charges, 36

Phantom protection in databases, 118

Photobook system, 52, 105, 124

Photographic stock houses, 19, 37

Photographs. *See also* Digital images; Documents; aerial photography archives, 169-175; attrition, 169; digital orthophoto quadrangles, 171-174; keywording newspaper photographs, 145

PICTION system, 144-148

Pictorial alphabets, 84

Picture Network Inc. (PNI), 19, 37

PinPoint system (Virage), 82-83, 92, 124-125

Planar harmonic homology, 133

Plane object matching, 124

Plane texture modeling in tree, 132

Planning systems. *See* Designing digital imaging systems

Platforms: CVEPS remote Web video editing, 99; Java-based applications, 91, 93, 106; Web browsers as common user interface, 18; Web browsers as delivery platform, 13, 17, 93, 106; X-Windows-based systems, 17

PNI (Picture Network Inc.), 19, 37

POSTGRES database, 106

Precision of retrieval, 104

Predetermined modeling schemes for data, 61

Preparing documents for scanning, fees for, 50

Preservation of materials. *See* Digital preservation projects

Pricing models for collection use, 36-37

Primitives: describing, 127; volumetric primitives in tree identification, 134

Print materials: preserving paper-base materials, 161; print model of rights administration, 33, 36; printed resolution compared to scanning, 163

Printing needs of systems, determining, 45

Processing images. *See* Content-based retrieval; Extracting data from images

Processors, computer, 12

Published reproductions, 32

Purchasing systems, 46

Purposes of digital imaging systems, 44-45

QBIC system (IBM): feature-based retrieval, 92, 105; non-object queries in, 124; shape similarity in, 81

QPE. *See* Query by pictorial example (QPE)

Quad-tree methods in image indexing, 116, 117

Quality of images: archival quality resolutions, 162-164; defining needed resolutions, 23-24; source notes in metadata information, 21-22, 54; transmissive quality resolutions, 163-164

Queries. *See also* Query features, designing in systems; *types of content retrieval*; Boolean searching, 14, 111, 112; browsing queries, 75, 79, 96-97, 98, 111; classes of queries, 63-64, 74-76; concept querying, 118-119; containment queries, 80; feature-based retrieval, 90; fuzzy queries, 73, 74; general search by location, 79; iconic matches, 124; keyword-based retrieval, 89; metadata-based queries, 75; natural language queries, 73-74, 145-148, 157; object-related queries, 80, 124; point and click querying, 14, 150; query by pictorial example (QPE). *See* Query by pictorial example (QPE); query by sample color or texture, 112, 124, 127-131; query canvases, 80, 83 fig.4, 95; search queries, 75; semantic queries, 80, 89; shape-similarity retrieval, 90; simple and complex queries in MARS system, 111-112; spatio-tem-poral queries, 75-76, 80-81; spoken language queries, 150; video retrieval functionality, 96-99

Query by Image Content system. *See* QBIC system (IBM)

Query by pictorial example (QPE): basing queries on sample images, 75; defined, 79; in MARS system, 106, 112; in PinPoint system, 83-84; using query keys, 89-90

Query canvases, 80, 83 fig.4, 95

Query decomposition of images, 93

Query features, designing in systems. *See also* Queries; classes of queries, 63-64, 74-76; concurrent access issues, 118; incremental refinement process, 18, 64, 74, 125-127; integrated queries (cross-media), 76; query tree processing in MARS system, 112-115; specifying available types during systems analysis, 45; speed of system response, 46; use of WordNet in queries, 145-146

Query features (MUSEUM), 66

Query keys. *See* Query by pictorial example (QPE)

Query trees (MARS), 112-115

Query-only features (VIMSYS), 78

Quotations for document scanning, 50

RADIUS community, 150

RADIUS model board images, 151

RAM imaging requirements, 12

Ramchandran, Kannan, 6-7, 103-120

Recall, measuring effectiveness of retrieval, 104

Refining queries. *See* Incremental queries

Refresh rates for monitors, 48

Regions in images: 2D regions, 122; extracting color and texture for, 127-131; extracting shapes, 109; flow regions, 131; in grouping process, 126, 131; region-growing techniques, 131; ribbons, 137

Reindexing images, 122

Relationships between primitives, 127

Relative location of image features, 95

Relevance feedback in queries, 25, 125

Repetition of tiles in images, 130-131

Reproductions of images, 32. *See also* Rights and use restrictions

Resampling scanned historical photos, 173

Re-scanning in document conversion bid, 50

Research Libraries Group: pricing model, 37; task force on digital preservation, 20

Researching images, current problems, 30-31

Resolution: archival preservation quality, 162-164; cost savings/resolution tradeoff, 171; data in VIMSYS model, 78; monitor requirements, 48

Resource sharing, 161

Retrieval. See Content-based retrieval; Extracting data from images; Feature-based retrieval; Object-based retrieval; Queries

Retrieval systems. See Digital imaging and retrieval systems; names of specific systems or projects

Reuse of images, 55

RIAO '94, 52

Ribbons (regions) in images, 137

Rights and use restrictions: image and reproduction definitions, 31-33; legal framework for image rights, 30; museum administration and negotiation issues, 30, 33; needs of rights holders and rights users, 35-36; notes in metadata information, 22, 54-55; pricing models, 36-37; print model of administration, 33, 36; reuse of images, 55; rights holders, determining, 30-33, 45; site licensing, 29, 34-35, 38

Rights holder's collective pricing model, 37

Rights reseller pricing model, 37

RLG (Research Libraries Group): pricing model, 37; task force on digital preservation, 20

Road detection systems, 148, 152

Roberts, J. L., 55-56

Rotation in feature extraction, 116

Rothenberg, Jeff, 165

Row, M., 47

R-tree method in image indexing, 117

Sandore, Beth, 1-10

Scalability of imaging projects: concurrent access issues, 118; development issues, 26; expandability of systems, 47; feature-based

image indexing impacts, 117; ImageQuery issues, 18; manual indexing issues, 104; text annotation issues, 104

Scale of images: scaling notes in metadata information, 21; scaling scanned historical photos, 173

Scanners: imaging requirements, 13; model data in metadata information, 21, 53; needs assessment, 46

Scanning images: aerial photographs, 170-171; quality of scans, 23-24, 162-164; service bureau bids, 49-50

Scene clustering techniques, 98-99

"Scholars' workstations" philosophy, 17, 26

Search engines, 71-72. See also Content-based retrieval; Queries

Search query class, 75

Searching. See Queries

Secondary index structures, 64

Segmentation: clustering, 110-111; image segmentation issues, 81; in grouping process, 110-111, 126-127; video retrieval, 86, 155

Semantics: adding to multimedia data, 73; in face retrieval databases, 84; in VIMSYS model, 76-77; semantic queries, 80; semantic-level content retrieval, 89, 144, 146

Service and support issues: imaging system vendors, 49; monitors, 48-49

Service bureaus, 49-50

Seymour (Picture Network Inc.), 19, 37

SGML tags in text records, 19

Shape data: as feature-retrieval property, 92; extracting, 65-66, 81, 93, 106, 109-110; in primitive descriptions, 127

Shape similarity-based retrieval. See also Feature-based retrieval; Query by pictorial example (QPE); domain dependence, 79; extracting shape data from images, 65-66, 81, 93, 106, 109-110; in facial database queries, 146; MUSEUM modeling, 64-68; people or animal identification, 135-139; query canvases, 80, 83 fig.4, 95; reliance on object geometry, 123-124; shape features in MARS system, 75, 109-110, 112; tree identification, 131-135

Shapiro's embedded zerotree wavelet coder, 114

Shot decomposition in video, 96, 97-98

Show&Tell system: architecture, 151; overview, 8, 148; querying, 150, 154; results illustrated, 149; speech recognition and language processing, 152-153

Signatures, digital, 20

Silver nitrate file negatives, 170

Simple queries in MARS system, 111-112

Single-image model of rights administration, 33, 36

Site licensing agreements, 29, 34-35

Site models, 150

Size of documents: in VIMSYS model, 78; special costs for scanning, 50

Size of files: estimations for scanned images, 162-163; image files, 12; in VIMSYS model, 78; scanning average newspaper archive, 164

Sketching shapes for queries, 80, 83 fig.4, 95

Skewed images, costs to correct, 50

Skin, identifying in images, 135-139

Smith, John R., 5-6, 89-102

Social concerns of digital images, 53-56

Software obsolescence, 165

Software tools. *See* Tools

Source images: source notes in metadata information, 21-22, 54; sources for new system input, 45; tracing for rights purposes, 33

Spatial information and relationships: absolute and relative location of features, 95-96; combining with feature-based retrieval, 92-93; describing in natural language input, 153; extracting color locations, 108; extracting texture locations, 109; importance in feature-based retrieval, 92; in image segmentation, 110-111; in VIMSYS model, 76-77; indexing methods, 117; *Show&Tell* system, 151-152; spatio-temporal information, 76, 80-81, 98

Special effects, detecting in video, 96

Speech recognition software, 148, 152-153, 155

Speed of display, specifying for new systems, 46

Spoken language descriptions: image annotation, 148-154; speech and language processing, 152-153; video annotation, 155-158

SQL language: ImageQuery support, 15; incorporating into databases, 117-118

Srihari, Rohini K., 8-9, 143-159

Stains on documents, 163

Standards: archival preservation scanning, 162; compression standards, 13, 47-48; Dublin Core standards, 20; file format standards, 47-48

Statistics-based methods in texture extraction, 116

Stephenson, Christie, 26

Stock houses. *See* Photographic stock houses

Storage systems for image collections determining capacity needs, 46; history, 11-12; resolution/space tradeoff, 171

Stories in video, organizing by, 98

Stream-based annotation of video, 52

Structural features on shapes, 65-66

"Stuff" vs. "things": materials vs. objects, 122-123; retrieving images based on materials, 127-131

Subscription pricing for collection use, 36

Symmetry of shapes (MARS), 109

Systems. *See* Digital imaging and retrieval systems; *names of specific systems or projects*

Systems analysis for imaging systems, 44-50; cost constraints, 47, 50; database software needs assessment, 45; determining legal issues, 45; display monitors, 48-49; file conversion assessment, 49-50; flexibility and expandability, 47, 117; image sources, 21-22, 33, 45, 54; image types to be included, 45; indexing/retrieval features, 46, 89; integration with other systems, 46, 117-118; lease, purchase or build decisions, 46; network requirements, 12, 46-47; performance criteria, 46; purpose, 44-45; scanning requirements, 13, 21, 46, 53; specifying search and query modes, 45; specifying topic domain, 45; standards for file formats and compression, 46, 47-48, 50; storage capacity needs, 46, 171; use pattern and user analysis, 45; vendor interview questions, 49

T-1 to T-3 wiring, 12
TAM (Turning Angle Method), 109
Tamura, Hideyuki, 109
Tape life expectancy, 165
Target tracking in video, 157
Technical imaging information, 21, 53
Temporal event queries, 75-76, 80-81
Temporal ordering of video scenes, 98
Temporal relationships in VIMSYS model, 76-77
Terminology issues in image cataloging, 24
Text records. *See also* Keywords; as collateral information for pictures, 144; as not scalable, 104; as separate module in ImageQuery system, 15-16; combining spoken word record with images, 148-158; combining text with feature-based retrieval, 106, 144-148; emphasis in data retrieval techniques, 60; for video segments, 155; inadequacy of, 121-122; keywording newspaper photographs, 145; MESL project text data dictionary, 38; need for, 56; needs assessment for new systems, 46; SGML tags in, 19; extracting texture data from images, 81, 82, 105, 106; for regions of images, 127-131; in grouping-process object retrieval, 125; in image segmentation, 110-111; in people or animal identification, 135-139; in primitive descriptions, 127; in tree identification, 131-135; periodic texture, 127, 130-131; querying by sample texture, 112, 124, 127-131; texture as feature-retrieval property, 92; tile repetition in images, 130-131
"Things" vs. "stuff": materials vs. objects, 122-123; retrieving images based on materials, 127-131
Thirty-Third Annual Clinic on Library Applications of Data Processing, 1
Three-dimensional objects: describing and comparing, 66-68; object-related queries, 80
Thumbnail images: defined, 33; ImageQuery system, 14, 15
Tile repetition in images, 130-131
Time Warner digital photo project, 51
Tools: database software needs assessment, 45; future development of tools, 26; ImageQuery links to external tools, 16-17; video editing tools, 96-99; VisualSEEk system, 93
Tracking: motion and moving objects, 157-158; repetitions of texture, 131
Training costs of new systems, 47
Transform-based methods in texture extraction, 116
Transmission image quality, 163-164
Trant, Jennifer, 3, 29-41
Trees, identifying in images, 131-135
Tuning queries, 125
Turning Angle Method (TAM), 109
TV-tree technique, 79
Two-dimensional images, 65-66
Types of digital images, 45

Universal Transverse Mercator projection, 171
University of Arizona Library, 19
University of California: Alexandria project, 105; DLI projects, 105; ImageQuery system, 14-18; Information Systems and Technology office, 14
University of Illinois: Map and Geography Library, 169-175; Thirty-Third Annual Clinic on Library Applications of Data Processing, 1
University of Michigan: MESL project data distribution, 38; Xenomania system, 84-85
U.S. Copyright Act, 32
U.S. Department of Agriculture, 169
U.S. Geological Survey: digital orthophoto quadrangles, 171-174; Web and FTP site, 175
Use patterns for systems, determining, 45
Use restrictions for images. *See* Rights and use restrictions
User interfaces. *See also* Queries; CVEPS video authoring, 99; Image-

Query system, 14, 17-18; MARS system, 106, 111-112; requirements, 78; scanning software, 13; virtual reality interfaces, 25; VisualSEEk system, 94

User profiles, 61, 62

Users: defining system's audience, 45; demand for multimedia content, 34; disparate backgrounds, 78; perceptions of image quality, 23-24; user terminology, 61, 62; user-assigned keywords, 24-25; user-supplied descriptions, 89; user-tuned queries, 125; varying interpretations of data, 61

User-tuned queries, 125

Vector graphics, 33

Veracity of images. *See* Authentication of images; Integrity of images

Verification constraints (*Show&Tell*), 154

Versions of images, 22

Vertices on shapes, 67

Video content retrieval: access problems, 85; architecture of databases, 85; CVEPS system, 91, 96-97; editing and authoring tools, 97-98, 99; feature-based retrieval, 90, 98-99, 156; functionalities needed for retrieval, 96-97; hierarchical video scene browser, 98-99; Media Streams (M.I.T.), 52; MMVAR system, 155-158; natural language queries, 157; scene clustering techniques, 98-99; semantic retrieval, 156; spatio-temporal retrieval, 75-76, 80-81, 98; spoken descriptions or collateral annotations, 155-158; story order retrieval, 98; stream-based annotation of video, 52; video bit rates, 100

Viewing images on future systems, 21

VIMSYS data model: domain knowledge, 85; features extracted from images, 77-78; image retrieval system use, 82; levels in, 76-77; overview, 5

Virage system: feature-based retrieval, 82-83, 92; Web site address, 124-125

Visual information systems (VIS). *See* Digital imaging and retrieval systems

Visualization module in video retrieval, 97-98

VisualSEEk system: combining feature-based and spatial queries, 92-93; overview, 5-6, 91-92; query formulation and processing, 95-96; system features, 93-94

Vocabulary control: in natural language input, 152; issues in image cataloging, 24; needs assessment for new systems, 46

Volumetric primitives in tree identification, 134

Wavelets: increasing browsing speed, 113-115, 116; wavelet sub-bands, 105

Web browsers: as clients, 13; as common user interface, 18; as delivery platform, 13, 17, 93, 106; CVEPS remote video editing, 99; searching disorderly image collec-tions, 121

Web site addresses: Candid system, 125; Cypress database, 130; MARS system, 106; MESL site, 41 n.12; U.S. Geological Survey, 175; Virage system, 124-125

Weighting features in searching, 83

Wiring requirements for imaging systems, 12

WordNet, 8-9, 145-146, 157

World Wide Web. *See* Web browsers Web site addresses

WORM life expectancy, 165

X-Windows-based systems: development of, 13; effect of Web development on, 17; ImageQuery system, 14

Zerotree data structures, 114

Zoom detection in video, 96, 97